The Sufficiency of Scripture

The Sufficiency of Scripture

Noel Weeks

The Banner of Truth Trust

THE BANNER OF TRUTH TRUST
3 Murrayfield Road, Edinburgh EH12 6EL
PO Box 621, Carlisle, Pennsylvania 17013, USA

*

© Noel Weeks 1988
First published 1988
Reprinted 1998
ISBN 0 85151 751X

*

*

Typeset at The Spartan Press Limited, Hants
and printed and bound in Great Britain by
Bell & Bain Ltd, Glasgow

In thankfulness for
GWEN
who has entered into
the reward for this
and many other labours

CONTENTS

*

ACKNOWLEDGEMENTS

Most books are joint projects in one respect or another. This book is a combined work in far greater degree than most. The people who have given me ideas and suggestions and sharpened my understanding of the issues are too many to name. When I needed to type the manuscript in a relatively short time, I was blessed with an army of helpers. I record their names with thanks: Lyn Richards, Karen Doedens, Lynette Bradshaw, Karen McConnachie, Helen Oste, Harry and Tessa Neyenhuis, Yvonne Rietsma, Ria Young, John Bradshaw, Yolanda Althuis, Henny van der Schoot, Robert East, Anita Ingolstadt.

The late S. M. Houghton perused the manuscript very carefully. His suggestions and corrections have added greatly to the clarity of the work. I am also grateful to John Muether, the librarian of Westminster Seminary, for producing the indices.

Noel Weeks
Sydney, Australia

INTRODUCTION

This work is a response to new elements in recent discussions about the Bible. There was a time when the lines were drawn between those who affirmed the infallibility of the Bible and those who denied it. In terms of that debate it made little difference whether the point at issue was the Bible's testimony on a historical question or on a doctrinal question. Those on one side felt an obligation to defend the infallibility of the Bible on both questions. Those on the other side felt free to doubt it on both issues.

It is my conviction that there has been a shift in the debate to the point that the older positions are no longer so clearly defined. As this shift is still in process it is difficult to categorize parties to the new debate. Indeed it might be unwise to do so as the picture is one of a spectrum of opinion rather than two opposing sides. Rather we may talk about two tendencies.

The first is the tendency to restrict the area of Biblical infallibility. The tendency is to limit it to religious questions, that is, questions which concern the heart of the gospel. One person might express this tendency merely by saying that the Bible is not to be made a textbook for science because its focus is on our salvation through Christ. Another might take this to the point of saying that the historical events described in the Bible did not necessarily happen as recorded, but that details of historical accuracy are irrelevant to the gospel. Another again might question whether the gospel had completely permeated and shaped the ethical and doctrinal teaching of the Bible.

It is this range of opinion that makes categorization difficult. It also makes obsolete the old distinction into fundamentalist and modernist (or, to use other terms, evangelical and liberal). The person who feels free to question the infallibility of the Bible in matters of science or history, or even of ethics, might still desire to be called an evangelical. He may claim a concern to bring men to see their need of Christ as Saviour and Lord.

The aim of this book is to take up and examine the issues and arguments in this debate. Such an aim is not easy to achieve without introducing emotive factors. Ultimately this is an emotional issue, as it is one on which people will feel deeply convinced. Hence emotion and conviction are unavoidable. Yet we achieve nothing by a mere quibbling match with those who have different convictions. For that reason I have chosen to begin by presenting a case. It is presented over against other positions but I have not chosen a particular author as a target. The aim is to deal with the issues.

We do not always proceed from theory to practice, from theological conviction to practical outworking. Often the development is in the reverse direction. A course of conduct which a person or group feels is right or inevitable will lead to the development of a justification for that conduct. Or a position which might otherwise make a strong appeal will be rejected because of real or imagined consequences. Hence I have chosen in the second part to take up some of the issues which have become interwoven with the question of the authority and accuracy of Scripture. These studies focus in greater detail on particular issues.

PART ONE

Basic Issues

Authority and Exhaustiveness

To decide whether the Bible is authoritative in a particular area we might proceed by two different methods. We might look to see whether the Bible claims authority in that area. Or we might see whether the Bible has the character of an authoritative source in that area.

Looking to the Bible itself may not seem conclusive because it does not employ the distinctions to which we have become accustomed. Its claims to authority tend to be general. It says that it is given to furnish a man for 'every good work' (2 Tim. 3:17). Is that meant in what we would see today as a more restricted 'religious' sense? Is it meant to include a man's preparation in 'secular' areas? Even more important is the problem raised by the 'religious'/'secular' distinction itself. The Bible does not talk in terms of that distinction. But our culture does. Should we place all that the Bible says in the religious column and see it as irrelevant to the secular? Are the 'good works' of 2 Timothy 3:17 only 'religious' works?

For the sake of the argument let us suppose that something broader than the narrow area left to religion in our day is meant. Let us say that the Bible was meant to be an authority in psychology or physics or history. How would you ever apply that in practice? How much of the laws and data of physics are found in the text of the Bible?

In following this line of thought we have come, without noticing it, to the second of the two ways I mentioned at the beginning of this chapter. We are now examining the Bible to see if it fits what we expect of an authoritative source. The model to which the Bible is being compared is some sort of science textbook. Is it a book that will contain all the laws and all the facts of physics? Clearly the Bible does not come up to that model.

Or does it? What would we demand of the final authority in physics? We would probably expect absolute accuracy and exhaustive detail. A book could hardly claim to be the final authority in physics if it lacked some particular fact or detail needed to understand one aspect of the physical realm. Thus one of the things we are demanding is exhaustiveness.

It is easy to say, 'The Bible is not a textbook of science', but what does that mean? In fact I think people mean very different things by that or similar formulae. It may be a statement of the obvious in that the Bible does not have the narrow range of subject matter that we expect of a textbook. It does not concentrate upon a particular subject to the exclusion of everything else. However, such a point is not worth making. Sometimes the point is made as an excuse for the Bible. It is meant to apologize for a lack of precision or accuracy in the Bible. It is said: 'Well, the Bible does not have the accuracy of a science/history textbook, but that is not its main purpose.' Here one is doing little more than stating the obvious. One is accepting, generally without realizing it, a certain standard of accuracy. It is the pin-point accuracy that is the textbook ideal. The logical extension of this line of thought is to exclude the Bible from any role in areas for which there are textbooks. If there are more accurate, more detailed, and more precise textbooks, why consult the Bible on these subjects?

So behind much of our thinking in these areas is the conviction that the Bible does not measure up to a certain standard. Many of those who are concerned with this problem are yet anxious to maintain that the Bible is our religious authority. When it comes to areas such as science or history they find that the Bible lacks the detail and precision to be an authority. It is not exhaustive in these matters. Yet in religion they want to use it as an authority. The problem is that the Bible is not exhaustive in matters of religion either. There are many questions on which there is no absolutely precise and detailed answer. Look at the controversies which have divided Christians over the centuries.

[4]

Surely the logical conclusion of this line of thought is that the Bible cannot be an authority in religious or ethical questions either. For in these questions there is not exhaustive detail.

This argument against the ethical or religious authority of the Bible is not often found in the form I have stated above. However, it lies behind an approach to particular questions that is very common today. On a particular question in dispute it will be claimed that the Bible does not treat every possible form of the question or problem. Often it will be argued that there are dimensions or aspects of the question that have developed or been recognized only recently. The conclusion is drawn, from this incompleteness of the Biblical data, that all that the Bible says is not really relevant to our discussion of the question. If the conclusion is not as radical as this it may merely be said that the failure of the Bible to treat every aspect of the problem makes it difficult to come to any firm conclusions.

To prevent confusion some clarification is necessary. Here, I do not mean areas in which it may be argued that the Bible says nothing at all on the whole range of the subject. (I will come back to this subject later.) What I have in mind are discussions of the following kind. It can be observed that the Bible does not treat the problem of psychological incompatability in marriage. Yet the Bible has teaching against divorce. It is then argued that the Bible's teaching against divorce cannot apply to divorce on the grounds of psychological incompatability, for that subject is not considered in the Bible. So the general teaching on divorce is called into question by the Bible's failure to supply teaching on a specific factor in a marriage breakdown.

Arguments of this sort really are built on the incompleteness of the Bible. They imply that exhaustive detail is needed before the Bible can speak authoritatively on any subject. Generally this argument will be applied only to matters of science or history which are thought to be peripheral to the Bible's main purpose. Yet logically the argument would be just as valid for all other areas. For instance, not every aspect of the 'gospel', in the narrow sense of that term, is treated in detail in the Bible.

The attempt to use the incompleteness argument to restrict the authority of the Bible to religious matters must lead logically to the use of the same argument against the religious authority of the Bible.

In our day a consideration or an argument that is seen as *new* has considerable prestige. It is often directly stated or implied that the element lacking in the Biblical teaching is one that would not have been known or appreciated in Biblical times. This whole point of the difference between our times and Biblical times will be treated more fully later. However for the moment I would like to ask whether the argument from incompleteness is a new argument. Are we the first to realize the Bible's lack of detail?

A MEDIEVAL ARGUMENT

Of course we are not! The 'incompleteness' of the Bible has been part of arguments against the exclusive authority of the Bible for a thousand years or more. One such Medieval argument forms a very nice illustration of the connection between the incompleteness of the Bible in matters of scientific detail and the understanding of Biblical authority.

Readers of the New Testament will be aware that the Pharisees made the tradition of the elders an authority alongside that of Scripture. That dependence on tradition was passed on to Rabbinic Judaism. However it was attacked both by Christianity and movements within Judaism itself. Sa'adya Ga'on, the eminent defender of Rabbinic Judaism in the 9th century AD, took up the disputed question of calendrical regulation. The regulation of the calendar had been a disputed question in Judaism before New Testament times. The Old Testament implies that the calendar was a lunar calendar, for a month begins with the first appearance of the new moon. The practical problem with a lunar calendar is that twelve lunar months are shorter than the solar year by about ten days and thirteen lunar months are too long.

The Bible sets the annual festivals of the Hebrews on a certain day of a certain month. It makes them also agricultural festivals with offerings of grain or fruits. However, it says nothing about how to regulate the calendar. A twelve-month lunar year will quickly fall out of phase with the solar and thus the agricultural year. The point will come when the prescribed offerings can no longer be offered as they have not yet ripened. Hence there must be a scientific regulation of the calendar, yet the Bible does not tell us how it is to be done.

For Judaism the correct regulation of the festivals was a matter of great importance. Sa'adya Ga'on argues that the lack of Biblical detail on calendrical regulation proves the need of some other authoritative source of truth. That source, he asserts, is the tradition of the elders. So Sa'adya Ga'on has turned the incompleteness of the Bible into a defence of the Pharisaic position on tradition. Questions of festivals and calendrical regulation are not burning issues for most Christians today. Christians would be reluctant to grant the validity of Sa'adya's argument and thus of the Pharisaic appeal to tradition. Nevertheless this whole Medieval argument is formally identical to many modern discussions.

The whole point of the preceding discussion is that there are ramifications to the argument from lack of scientific detail that are seldom realized by those who use this argument today. The argument can be used to justify any sort of extra authority beside the Bible and has been so used in the past. It is equally valid against the religious and ethical authority of the Bible.

Many issues raised so far will need detailed discussion. And only one issue can be discussed at a time. We have seen the claim in 2 Timothy 3:17 that the Bible equips a man for 'every good work'. We have also been forced to face the fact that the Bible's treatment of ethical or theological matters is not exhaustive in every detail. That raises a question. Even those who do not accept the authority of the Bible must concede that its authors intended it as a code for human conduct. How could it operate as such a code without being exhaustive? The raising of this question makes us ask how the Bible functions to direct conduct without being a multi-volume work covering every conceivable situation. It will also raise the question of whether we are right in expecting an authoritative source to say the last word on every detail of a subject.

The Form of Biblical Teaching

We have seen that one form an authoritative source could take is to cover every last detail of every aspect of a subject. That is the ideal to which some authors of definitive textbooks have aspired.

There is another possible way. Seeking for exhaustive detail means a work so voluminous as to be practically impossible to produce or print. The other method chosen by those who have sought to say the last word on a subject has been to try to cover everything by means of a few general principles, rules, or laws. The belief then is that everything can be deduced once these general principles are understood. Thus the two possible approaches are at opposite extremes. One tries to state the case to the last minute detail. The other tries to sum up everything under a few general principles.

Both approaches depend on a belief and a hope. The attempt to obtain exhaustive detail depends on believing that it is possible to exhaust a subject and to cover its every detail. Those who would reduce all to a few general rules or laws believe that all the complexity of human life and experience can be subsumed under a few general laws. I will return later to the question of whether these hopes are reasonable.

THE FORM OF BIBLICAL LAW

For the moment, the significant fact is that the Bible does not subscribe to either the approach of exhaustive detail or that of pure and general principles. The best example is the laws of Sinai and/or the laws recorded in Deuteronomy. Here we have an attempt to set forth rules to govern the community and personal life of Israel.

The first impression of the Sinai and Deuteronomic covenants is of a mass of detail. Yet we also have general principles, the most obvious being the ten commandments. Is the Biblical approach, then, an attempt to give both general principles and exhaustive detail? While there are more general laws, their existence does not make laws on matters of detail useless.

The interaction of more general laws and laws covering more restricted circumstances is clear in Exodus. The ten commandments are given in Exodus 20. Following the ten commandments come laws that deal with matters of the application of those commandments. In Exodus 20:22–26 we find laws which give an amplification of the second commandment. To forbid the worship of idols is one thing. But if Israel were left only with this general principle they would not know the form their sacrifices were to take. Such details as the form of the altar (vv.25,26) cannot be logically deduced from a prohibition of idolatry. Many other considerations like the Biblical concern for modesty also come into play.

Another good example is the amplification of the law on stealing in Exodus 22. The eighth commandment does not contain in itself any indication of appropriate punishment. Hence this matter must be spelled out in a more specific law. There is also the problem of overlap between the sixth commandment against murder and the eighth commandment against stealing. Is the killing of a thief a case of murder? Exodus 22:2,3 make a distinction. A thief killed in self-defence when he is in the act of breaking into a house has not been murdered. However, when self-defence is not in question, but a person later takes revenge on a thief by killing him, then that is murder. Verses 5 and 6 show that to cause the loss of another's property through negligence can also be regarded as a form of stealing. Another area of difficulty is loss of property held by another under a form of safe-keeping, loan or hire (vv.7–15).

Clearly these laws attempt to clarify the application of the eighth commandment. Some of them deal with very specific matters. Yet it could not be said that they attempt to be exhaustive. It is easy enough to think of obvious cases that are not covered. Verse 6 seems from its wording to deal with the case of a fire which gets out of control through negligence.

Deliberate arson is not given a specific law. Could we then say that, as far as the Bible is concerned, arson is not wrong? I doubt if anybody would say this, because if the negligent lighting of a fire is wrong, surely the deliberate starting of a fire is even more wrong.

This particular example makes an important point. The Bible often does not restate the obvious. What it states, as in this case, is the law in situations where it might be uncertain whether the law applies or not. Where the application of a general law is not in any reasonable doubt, there is no need to make the law more specific.

Thus Biblical legislation is not shaped by any abstract philosophical desire to reduce everything to a few general principles or to formulate a rule for every last detailed case. It is shaped much more by functional considerations. The general laws are clarified in matters of detail to avoid possible confusion.

A moment's reflection will make it clear that this is the obvious approach. A comprehensive and exhaustive work would be so voluminous as to be practically useless. A work devoted only to the most detailed legal principles would leave the people of God uncertain as to the implementation of those principles. It is not out of practical considerations that people expect legislation in exhaustive detail or reduced only to very general principles. It is out of abstract philosophical commitments that will be considered in more detail later.

While the more specific commandments are not simple logical deductions from the general commandments, they generally embody the principles of those commandments. It is often possible to see a more general concern behind a number of quite varied specific commandments, even when that more general concern may not be specifically stated. For example there is the command that one must not prevent an ox threshing grain from helping itself to the fruit of its labours (Deut. 25:4). And there is the prohibition against withholding a hired man's wages (Lev. 19:13). Both of these proceed from a concern to allow a worker to enjoy the fruit of his labour. Hence Paul may see the law on oxen as supporting his argument that the preacher of the gospel is entitled to remuneration (1 Cor. 9:6–11). As he mentions elsewhere, it is a case of the principle stated by our Lord: 'The labourer is worthy of his wages' (1 Tim. 5:18; Luke 10:7).

This example is given to warn against another misunderstanding of Biblical legislation. There is in the field of religion and ethics a bias against detailed rules. This bias is partly understandable as a reaction against unbiblical legalism or rigidity. It can also be motivated by a desire to claim conformity to the spirit of Biblical law while breaking its specific provisions. Where this attitude prevails there is an antipathy to the study of the details of Biblical legislation. Often this antipathy is mixed with a profession of adherence to the principles, especially the principle of love. Yet this whole attitude to the details of Biblical law ignores the fact that one must know the details to catch the principles that motivate those details. Just as not every general command is spelled out in every detail, so a series of specific commands may embody a principle that is not given a more general expression.

From this consideration of the form of Biblical law it is obvious that some popular approaches are at variance with the Bible. An obvious case is what has been called 'Situation Ethics'. Some aspects of this teaching will have to be considered later. What concerns us at the moment is the attempt to take the general Biblical teaching on love and to detach it from the more specific Biblical teachings. It is held that 'love' may require the breaking of any of the other commandments in specific situations. The commandment to love is absolute. The other commandments are 'optional'. They may have been appropriate expressions of the commandment to love in certain restricted and dated situations. They are not necessarily appropriate in modern situations. Rather the individual is to deduce for himself the appropriate expression of the law of love in a particular modern situation. Such is the teaching of 'Situation Ethics'.

There are many grounds of objection to this teaching. In the present context I would simply point to its understanding of the relation between the general commandment to love and practical ethical decisions. It sees these decisions for more specific situations as deducible from a general commandment. It is certainly true that the other commandments are an expression of love (Rom. 13:8–10), but they do not all follow as simple logical deductions from the command to love. This is true both of the Old Testament commandments and the commands given to believers in the New Testament. If all could be logically deduced from a general command, there would be no need for the specific commands already noted in Exodus.

The practical effect of making all ethical decisions logical deductions or inferences from the law of love is to reduce man's need for divine instruction. He needs to be told only one thing, to 'love', and he will work all the rest out himself.

Defenders of 'Situation Ethics' often like to brand their opponents as woodenly inflexible, concerned with the letter of Biblical law rather than with the loving approach in difficult and complex modern situations. Yet the Biblical law that Situation Ethics rejects is much more practical than Situation Ethics. It gives guidance on the implementation of the law in specific situations. It was not so academic and divorced from everyday reality as to imagine that all could be deduced from a simple general principle. Clearly, Biblical law is motivated by a very different spirit than Situation Ethics. It is not concerned with giving man maximum freedom to do as he thinks fit. It is concerned to show him that practical implementation of the law of love that is pleasing to God.

While Situation Ethics errs in ignoring the importance of the more specific Biblical commands, there is also the danger of ignoring the more general principles. It is on this ground that Jesus condemned the Pharisees (Matt. 23:23). One also meets an ignoring of general principles in the common argument that the absence of a specific command means that there is no Biblical teaching on a subject. Paul who built an argument for paying evangelists from a law on oxen had a far better appreciation of the structure of Biblical law. He did not need a specific commandment on pay for evangelists because, as he himself says, God did not give the command just for the sake of oxen (1 Cor. 9:9,10).

The point of this consideration of Biblical law is that you cannot expect the Bible to conform to the textbook image on ethics. It does not aim to express every detail or to reduce all to a few abstract principles. The mixture of more general and more specific commands is dictated on the whole by practical considerations. Where ambiguity or uncertainty exist we are more likely to find a more specific commandment.

Does this mixture of general and specific apply only to Biblical law? What about the doctrinal teaching of the Bible? There is quite a variety in the doctrinal teaching of the Bible. Some topics are treated in great detail and others receive far less detailed treatment. One may compare, for example, the detailed treatment of salvation in Romans, Galatians, and Ephesians with the far briefer treatment of Christ's incarnation in Philippians 2. The reason for the difference is perfectly plain. Controverted and disputed doctrines received more extended treatment. In this respect there is a similarity to the legal portions of Scripture which go into greater detail on matters where there may be uncertainty. Also, as in the legal sections, there are logical links in matters of doctrine but no attempt to deduce all doctrines from one basic doctrine.

Biblical theology is thus different from rational theologies which try to deduce all from a few abstract ideas. Its God is a living and personal God, not just a rational concept.

Misunderstanding of Biblical theology, as though it were a rationalistic theology, is evident in some arguments about the importance of this or that doctrine. For example it has been argued that the virgin birth of Christ is really unimportant in the New Testament because it is so seldom mentioned. The person who uses such an argument is working with the concept of a Bible written like a textbook with the most important matters coming first and being given the most space. In books written to instruct believers in the way of godliness, frequency of mention has much to do with the controversies of the time. Hence the argument for the unimportance of the virgin birth seems plausible only if we picture the Bible as something it is not. That people can propound such arguments and not be immediately howled down as ridiculous shows how our expectation of the way a book of religion should be written colours our understanding and use of the Bible.

This consideration of the form of Biblical teaching in ethics and theology is all aimed to make one simple point. You cannot conclude that if the Bible says relatively little about a subject, it says nothing about that subject. Yet such is the power of this way of thinking that some people conclude that the textbook argument settles all questions. Generally it is not even put as an argument. It is put as a categoric fact: 'The Bible is not a textbook of science/history/ethics, etc. Hence our thinking in science/history/ethics, etc. may be completely unbiblical.'

It has already been argued that the Bible's mode of teaching often uses a mixture of general truths and specifics rather than aiming at comprehensive detail. The real question is not: does the Bible give every last detail in science/history/ethics, etc? The real question is: does the Bible say anything, whether in general or in detail, relevant to science/history/ethics, etc?

To ask this last question is to answer it. Indeed the textbook argument would not need to be employed if there were obviously no Biblical passages pertaining to these disciplines. That we can point out passages that seem relevant for science does not of itself determine the meaning or importance of these passages. All it means is that we cannot refuse to consider them.

ꙮ 3 ꙮ

General and Special Revelation

Often the textbook argument is reinforced by drawing a sharp distinction between general and special revelation. General revelation means what may be learned of God from the creation. Special revelation means God's verbal communicating to man, especially through the Bible. It is argued that what we know through science is part of general revelation. Hence it has the authority of a divine revelation. Particularly in matters of science (but some would include other areas as well) it is this general revelation which is to be treated as the authority.

A common extension of this is that what are called scientific 'laws' are equated with the 'laws' by which God controls the world. By knowing these laws we know the ways of God.

Sometimes by implication, sometimes directly, the certainty of what we may know by general revelation is contrasted with what we may learn from the Bible. Since general revelation is often taken to be synonymous with science, this amounts to a contest between the Bible and science. Science, which supplies so much more detail, naturally wins easily.

Just because such views have become popular they should be carefully examined. Is there any real basis for thinking that general revelation is the same as what we learn today from what we popularly call science? Are the laws of science the laws of God?

What does a person mean when he says: 'We should learn about this or that, not from the Bible, which is a book of religion and not of science, but from God's general revelation'? Behind what he says, there often lies a conviction that what is popularly called science must be right. The idea of the infallibility of 'science' is probably declining somewhat in our day, but it has been a widely-held conviction. However, for the Christian this 'infallible' source of information in science has to be correlated with another source, namely, the Bible. Furthermore the Bible can claim a certain authority as the Word of God. To prevent conflict between these two authorities some divide the field of knowledge between them. This effective restriction of the area over which the Bible may claim authority has to be justified. The justification is that science is concerned with God's general revelation.

SCRIPTURE ON GENERAL REVELATION

There are a number of Biblical passages which refer to the revelation of God through the things he has made. We note in particular Psalm 19:1–6; Romans 1:18–20; Acts 14:15–17. According to these passages the creation can teach us God's glory and his handiwork (Ps. 19:1), his eternal power and deity (Rom. 1:20), and his goodness to his creatures (Acts 14:17). The obvious, yet overlooked, thing in all these passages is that general revelation is a revelation of *God*. What is popularly called science makes very little if any reference to God. The whole tendency of its development has been to exclude God more and more.

Where there has been some realization of what the Bible actually says about the revelation through the creation, the claims for science have often been somewhat modified. It will not be claimed that the findings of science are synonymous with general revelation. Sometimes all that is said is that science studies God's general revelation. It is claimed that, as the study of general revelation, it should be granted as much respect as theology which studies God's special revelation.

Formally this may be correct, but if it is, there is a consequence which should follow. The first and most basic conclusion of science should be the character of the God who made the world. For we have seen that according to the Bible the character of the God who made and rules the world is what the creation reveals. To avoid the inconvenient fact that science, as we know it, largely ignores God, there are various excuses. The most common is to say that science is concerned with how the cosmos operates, not with how it began or why it

[16]

operates as it does. These various approaches will be looked at in more detail later. For the moment we are concerned with the basic fact. Suppose we had a theology which missed a basic point of the Bible; a theology which, for example, ignored the fact that God 'is and that He is a rewarder of those who seek Him' (Heb. 11:6); would we think that theology a valid study of God's special revelation? Of course we would not! How can a science that ignores the existence and attributes of the creator God be called a valid study of God's general revelation?

In asking this question I realize that there are those who would defend a task for science which ignores God. That is not my immediate concern. My concern here is those who want to make science an authority for Christians on the ground that it is studying God's general revelation. Since science, as we know it today, misses the main point of God's revelation through the creation, it could hardly be said that it should be regarded as an authority by a Christian.

This leaves open the possibility that there could be a very different science which would not ignore the revelation of God himself through his creation. What could that science be expected to learn from the creation? We have already seen the things about God which it might be expected to learn. Compared with all that the Bible teaches, it offers very little information. Many people have wanted to solve controversial questions like the nature of creation, the causes of homosexuality, etc., from a study of creation rather than from the Bible. Clearly they expect to learn something very certain and definite other than the nature of God. What right have they to expect more definite answers to such questions from a study of creation rather than from the Bible?

The passages which actually deal with revelation through the creation give no encouragement to that hope. In itself that is rather an argument from silence and has no great weight. However, it is interesting and instructive to see what those passages are teaching.

Psalm 19 is the most interesting of them, for it deals successively with what is taught by the creation and what is taught by the revealed law of God. The creation is described as being able, even without words, to reveal the glory of God through the things he has made. This revelation is made, not to

Israel only, but throughout the earth. From there the psalm goes on to talk of the sun. In the second part, on the law of God, we are told that it is the commandments which teach, guide, and protect the believer from error. The claims for what may be learned through the law of God are much more varied, detailed, and comprehensive than the claims made for the revelation through creation.

What rôle does the mention of the sun play in the earlier part of the psalm? I think that a comparison is being made. The sun performs its function as light-giver without wavering or disobedience. It acts as someone does who finds joy and enthusiasm in obedience. In a similar way the psalmist finds the written Word of God a joy 'rejoicing the heart'. Thus both sun and believer act as willing and obedient servants to God. I am inclined to this interpretation by the fact that the same thought appears in Psalm 119:89–96. Here it is explicitly said that the heavens and the earth are established according to God's commandments. All things are established according to God's commandments, for all things are servants to God. Immediately following this, the writer identifies himself as a servant of God who is preserved by God's law.

The thought that emerges from these two psalms is that all creation is under God's law. The believer finds the path of obedience in God's written law, the heavenly bodies find it in God's commands to them. Notice then that these passages which are often pointed out as passages teaching general revelation, emphasise the importance of God's word for the believer. They do not teach the believer to look to the creation and away from the revelation of God in his word. Rather we should see the obedience of the creation to its glorious Lord and also submit ourselves to the commands of that Lord.

The two main New Testament passages dealing with God's general revelation, Romans 1:18–32 and Acts 14:15–17, are largely concerned with the rejection by man of that revelation. Men have not received, embraced and acted upon that revelation. The first thing they would have done had they received it would have been to turn from the work of their own hands and to worship and serve the Creator. Like the psalmists, Paul's main point is not to direct men to a scientific study of natural phenomena. His concern is to direct them to the truth

[18]

that God has revealed in a different way (Rom. 3:21,22; Acts 14:15).

Thus, the passages on general revelation must be rudely wrenched from their contexts to be made a basis for an appeal to human science as an authority. In context they show the importance of God's special revelation to man.

THE AUTHORITY OF APPEALS TO THE CREATION

In addition to this we have in the New Testament an extended treatment of the question of authority. Paul in his letter to the Colossians speaks directly to this point. Paul's argument is quite simple. All was made by Christ (Col. 1:15–17). Hence we should turn to Christ as our authority (Col. 2:1–23). Revelation through such other mediums as angels, visions (2:18), philosophy and tradition (2:8) are rejected. The authoritative source is Christ. How does the authoritative Word of Christ come to the Colossians? – through their Christian instruction (2:6,7)! The whole point of what Paul is saying is to prevent their allegiance to false teachings, and to secure their allegiance to the apostolic teaching.

Some may object that an argument against first century false teachers is hardly relevant to modern debates over science. But look at what Paul actually says and the structure of his argument. Paul's opponents had access to information which in some sense came from creation. They appealed to philosophy (2:8) and probably to visions mediated through angels (cf. 2:18 with Heb. 1, which seems directed to the same heresy). They may even have gone further in their appeals to creation. We are not sure of the technical meaning of the phrase translated 'elementary principles of the world' in Colossians 2:8. Since these principles are said to be 'of the world' (or 'cosmos') they probably have some reference to principles people claim to deduce from the cosmos, or to see in the cosmos. Over against this information derived from the creation or parts of it, Paul sets the One who made the whole world, and indeed all worlds.

Paul does not accept their deductions from creation as correct. In passing he refers to them as 'empty deception'. However, his argument does not take the form of arguing that there is a better philosophy or a better deduction from man's experience, or better angelic revelations. He does not need to do so. His appeal to Christ as the source of all wisdom (2:3) makes trivial the wisdom man has sought to derive from the world.

How are men brought into contact with that wisdom? It is through the apostolic teaching. Once again Scripture, when it considers the matter, directs us to special revelation.

It would be quite simple to construct an argument similar to Paul's to deal with a modern debate. Suppose the musings of a certain group of people upon created phenomena lead to a conclusion at variance with Scripture. It is claimed that these conclusions derive from a study of God's world and therefore have authority. The counter-argument is an appeal, not to human musings on a part of creation, but to the wisdom of the One who made the whole creation as that wisdom is revealed in Scripture. Certainly somebody may object that the wisdom of Christ the Creator was not revealed to the apostles. However, that is another argument. He is not then finding ground in Scripture for an appeal to creation's general revelation. He is directly contradicting what Scripture says.

Thus an argument identical in form to Paul's argument can be made against any appeal to creation in opposition to Scripture. Some would seek to blunt such an argument by the claim that the Bible cannot have relevance to matters that are loosely called 'science'. However such an argument would tell just as well against Paul as against any argument built upon Paul's model. Paul was arguing against a philosophical point of view which made some sort of appeal to 'the elementary principles of the world' (2:8). The 'science' that Paul combated was certainly different from modern 'science'. Yet what is at issue is not the form of the 'science' or 'philosophy', because Paul does not attempt a point-for-point refutation. What is at issue is the right to appeal to the fuller wisdom of Christ against any human wisdom based upon man's contact with the creation. If we cannot appeal to God's special revelation to refute philosophies about creation, then Paul was wrong in his appeal to the special revelation of Christ.

The same point can be made another way. Paul, confronted by a philosophy which claimed in some sense to derive information from the cosmos, shows no awareness of the fact that Scripture cannot speak on such subjects.

Some will object to the use I have made of Colossians on another ground. They will say that the issue at Colossae was merely a matter of Jewish food laws and calendrical questions. The issue is one of the relation of the Old Testament ceremonial law to believers. Hence it is quite irrelevant to the question of the Bible and science.

However, that ignores what Paul says and the whole force of his argument. In Galatians, Paul argues the relation of the old and new covenants. The writer to the Hebrews, dealing with a very similar problem, deals with it largely in terms of the old and new covenants, though the created nature of angels is also stressed (Heb. 1:7). Colossians is not Galatians or Hebrews. In Colossians the argument is about wisdom and its source. The reason for the difference is obvious from the letter itself. The heretical teaching endangering the Colossians not only appealed to the Old Testament or the tradition of the elders. It appealed also to philosophy and the 'elementary principles of the world'. Just what form this appeal took we may not know. However, that gives us no excuse for banning everything distinctive in the argument of Colossians and reading it as though it were Galatians.

We shall see as we proceed that it is very difficult to keep the 'scientific' and 'religious' realms apart. One reason for this difficulty is that people try to support religious positions by appeal to other authorities. Science, philosophy, tradition, or 'common sense' may be appealed to in varying degrees, depending on what is held to be authoritative in that particular community. This appeal to another source of proof for a position is not just a phenomenon of our day. New Testament Judaism was also being influenced by the secular wisdom of its day. It would be surprising if that were not so. The significant thing is Paul's reaction when faced with the appeal to secular wisdom. He did not try to separate 'religion' from the domain whence philosophy drew its 'wisdom'. Rather he asserted the superiority of Christ over that domain. And he asserted that the wisdom of Christ is known via revelation. Hence it makes no difference if 'religious' questions like food taboos and calendrical questions were involved. Paul's argument still breaches the wall that some would try to erect between religious and secular questions.

[21]

There are some who would argue that, since Paul links 'philosophy' and 'empty deception' (2:8), he was only attacking philosophies that could be described as 'empty deception'. That means that other philosophies, including natural philosophy (or 'science' as it is more commonly called now) are not necessarily included. Hence one could argue that the right sort of human reasonings on creation do have authority for us. This argument can come in various forms. It can take the form of a blatant defence of philosophy even when it contradicts Scripture. Or it can be more subtle, seeking to re-interpret away any Scripture passage that might contradict a cherished philosophical or scientific 'truth'. It can be coupled with the argument mentioned earlier that science brings us to understand God's laws.

Paul was not addressing the general question of philosophy as a discipline. One could just as well argue that his coupling of philosophy and empty deception shows his opinion of all philosophy. I think the argument between these two possibilities would be unproductive and inconclusive because Colossians was not primarily interested in the varieties of philosophy. It was primarily concerned with the superiority of Christ over all these varieties.

Rather let us consider the more substantial issue. Have we any reason to believe that man can know the laws by which God rules the world? The Bible teaches clearly and emphatically that we do not know them. That is the main thrust of God's answer to Job.

MAN'S KNOWLEDGE OF GOD'S COMMANDS

Job's misfortunes were not his only concern. He had problems with God's government of the world. In questioning God's government he was forgetting his place as a creature. God's answer reminds Job that he is not God. It is not Job who rules and commands the universe.

In the course of an interrogation aimed at bringing home to Job that he is not God, God asks (in Job 38):

38:31 'Can you bind the chains of the Pleiades,
or loose the cords of Orion?

32 Can you lead forth a constellation in its season,
  Or guide the Bear with her satellite?
33 Do you know the ordinances of the heavens,
  Or fix their rule over the earth?
34 Can you lift up your voice to the clouds,
  So that an abundance of water may cover you?
35 Can you send forth lightnings that they may go
  And say to you, "Here we are"?'

Clearly, all these questions demand the answer 'No'! Especially
significant is the question of verse 33, 'Do you know the
ordinances of the heavens?' Since 'ordinance' occurs throughout the Old Testament as a synonym of 'law', we have here a
reference to the law of God which governs the heavens. God
points out that Job does not know these things. It is also
important to see what is parallel to knowing the ordinances of
the heavens. It is fixing their rule over the earth.

Verse 34 makes this point somewhat clearer. If one knows
the commands that God addresses to the clouds, then one could
address those same commands to the clouds. One could
command the clouds to rain and they would have to obey.
Hence to know the command which God addresses to the
creation is to have the power of God to command the creation.
Knowledge and power are closely connected throughout God's
speech to Job.

Does man therefore know the law of God by which he rules
the non-human world? There is a simple way to answer that
question. Who but God can command the clouds to rain? If we
cannot command the creation as God does, then we do not
know his law.

Some will object to basing an argument upon this passage.
They will say that this is a poetic passage. It certainly is, but
does that mean that it cannot say what it clearly says? Is the
Lord not our shepherd because Psalm 23 is poetry? Poetry still
says something!

Let us suppose that God did not mean to deny to Job the
understanding and power of God. Suppose that is just the
meaning we got because we wrongly read poetry literally. Then
what does God say to Job? We can imagine all sorts of things he
might have said, but we cannot get them out of the actual
words. The words, poetry or no poetry, speak very clearly.

Further, let the man who wants to dismiss this passage in order to claim that he knows the law of the universe, answer God's question. Do you command the clouds? Does the lightning obey your voice? If not, then you cannot claim to know the law of God.

This passage is relevant to the view mentioned earlier, that the study of creation teaches us God's laws. Do what the modern scientist formulates as 'laws' correspond to the laws of God by which God commands the creation? A way of answering that question is provided by God's answer to Job. Try saying $E = MC^2$ and see if anything happens! In other words, knowledge of God's command gives power because that command is a powerful command that the creature must obey. If the knowledge of and the speaking of our scientific 'laws' do not produce obedience in the creation, then we cannot say we know God's law.

There is another reason why we should not dismiss God's answer to Job as mere 'poetry'. That is because its perspective is quite in agreement with the rest of Scripture. Failure to understand what Scripture says about the relation of God to his creation will not only affect our understanding of general revelation. It will also distort our understanding of Scripture.

Before we take up that point, the connection between what has been said in this chapter and the previous chapter needs to be made clear. The previous chapter dealt with the 'textbook' expectation. That is, that an authoritative source would have to be exhaustive in its knowledge and detail. In this chapter we see God criticizing Job. God asks whether Job's knowledge is exhaustive and comprehensive. That makes us look again at the expectation that an authoritative source must be all-comprehending. Can human knowledge ever be so comprehensive? Is it Scripture that tells us that we must expect universal knowledge in an authoritative book? It certainly is not! That expectation comes when man tries to replace God's wisdom with man's own wisdom as the measure of all things. A consequence is that man's wisdom has to be like God's wisdom, complete and comprehensive. Human wisdom will never meet the requirement because man is not God, as God reminded Job. Hence incompleteness and lack of exhaustive detail cannot be used to rule out the Bible as an authoritative source. Accordingly the Bible is not ruled out as an authority in matters such as science or history by its lack of completeness. The 'not-a-textbook-of-science' argument against the Bible sets up a false model of authority.

Ꮼ 4 Ꮼ

Providence and Scripture

Psalm 119:90b,91 says:

Thou didst establish the earth, and it stands.
They stand this day according to Thine ordinances,
For all things are Thy servants.

The earth stands firm because God commanded it, and still commands it to do so. The relationship between God and the earth is thus a covenant relationship. It is between the Lord who issues commands and the servant who obeys. This same idea is found elsewhere in Scripture. Jeremiah 31:35,36 speaks also of the covenant relationship between God and the sun, moon and stars. The light provided by the heavenly bodies is certain because they obey the ordinances of God. This same certainty of the covenant relationship between God and the creation is stressed in Jeremiah 33:19–21.

Thus the picture in Job of the creation as the covenant servant of God, obeying his commands, is not just restricted to that book. It is the uniform picture of Scripture. It is important to note that according to Jeremiah 33:20 and 31:36 this covenant relationship produces stability. God's covenant ordinances cannot be broken.

Thus there is stability and regularity in the creation because God's commands maintain that stability and regularity. Our whole culture is very much influenced by the belief that the stability and regularity reside in the creation itself. The universe is thought to operate according to 'laws' which are built into the structure of creation and are thus unchangeable. There is something of the mentality of idolatry about this point of view. It places in the creation what properly belongs to the

[26]

Creator.

The difference between the Biblical view and the common non-Christian view can be very simply illustrated. Suppose a soldier were marching to and fro on sentry duty. The point at which he turned and marched back was determined by his commanding officer. Whether the commanding officer gave him a command at the beginning of his watch or gave him commands on every beat makes no difference for the purpose of the illustration. The regularity of the sentry's beat and his turning points are determined by the command of his officer. Suppose somebody were to watch the soldier and ignore the commanding officer. He could then say that there is a 'law' inherent in the soldier that he will march so many paces and then turn. Which is the real law governing that soldier? Is it the command of the officer or the description of his march given by the observer? Following God's question to Job in 38:34 we can answer that question very easily. If the commander says, 'about turn', then the soldier will turn. If the observer says, 'He marches twenty paces and then turns', it will not make the soldier turn.

The regularity of creation, its conformity to 'law', is not inherent in creation. It comes from its Lord whose command brought it into being and whose command maintains its regularity. As long as the commander is ordering his servants to do what they have always done, it may not seem to make much difference whether the order is inherent in creation or is maintained by God's commands. However, there is a point where it makes a great difference. That is when God, as a sign of his power and authority, gives an unusual command. Generally we call these miracles.

Where the belief in a law inherent in creation itself has spread, there has been opposition to the idea of miracle, or of any divine influence upon the creation. Creation becomes a law unto itself and God is resisted as an intruder.

THE INFLUENCE OF DEISM

In the 'Christianized' version of this philosophy, God is made the originator of the law-bound creation. Once he has done that, he has no more function. To act on or speak to creation would be to break his 'own' laws. This notion, commonly called Deism, is one of the most pervasive influences in the modern Western church. The personal, active, speaking God is rejected and in his place is substituted a logical first cause.

Sadly, many Christians have tried to meet this challenge by conceding the truth of the Deist picture in some sciences but rejecting it in others. Thus they might concede that the non-Christian astronomer knows the laws of God for the solar system but try to reserve a rôle for God in biology. Or they concede biology but try to make the conversion experience a psychological miracle immune to secular psychological explanation. Hence arises what has been called the 'God of the gaps' mentality where God was reserved to be an explanation of those areas not yet reduced to 'scientific' explanation. Of course the gaps became less because more and more order was found in creation.

Once one area of creation is seen as autonomous, with its laws inherent in itself, then the battle has been lost. For the personal, commanding, speaking Lord of the universe has been rejected. That there is order and regularity in creation is no problem for the Christian. That order should be found in more and more areas is no problem. What is a problem is the unwarranted assumption that the order resides in creation itself.

The personal God commands regularity. However, there will be a time, as there has been in the past, when his commands will be different. Peter deals in 2 Peter 3:1–13 with those who argue against any intervention by God in history. They argue for unchanging processes in creation: 'all continues just as it was from the beginning of creation' (3:4). Peter points out that their belief is refuted by one obvious fact: the flood. Similarly there will be a day when God will command destruction in another way – by fire.

The Deist world-view has problems besides 'miracles'. It has problems with any activity of God in relation to creation; any speaking of God that is different from the more usual commands which he gives to creation. Historically this has created two particular problems, besides an embarrassment with Biblical miracles. They are with conversion and the inspiration of Scripture. Orthodox Christian doctrine affirms that with both of these the Holy Spirit exerts an influence upon the humans involved (see John 3:3–8; Eph. 2:1–7; 2 Peter 1:20,21). The Deist's god cannot do that. All he can do is start processes in action at the very beginning and then stand back and watch the consequences of those processes. Hence conversion or regeneration must be seen by the Deist as an outworking of normal psychological processes similar to those that produce any other change of mind. The writing of Scripture cannot be different from the processes involved in the writing of any other book.

Note that the crucial question is not whether human agents are involved in either case. The crucial question is whether those agents come under an influence from God. The crucial question is whether God acts and whether there is a result in the creation. It is whether the God who once brought creation into being by the Word of his mouth, can still speak to creation and produce results by that speaking.

One of the consequences of what has been considered here is that there is a connection between the doctrine of providence and that of Scripture. There are also connections between our understanding of conversion or the last things and our understanding of Scripture. Denial of the ability of God to act or speak with respect to creation means that miracles, inspiration, regeneration, providence, all have to be understood in a different way.

It also means that God becomes a distant God. He is significant only for creation. Such a God cannot answer prayer. In other words, Deism produces a religion in which there is little personal fervour because its god is a force or a logical starting point. It is not the personal acting and speaking God of Scripture.

Whenever people who adopt a Deist perspective claim that Scripture is a work of man not distinguishable in origin from other human literary productions, they do not merely influence our understanding of Scripture, but ultimately change the whole shape of our religion.

There is order, regularity, and continuity in history, yet also change and newness because God's command controls all. A proper understanding of this subject is essential not only for our understanding of providence, but also to enable us to understand the progressive way in which God has revealed himself throughout history.

[29]

Ꮬ 5 Ꮬ

The Bible and Technical Precision

So far we have looked at some of the assumptions often made in discussions about the Bible, and in particular at the expectation that 'textbooks' alone, as authoritative works, show a particular standard of authority. Exhaustive detail, it is claimed, is to be looked for in an authoritative work. The problem is that only God has such exhaustive knowledge. When man sets out to replace God, he has to pretend to have some of the attributes of God. Omniscience is one of those attributes. Once people start thinking in this way, then they will set that standard up as their test of an authoritative book. The Bible obviously does not pass that test.

As people are inclined to expect scientific works, particularly, to have these characteristics, they use this argument mostly to exclude the Bible as an authority in science. However, as we have seen, the same argument could be used against making the Bible an authority in any area. We have also seen that the Bible regards the apostolic revelation as having greater authority than any wisdom derived from the creation. That is because the apostolic revelation comes directly from Christ, the source of all wisdom. Everybody knows that a piece of wood can be burned to yield light. What is the source of the energy in the wood that can be turned into light? Its ultimate source is the light of the sun. However one would not replace the sun as a light source by the wood, simply because the energy stored up in wood comes ultimately from the sun. It is just as foolish to try to replace Christ, the source of creation and wisdom, by human wisdom derived from the creation. That is the argument Paul develops against making human philosophy our authority.

[30]

Now we need to spell out the consequences of the points that have already been argued. When exhaustive knowledge is made the standard of truth, that is understood as being not only exhaustive in terms of extent but in terms of detail. Very technical, precise, detailed descriptions are seen as being more 'true' than general descriptions. This way of thinking is encouraged by the idea that detailed statements of the 'laws' of science allow an insight into the mind of God. Hence the mathematical, technical descriptions are felt to be 'true' in a way in which ordinary language is not true.

This attitude is partly connected with the hope that the more precise, detailed, and mathematical study of the world will reveal the final 'law' which will make the processes of the world fully comprehensible to man. Man would then know as God knows, and be able to command the creation as God does. This hope has not been realized. We have found that on whatever microscopic or macroscopic scale we investigate the creation, there is order and there is also mystery. In that sense a precise scientific description may be a relatively accurate description. But it is not the final description. And one can say the very same thing about descriptions couched in ordinary language. They are true as far as they go, but they do not say everything.

The claim for a special priority, a special claim for trust-worthiness, to be accorded to precise technical language really rested on the belief that it approached closer to an ultimate statement, that is, to a statement which would explain, or potentially explain, everything. If such a statement is possible only for God, then the situation is considerably changed. Precise technical statements are functionally useful in certain situations. But, of course, statements couched in ordinary language are also functionally useful. Neither, then, has special status.

THE BIBLE AND ORDINARY LANGUAGE

How does all this relate to the Bible? The Bible is written in ordinary language. It does use technical or specialized vocabulary in sundry places but on the whole it is written in ordinary language. Going back at least to Philo in the first century AD, those who have wanted to make Scripture subservient to a non-Christian philosophy have seized upon this fact. They have argued that the real, deeper truth is in their technical and erudite philosophy. The Bible, being written in the language of ordinary people, cannot have an authority superior to that of philosophy. It is rather a lesser truth, written in ordinary style as a condescension to the unphilosophical. Today it is claimed that science has replaced philosophy as the ultimate truth, but the argument is the same.

We have seen how Paul refutes the claim of philosophy to priority over Christ's revelation to his apostles. The same argument would also refute any claim that science is more true than Christ's revelation to the apostles. Knowing this, we can now reach the same point as has been argued in another way. Paul argues in Colossians that the apostolic revelation, not philosophy, is the authority. We know that revelation is in ordinary language because we have it in our Bibles. Here is a case where ordinary language has greater claim to wisdom than esoteric, technical language. That is not to say it is wrong to use technical language. It is a question of authority. The general assumption is that philosophy or science, being more precise, detailed, or jargon-filled, must have greater authority. Scripture itself rejects that assumption. We have already seen why it is that an authoritative work can be in ordinary language. There is no final key to the secret of the universe whose possession will make man like God. Scientific or philosophical language is not closer to the ultimate truth simply because of detail, precision and jargon.

This means that the Bible can generalize, can use approximation, and at times fail to specify detail. Yet it is still authoritative.

∾ 6 ∾

Imprecision and Error

It is obvious that the Bible uses approximations. Sometimes these have been used as proof of the fallibility of the Bible. An example would be the dimensions of the laver in Solomon's Temple. These are given as a diameter of 10 cubits and a circumference of 30 cubits (1 Kings 7:23). Obviously this involves an approximation of 3 for π. This has been used as evidence for error in the Bible.

Since π is an infinite non-repeating decimal any figure given is technically in error. What we see here is simply the fact that the Bible, as already said, is not written in terms of precise technical language. If it were so, the whole of the Bible would be taken up in giving the 'correct' dimensions of the laver. God has chosen to reveal himself in ordinary language. Hence it is ordinary language which has privileged status.

Granting privileged status to ordinary language will not please those who have sought to boost their own status by the use of a complex jargon. Yet God chose to reveal himself in ordinary language. Technical disciplines are still possible but they are under the authority of a revelation in ordinary language, not vice versa. By not becoming lost in technical detail the Bible can be a general authority. As the example of the laver shows, a work that depends for authority on completeness and 'accuracy' of detail would never finish giving the details about just one thing. To judge the Bible because it does not come up to that standard is self-defeating. No human can come up to such a standard.

Another frequently cited example of error is Matthew 27:9. Here a quotation from the prophet Zechariah is said to come from Jeremiah. Of course we could always explain it away as a

[33]

copyist's error but a much more likely explanation exists. We have a number of indications of a tendency within Judaism to regard Jeremiah as the first work of the prophetic corpus, not Isaiah as in modern printed Bibles. We have abundant evidence of the tendency to name a corpus of works after the first work in the group. Hence 'the prophet Jeremiah' may have been simply a way of saying 'in the prophetic books'.

Let us grant this explanation just for the sake of the argument. It is, of course, a departure from precision to call a group of books after the first book in the group. It is the sort of departure from precision common to language. Yet, for those who know the language and its usages it is quite unambiguous.

Is Matthew 27:9 an instance of error? The answer is completely a matter of definition. If you insist on a certain sort of precision, it is erroneous. However, such precision cannot be insisted upon once we grant that God chose to use ordinary language. The so-called 'error' is really not in this particular instance. It is in God's choice of the language to use. Then we are back with the whole point of whether technical language has privileged status over all other language.

Another example of the same sort of problem is found in Leviticus 11:2–6. Several animals are said to chew the cud but not divide the hoof. They include the rock hyrax and the rabbit. (Perhaps the hare is meant rather than the rabbit, but it does not matter greatly in this discussion.) Both would today not be classified as ruminants and hence would be deemed not to chew the cud. Perhaps the solution lies in a problem of translation, and the animals concerned are not the rock hyrax and the rabbit. However that does not appear a likely solution. Perhaps there is a reference to the rabbit's passing of partly-digested faeces which are re-ingested. However this seems a rather extreme way out of the difficulty. For the sake of the argument let us ignore these proposed solutions to the problem.

It has been frequently pointed out that these animals make movements of the mouth that look like chewing the cud. Hence the suggestion that herein lies the explanation of the Biblical statement. Once again we will take this as being the explanation.

How then do we interpret what we have discovered? Some people see it as evidence of error in the Bible on a scientific matter and hence proof that the Bible is not to be made an authority on such matters. Others, in reaction to that possibility, would reject what has been suggested here as the most likely possibility. (They may be right in this case but there would be other similar problems in other passages.) Some would see it as an error, but to be excused because of the Bible's resort to popular language.

As there is what many would call an 'error' this case may seem different from those previously considered. Is it really so? Does it not come down to the way one chooses to classify animals? Our classification systems are very much based upon what dissection reveals to be the structure. Perhaps another Biblical example will make this clearer. In 1 Kings 4:33 Solomon is said to have spoken of trees, 'from the cedar that is in Lebanon even to the hyssop that grows on the wall'. This has been used as evidence that the Hebrews followed the 'primitive' system of botanical classification according to size, whereas the modern botanist uses a 'scientific' system largely based on the structure of the flower. Of course, the attempt to deduce the Hebrew botanical classification system from this passage is absurd, but once more for the sake of the argument, let us accept it. The issue then becomes: plants can be classified according to size or plants can be classified according to flower shape. Both ways yield a system which has some order and some anomalies that will not fit neatly into our boxes. In other words, both systems are dealing with an ordered creation which yet has more diversity than our rigid classifications. Why is one system of classification deemed 'primitive' and the other 'scientific'? There is a long and a short answer. The long answer which takes us back through Greek philosophy's influence on the early botanists would probably embarrass the modern 'scientific' botanist. The short answer is all that is needed for our purposes. One system classifies plants according to their obvious external appearance. Another does so by dissecting their flowers. We are conditioned to think that one reveals a more real and basic system than the other. Classification by dissection has priority over classification by appearance.

Yet we must ask whether our assumptions are necessarily correct. If classification by flower-structure yielded the rationalist's dream of a complete, consistent, and elegant scheme we might give it priority. The botanist is well aware that it does not. It is another case of a functional system which is not the final system.

Much the same applies in the case of the 'cud-chewing' animals. Does one classify them according to appearance or does one classify them by cutting the animal open to reveal anatomical structure? Both systems are functionally useful.

Note clearly, that I have not said that calling these animals cud-chewers is a concession to the unphilosophical and un-scientific. Rather I have questioned the idea that there is only one basis on which you can put animals amongst the cud-chewers.

All the things I have considered in this chapter have seen frequent service as proofs of 'error' in the Bible. That use betrays a rationalist mentality which demands a standard of exactness and precision which the Bible fails to meet. That then becomes proof of error, or with some, proof that the Bible has no relevance in scientific, scholarly matters. There is, of course, another way one could view the Bible's failure to 'pass' the test. It could be proof not of a problem in the Bible but of a problem in the test.

What does a person really say when he objects to the Bible because it fails such a rationalist test? He really says that he refuses to consider the possibility of the Bible being an authority. He refuses because he already has an authority in a rationalist sort of precision. The conflict between the two authorities did not lead him to debate which was right. It led him to reject the Bible in terms of the authority to which he already clings.

∞ 7 ∞

The History of Revelation

In recent discussions about the Bible, a major consideration has been whether certain of its teachings reflect ideas or customs of the times in which it was written. Such teaching would be relevant for that time but not for our time. Examples suggested would be the use of Near Eastern myths in the story of creation, or the supposed conformity to popular views of the role of women in the New Testament.

Such suggestions of material in Scripture no longer relevant for our times gain plausibility from the fact that already in Scripture some material is considered no longer binding. The New Testament sets aside many Old Testamaent ordinances. Cannot we do the same, not only with the Old Testament, but also with the New Testament?

Carried to its logical conclusion such an approach could leave us without any authoritative Scripture. At the most, Scripture becomes an example of the way people have tried to interpret their circumstances religiously. None of their interpretations have authority for us. All that is relevant for us is an example of an attempt.

Often we do not face such consistent applications of the idea. What we face is a selective use of the idea. Passages of Scripture which contradict the 'wisdom' of our age, as for example the accounts of creation, are dismissed in this way. Similarly teachings, such as those on sex and marriage which are not in vogue today, are regarded as relevant to their own times only.

This rather arbitrary selection of the material to be treated as 'out-dated' would not impress the impartial observer. Clearly, respectability in the eyes of the world is more important here than any principle. However, we must ask a question: are there

[37]

any principles we can learn from Scripture as to when an ordinance or a teaching should be considered no longer binding?

It is clear that time itself does not render commands obsolete. When the Pharisees quote an ordinance of Moses regulating the abuse of divorce, Jesus appeals to the original creation order (Matt. 19:3–8). If time were the sole issue, the situation in Moses' time, being closer to New Testament times, should have greater authority than the original order. Clearly, in the view of Jesus, it does not.

Similarly Jesus criticizes the Pharisees for setting aside commandments (Mark 7:8–13). It is not simply assumed that a commandment addressed to a former age has lost its validity.

THE HISTORY OF REDEMPTION

Yet there *are* commands set aside in Scripture. Under what circumstances does this happen? The first, and in many ways most instructive, example is found in Deuteronomy 12:20–22. In Leviticus 17:3–6 it was commanded that any animal killed for food had to be brought to the tabernacle and offered as a peace offering. When Israel took possession of Canaan some of them would be too far from the central sanctuary to do this. Hence the command is changed. However, note carefully the circumstances which lead to a change in the command: 'When the Lord your God extends your border as He has promised you' (Deut. 12:20). It is God's fulfilment of his promise that brings Israel into a new situation where a new law applies. Similarly the law change in the New Testament age is linked to God's fulfilling of his promises in sending the Messiah.

We should note, however, that this new situation does not involve the change of all laws. When Israel entered Canaan only this one law was changed. Clearly the change of situation did not affect the other laws. The prophets pointed out that it was disobedience to the law of Sinai which brought the judgment of God on Israel.

Similarly, while the coming of Christ brought a much greater change in law, yet it did not involve a complete sweeping away of the old law. Hence Paul can quote Sinaitic law as still valid for the Christian community (Eph. 6:1–3; Rom. 13:8–10). The connecting of these commandments with love by Paul does not invalidate them but rather affirms them, because to break them is to go against love. Clearly with respect to many of the commandments the situation has not been changed.

In all these changes of commandments it is not change in ideas, or change in contemporary standards, that leads to a change of law. It is God's action as he, in fulfilment of his promises, brings his people into a new situation. God alone changes law. 'There is only one Lawgiver and Judge, the One who is able to save and to destroy' (James 4:12).

In many of the cases where the argument is presented that Biblical commands simply represent the ideas of Biblical times, the argument itself is false. The Biblical standards were unpopular then as well as now. All that has changed is that certain elements of the church are unwilling to take an unpopular position. However, let us for the sake of the argument assume that in all these cases there has been a change in customs or ideas since Biblical times.

The reasons for change in the law that we see in the Bible lie in changes in the history of redemption. It is God alone who brings changes in this history. The power to redeem and the right to change law lie together. Change in customs and ideas in the general community, while under the general providential oversight of God, involve the actions of man. The general history of culture is not to be confused with the history of redemption. However, when it is said that changes in culture can change law, then the history of human culture is confused with the history of redemption. Man is given a prerogative that belongs to God alone.

The logic of this confusion will work its way through the whole theological system. It leads to the conclusion that changes in human culture are redemptive. And that is an idea we have already encountered. It is affirmed by many that if man is given the freedom to live without law, especially laws in the sexual and marital domain, this will solve many, if not all, of his personal and psychological problems. Once again redemption from the human problem and law-change are being connected. Even the unbeliever cannot escape the use of Biblical theological structures and connections. Similarly, the belief that advances in science and technology will solve all mankind's problems is closely connected with the idea that these discoveries have rendered obsolete the Biblical world-view.

Of course, people who are arguing that this or that Biblical command or teaching is merely the product of its time do not see all the implications of what they are saying. Their concern is merely to avoid an issue in which the world condemns the Biblical teaching as foolish. Nevertheless they also cannot escape the logic of the connection between redemption and law-giving. The more they give to man the power to alter the laws and teaching which God has given, the more they will grant that man has the power to redeem himself. Ultimately the gospel is at issue.

Ꮼ 8 Ꮼ

The Perfect Translation

We have seen that when man tries to place himself in the
position of God, he has to aim at complete and perfect
knowledge in all areas. Thus we have a rationalism in which
man sets up exhaustiveness as his standard of truth. If the truth
is not given in exhaustive detail it is declared not to be the truth.
But if the rationalist were to apply this test to his own statement
he would himself fail. Yet rationalistic tests are commonly
directed only at 'enemies', particularly at Christians.

We will meet many examples of this sort of thinking as we go
along. For the moment we are concerned with the claim that it
is impossible to have a perfect and completely accurate knowledge of what the Bible says.

There are many forms in which this attack can come. It is
sometimes argued that we do not have a completely accurate
knowledge of Scripture because there may have been errors
made by copyists. Or it can be argued we make use of Scripture
in translation, and that no translation can possess the exact
force of the original. Or perhaps it is argued that it is impossible
to know exactly what an author had in mind. Any interpretation involves uncertainty.

From this it is then argued that the whole idea of an
authoritative Scripture has been undermined. Yet this whole
argument is built on the premise we have already examined,
that is, that no approximation, no matter how small, can be
correct or have authority. The only alternatives are absolute
precision or no authority whatsoever.

Actually, this view is easily refuted if the authority of Jesus or
of the apostles is taken seriously. For they used translations of
Scripture, quoting it in Aramaic (Matt. 27:46) or Greek (Acts,

passim). The whole argument against the possibility of an authoritative Scripture is an argument against Jesus. He used Scripture as an authority. But he used a translation. Already by his time there were differences in the manuscripts of the Old Testament and the argument that one cannot perfectly understand an author would apply against him as much as against us.

The reality is that the convicting, converting, and sanctifying truth of Scripture comes through in spite of human errors in copying, translating, and even in spite of misconceptions. That in itself is proof that Scripture is not a rationalist truth which depends on total precision.

᠗ 9 ᠗

Words and Meanings

Taken to an extreme, the argument of the previous chapter might be thought to make the actual words of Scripture irrelevant. If the truth comes through, in spite of the mangling of sundry words by copyists and translators, are the words really important?

A similar question is raised by attempts to find a basic intent behind certain Scriptural teachings which may not be expressed in the words or even run counter to the words. I refer here not to the difference between literal meaning and actual meaning in parables or literary figures. I mean the attempt to discern an intention behind the passage that does not find adequate expression in the words used.

We have seen that Jesus and the apostles used translations. Yet they also made frequent appeal to the very words of Scripture and built arguments upon the actual wording. While appealing on occasion to the very words of Scripture, Jesus could also, on occasion, be very critical of the Pharisees for missing the overall message of the Scripture.

The appeal to the actual words is not set against the appeal to the fundamental meaning or intent. How do we explain the appeal of both to overall meaning and specific words? How do we explain appeal to specific words and phrases by people who are happy to use translations and to paraphrase?

It is common in non-Christian thought to see here incompatible alternatives. We encountered in the previous chapters some of the reasons for this, including the belief that truth can be found only in absolute precision and exhaustive detail. There is also a non-Christian reaction to this rationalist view. The irrationalist will often deny that truth can be expressed in words at all. When this idea influences Christians, then we have the notion that the real truth of Scripture is something which lies behind the words and may be so different from the words that it is actually contrary to what the words say. There is a glaring contradiction here. If the Bible writers were unable to put this truth into words, and their words obscure it, how is it that the irrationalist is able to put it into words? Really the irrationalist denies his own principles once he attempts to say what this truth is.

Clearly Jesus was not an irrationalist or a rationalist. Instead of approaching Scripture with these assumptions let us rather try to understand his approach to Scripture.

JESUS' USE OF SCRIPTURE

As good a point as any to start with is his argument against the Sadducees (Matt. 22:23–33). The whole Sadducean argument was an attempt to demonstrate the logical absurdity of life continuing after death. Jesus refutes them by quoting God's self-identification to Moses (Ex. 3:6) 'I am the God of Abraham, and the God of Isaac, and the God of Jacob'. On the face of it, these words seem to say nothing about life after death. Hence it is clear that Jesus' argument takes in more than the bare words. Indeed to make sense of it we have to know two things. One is that the words were spoken to Moses long after the patriarchs were dead. The second is that the phrase or idea 'to be the God of' is used with a particular sense in Scripture. It is used to mean that God is the covenant God of that party. It means that a covenant exists between God and that person (e.g. Lev. 26:12). A covenant exists between two parties. It cannot exist where one party is dead or non-existent. Hence if God is the God of the patriarchs, then the patriarchs must be alive. Hence the explanatory comment in Matthew 22:32: 'He is not the God of the dead but of the living.'

For the argument of Jesus to have force, a precise form of words had to be used in Exodus 3:6. It had to be a phrase of definite meaning and there had to be no limitation of the covenant relationship to the past time of the patriarchs' lives. Further, the words had to be spoken to Moses, that is, after the patriarchs' deaths. In that sense the appeal of Jesus is to the very words.

Yet these words derive their particular and highly significant meaning only from the usage of words throughout the Scripture. In that sense the appeal of Jesus is to words seen in the whole context of Scriptural usage.

Words have meanings, sometimes precise, highly significant meanings. A word does not exist by itself; it belongs in a pattern with other words. Clearly what is involved here is not a view which would make the individual word or phrase complete in and of itself. Neither is it a view which would see the particular as meaningless because only the mass has meaning. It is simply a correlate of the Biblical world-view. We can illustrate by taking the example of man. An individual man has significance as the creature of God. He is not a cipher to be swallowed up in the whole. Yet man was not created to exist for himself. He was created to live as part of a community.

APPEALS TO THE LITERAL WORDING

Hence occur the arguments of Scripture which appeal to specific words or even forms of words. A good example, though a much debated one, is Paul's argument in Galatians 3:16. There Paul argues from the use of the singular noun in the phrase 'and to your seed' in Genesis 13:15 etc. It is objected that Hebrew uses the singular when referring to human descendants and the plural only when referring to plant seeds, just as in English. The whole objection to Paul's argument rises from a failure to share Paul's high view of Scripture. A particular wording is not accidental. Paul's argument has to be considered along with another fact. If the original promise had wanted to make clear that it had an individualizing reference, that is, if it referred to each individual Israelite, then there are ways this could have been said in Hebrew. Different words could have been used. However, the text fails to use an individualizing term. It uses instead a singular. Paul sees that there was a reason for the use of this singular. It was so that it could point to the one who is the embodiment and recipient of all the promises – Christ himself!

The building of arguments based on the very words of Scripture presupposes a very tight and definite control by God over the production of Scripture. Forms of expression are not accidental. They are controlled by God. The person who would limit inspiration to the general ideas of Scripture, if as much as that, cannot understand such use of Scripture.

Yet for all the detail and particularity of Scripture, it can be summarised as having a general sense and direction. Jeremiah could summarise the general tendency of the prophetic word of judgment (Jer. 28:8). Jesus could say that the Scripture testified of him (John 5:39). The thing to remember about these appeals to the general teaching of Scripture is that these general teachings come to expression in words. There is no appeal to a doctrine which could not be expressed in words, or which the writers could not properly formulate. Instead the appeal is again and again to the very words of Scripture. Certainly we have to understand the teaching of the rest of Scripture in order to understand the appeal to the very words. However the appeal to the words is still there.

It is the connected character of Scripture which allows the truth to come through in spite of mistranslation or miscopying. Truth is not stated in one place only. It is stated repeatedly. A knowledge of the structures of Scripture enables one to understand a passage obscured by mistranslation.

ꙮ 10 ꙮ

The Bible and the Historian

In our sixth chapter we considered some passages which often are included amongst those cited as erroneous when somebody wants to prove that the Bible contains error. Yet there are quite a few others, including some which particularly concern the historian. Basically what the historian is concerned about is the conflict of sources.

CONFLICT BETWEEN SCRIPTURE AND OTHER SOURCES

Sometimes a claim of error is made because the Biblical text disagrees with a non-Biblical source. An example would be the question of who captured Samaria. 2 Kings 17:3–6 gives the credit to Shalmaneser (V). However his successor Sargon II claimed it. (We lack inscriptions from Shalmaneser V.) Here is a case of conflict between Biblical text and extra-Biblical text. Do we assume error in the Biblical text? Some historians have done so. The historian, however, if faced with a clash of sources, should suspend judgment, unless he has a ground for judging one text to be intrinsically more reliable than another. In this case, because the record of the capture of Samaria does not occur in the earliest version of Sargon's Annals, we have reason to doubt the reliability of the Annal which claims the capture of Samaria. Nevertheless the question remains: where there is a conflict between a Biblical and an extra-Biblical source, does the Bible have an intrinsic reliability?

That is equivalent to the question: does the inspiration of Scripture include its historical aspects? The general statements of Scripture as to its own inspiration and truth are well known (e.g. John 10:35; 2 Tim. 3:16; 2 Peter 1:20,21). The question is:

can this inspiration be restricted to a 'religious' dimension and does it guarantee historical accuracy?

We have no statements in Scripture which would exclude historical details from the scope of inspiration. We have arguments however based on the historical detail of the Old Testament. In Matthew 12:3,4 Jesus argues from David's act of entering the tabernacle and distributing the shewbread amongst his followers. Jonah's experience of being in the belly of the sea monster is cited as an example in Matthew 12:39–41; that of the Queen of Sheba in 12:42. Stephen's address in Acts 7 and Paul's in Acts 13:17ff. are both built upon recitations of significant events in the history of Israel. Paul builds his key defence of justification by faith in Romans 4:1–12 on the historical detail that Abraham was justified by faith before he was circumcised. A similar argument from the chronological order of events comes in Romans 9:10–12. Hebrews is full of arguments from Old Testament history. James used the prayer of Elijah as an example in 5:17,18. Peter cites the instance of the world being destroyed by the flood as the conclusive refutation of those who deny that God intervenes in the history of the world (2 Peter 3:3–6).

Such examples could be multiplied many times over. One therefore has to say that Jesus and his apostles built precedents and arguments upon details of Old Testament historical narrative, just as they did upon other parts of the Old Testament. To say that inspiration and reliability did not extend to the historical sections of the Old Testament necessarily leads to an accusation that Jesus and the apostles built arguments on a false basis.

Furthermore we have from the New Testament some knowledge of what the New Testament historians were trying to do. The introduction to Luke's Gospel is very clear in saying that Luke set out to do a careful work of historical research. One cannot say that the details of history lay outside of his interest.

Furthermore, one cannot say that such details are irrelevant to the religious concerns of our salvation. For Luke says the purpose of his historical investigation is 'so that you might know the exact truth about the things you have been taught' (1:4). The Gospel is through and through concerned with events that have occurred. Luke's concern to pin down the census at the time of Jesus' birth (2:2), his careful dating of the beginning of the ministry of John the Baptist (3:1,2), are not the work of a man who believed matters of historical dating were peripheral and irrelevant to the central religious truth of the gospel.

Peter presents a very similar line of argument. He says: 'For we did not follow cleverly devised tales when we made known to you the power and coming of our Lord Jesus Christ, but we were eyewitnesses of His majesty' (2 Peter 1:16). Peter rejects the idea that the apostles had clothed religious truth in an attractive story. It is not a fable but an eyewitness account. He goes on in the next verses to give a specific instance of such a witnessed event in the life of Christ. Once again, it cannot be said that he saw the events as irrelevant to the gospel and the accuracy of what was reported as of no concern.

What follows this defence of the accuracy of the events recounted is also of great significance (1:19–21). The witnessed events of the life of Jesus confirm the reliability of the prophecies which foretold them. Hence the Old Testament itself is also confirmed in reliability. It is not a case of the New Testament being confirmed to the detriment, by comparison, of the Old Testament. The attitude which would make the inspiration of the New Testament of concern but the inspiration of the Old Testament of little moment is not found in Peter. Rather the historical reliability of the gospel record lends greater credibility to the prophetic word of the Old Testament. That reliability is only to be expected, says Peter. For the prophecies of Jesus were not a matter of the prophet's own wishful thinking. They did not arise from his own imagination and interpretation. The prophets spoke because they were moved by the Holy Spirit to do so.

This raises another important perspective on Scripture and history. Scripture has a predominantly prophetic character. Events occur as prophets have foretold. Before things come to pass, God declares them beforehand through his prophets (Isa. 48:5; Amos 3:7). Indeed, the test of a true prophet is that what he says comes to pass. If it does not come to pass, then he is a prophet who has spoken presumptuously and not from the Lord (Deut. 18:22).

It is impossible for Scripture to be indifferent to historical events when those events are a fulfilment of prophecy. Similarly those events are also demonstrations of the faithfulness of God to his covenant commitments. Historical events demonstrate that what he has promised comes to pass. To remove the historical from the concerns of Scripture is to remove what demonstrates the faithfulness of God.

Thus there are many reasons for believing that inspiration extends to the historical details of Scripture. Hence, we do have a reason for believing that the Biblical account has an intrinsic historical reliability. When it is a case of a conflict between Biblical and extra-Biblical sources we have to decide in terms of the source which is more reliable. There has been a tendency on the part of some to treat any such conflict as evidence for errors in the Bible. Some who would not put it so strongly would yet say that it is evidence that Biblical writers were unconcerned about matters of historical accuracy. When people do this they have virtually assumed that the Biblical text is the unreliable one. It is striking that people are willing to do so when that assumption runs contrary to the Scripture's own claim to inspiration, and to the many instances where the Scripture has proved the more reliable source.

Those who like to argue for errors in the Bible might well argue that until such conflicts are all resolved, the historian cannot claim that the Bible is without error in historical matters. At the most he can suspend judgment. And certainly a claim for historical reliability for the whole of Scripture is not an instance of suspended judgment.

People who argue this way are driving a wedge between what a man might think as an historian and what he might want to believe as a Christian. Some would even go so far as to say that while as a private Christian he may believe certain things, as a professional historian he has to be ruled by the rules of historical evidence and argument. Such evidence may call in question what he believes as a Christian.

We saw in Chapter 3 that Paul argued against those who would make a knowledge of the world, gained from the world itself, of greater authority than the revelation of Christ. Certainly that relevation came through men, but such was Paul's view of revelation that he did not see that as a problem. A similar argument to Paul's could be constructed with respect to history. Is our authority for history to be based upon our human view of history, or upon revelation from the Lord and director of history?

It comes ultimately to a question of authority. Can the historian say that as a professional historian he is free from the necessity of submitting his judgment to God's revelation? We face here a question broader than that of historical 'errors' in the Bible. It becomes a question of whether the 'professional' conduct of a Christian is removed from the authority of God. The only way such a position could be defended would be if the Bible said nothing at all relevant to the historian. We have already seen that it says much that is relevant to the historian, both in giving historical detail and in developing a structure within which history is to be viewed. Thus the historian cannot plead that God's Word has no bearing upon his professional work. Hence in that area also he must yield to the fulness of wisdom of the Lord of history.

We will not always be able to explain the reason for the difference between Biblical source and extra-Biblical source. That problem will not be unusual to the historian, and especially the ancient historian. Our sources are so incomplete that we very frequently find apparent conflicts in them. Often it is because, having an incomplete picture, we misinterpret them. Happily with the Biblical text we have the valuable help of a measure of internal cross reference and back reference. This helps to resolve some of the problems. With extra-Biblical sources we often lack this.

Perhaps one example will illustrate the problem. In Exodus 1:11 we are told that the Israelites were commanded to build the city of Raamses in Egypt. The historical problem is this. If we work from the information in 1 Kings 6:1 that the Exodus occurred four hundred and eighty years before the building of the Temple, then we reach a date for the Exodus *c.*1440 BC. our problem is that we do not have evidence of a city called Raamses in Egyptian sources until the Nineteenth Dynasty *c.*1300 BC.

One way to solve the problem is to say that the Bible is using a later name for a city known by another name earlier. But this does not resolve our problem because we then have difficulties with Biblical statements ascribing the book of Exodus to

[51]

Moses. Often the problem is solved simply by ignoring or explaining away the four hundred-and-eighty year date of 1 Kings 6:1. However, attempts to place the Exodus later simply create other problems with the chronology of the Judges era, especially Judges 11:26.

Is the Biblical text in error? There are all sorts of possible solutions. We can question the date we assign to the Nineteenth Dynasty and rearrange all of Egyptian history. This has been attempted, but not in a convincing fashion. We could suggest a later copyist's substitution of the later name for the earlier name. Perhaps the city was called Raamses long before the Nineteenth Dynasty, but we do not read of it in our existing Egyptian sources before the Nineteenth Dynasty.

This sort of problem with nothing but hypothetical, unprovable solutions is common, even where the Biblical text is not concerned. It may not be the image the historian likes to present of his discipline, but it really is full of unresolved clashes between sources.

We have seen that the non-Christian has tended to accept comprehensive knowledge as the test of truth. When he works in that framework, he has to present himself as knowing almost everything. Otherwise he would, by his own definition, not even be close to knowing the truth. Hence the projection of the image of the 'expert' as having wide and comprehensive knowledge. The non-Christian is unable to admit frankly that the gaps in his knowledge are huge. Hence, the impression is given that our knowledge is certain and comprehensive. If it is so final, then there is not much hope of a new discovery changing our picture completely and removing the historical problem which concerns us. Hence discrepancy between sources is not treated just as a consequence of our incomplete knowledge. It is treated as an unresolved conflict, and therefore historians jump, quite unjustly as we have seen, to the conclusion of historical error in the Bible.

If we openly admit the poverty of our knowledge, then we are not so willing to jump to the conclusion that no resolution of the discrepancy is possible. One of our problems in the particular example cited is that we have very little knowledge of the area in which Raamses was sited from the period before the

Nineteenth Dynasty. Even if the discrepancy were between two extra-Biblical sources, that fact should make us hesitate before jumping to the conclusion of an error in one source.

When the historian is seen as competent to pronounce on errors in the Scripture, then very partial, and often misconstructed, human scholarship is being given too much credence.

Often, the objection to the historical accuracy of Scripture is based, not upon conflicts between Scripture and other sources, but upon problems within Scripture itself.

BIAS IN SCRIPTURE

One such problem is the accusation that Scripture is a biased, tendentious, and non-objective source. It does not present all the information available but makes a biased selection of the data. It could be retorted that there is no such thing as an unbiased historian but that counter would leave Scripture as merely one biased account amongst many.

Rather we should note that this criticism proceeds once more from the image of comprehensive knowledge. The Bible is held at fault because it does not tell everything. The charge excludes the possibility of a presentation which is partial, yet accurate. Unquestionably the author is choosing out of the mass of events those which to him are most significant. Is that to be condemned?

Let us take one example. The record of the life of David is biased towards giving a disproportionate treatment to the years that David was the true but rejected king of Israel.

Several chapters are taken in introducing David as the champion of Israel and the anointed ruler (1 Sam. 16,17). Then there are several chapters describing Saul's rising jealousy (18,19). There follow at least a dozen chapters concerned with David the fugitive. The section describing David's victories as king, extensive as those victories were, amounts to only a few chapters and these are balanced by the section devoted to David the fugitive from Absalom's rebellion. Hence David as a fugitive receives disproportionate emphasis, especially compared with David's victories, which formed the basis of Israel's empire. If one turns to the psalms of David there is a similar disproportion. A large group of these psalms is concerned with David as the one threatened by enemies and close to death.

The interesting thing about this portrayal of David in the historical section and in the psalms as the true but rejected king of Israel is that it forms the pattern for Christ as the rejected king. Christ quotes from David's psalms to picture his own betrayal and rejection.

Was the historian of 1 and 2 Samuel wrong in giving such disproportionate attention to David the fugitive? He was at fault if equal attention has to be paid to every year of a person's life. He was at fault if the important thing about David is what the secular historian would see as important, namely his military successes. He is not at fault if the purpose of Scripture is to point to Christ and if that is the truly important thing.

The secular historian may say that the Biblical historian made wrong choices in his portrayal of David. But the Christian historian may not do so, without calling in question the whole function of Scripture to testify to Christ.

This concentration upon Christ is sometimes used as the ground for saying that Biblical history has a very narrow 'religious' concern. That is not our concern at the moment. Rather the concern is whether the Biblical history can fairly be accused of bias because of that focus. It resolves itself into this question: was David's foreshadowing of Christ historically significant or insignificant? If it is significant, then the historian was right to emphasise it. If not, he was wrong. Surely the Christian verdict is that it was of the greatest importance.

Thus, questions about whether the Scripture is biased in its selection of material turn to questions about what is really important in history. In practice the secular historian does not give every fact. He makes a selection according to what seems to him important in history. The Bible writer also makes a selection which is dominated by the priorities in God's unfolding plan. The selection of material to report is not evidence of lack of interest in history or in historical accuracy. It is evidence of different priorities to the secular historian. Behind the objection to the selection of certain items for emphasis there can be a belief that there is nothing important in history. There are no themes which make history significant. The modern view of history is laced with contradictions. It sets up exhaustive detail as its goal. It supposedly avoids personal interpretation and bias on the part of the historian. Yet historians do not write books which narrate one unconnected fact after another. The material, even if given in fair but never exhaustive detail, is selected. Some criterion guides that selection. It may be belief in the priority of social forces, of ideas, of politicians, and so on. Yet it is still a selection. One cannot say: 'The Bible is not history as we would write it; it is selective.' One has to say: 'Its principles of selection are different because it has a different view of what is really important in history.' Its view of what is important reflects its understanding of God's plan. The Christian cannot say: 'I accept what the Scripture tells me about Christ, but I cannot accept its historical narratives because they are biased in their presentation of material.' For the 'bias' is determined by what the Bible teaches about God's plan of salvation. Once more the real debate is about the truth of the gospel.

It may be objected that the choice of the Biblical treatment of David as an example was not a representative one. If the example had been, say, Omri (1 Kings 16:15–28), a different picture would have resulted. For it has been charged that Omri, the founder of an important dynasty in Israel has not had his accomplishments adequately recorded. Once again the charge reflects a different principle of selection. David too did not have his accomplishments dwelt on at length. For with Omri, as with David, the text is not dominated by belief in the priority of political-military accomplishment. It is dominated by belief in the priority of God. Omri's relationship to God is most important.

Sometimes the rejection of the Biblical principles of selection will be more forthright and blatant. It will be claimed that the historian cannot consider God. His approach has to be entirely secular. In this claim we see the working of the world-view which was considered in Chapter 4. That is the consequence of a more and more secularized Deist belief. God is first restricted by his 'laws' from any involvement in the world. Then this impotent god is regarded as unnecessary. To that it must be answered that God is not impotent. If He were so, we would still be dead in our sins. It is sheer matter of fact that God has been and is active. The failure of the historian to consider God is not a legitimate mark of his trade. It is a consequence of his being conformed to the world of unbelief.

The ability of writers to escape with the superficial dismissal of the Biblical history as 'Not the way we write history today' must also be considered. It is also the product of secularization. Just as God as the author of salvation has been rejected in favour of man, so our view of eschatology has changed. Man will bring in the perfect age by his accomplishments. Hence, whatever modern man does that is different from former ages must be right. Certainly, 'modern man' has proved a false Messiah, and there is increasing criticism of the misery and danger this 'salvation' is producing. Nevertheless, men abandon their idols reluctantly. Those who may now be criticising the god 'human technology' are still adhering to the god 'human secular scholarship'. The bomb may be bad, but secular historiography is still considered good. When we reject such secular hopes and confidences we do so because of the gospel. God alone saves. Hence we do not accept this blind confidence in man and human scholarship.

'CONTRADICTIONS' BETWEEN BOOKS IN SCRIPTURE

A second area where supposed historical problems are found in Scripture is the area of supposed internal contradictions. These contradictions may be found between different authors or may be found within a book. They are commonly explained as due to the author's indifference to historical accuracy or to the book being composed of different sources combined without concern for harmonization.

Along with this concern to detect and highlight such contradictions there often goes a contempt for harmonization. Many handbooks have been produced which attempt harmonizations of troublesome passages. These are dismissed with disdain or not even considered.

It is not easy to come to a balanced judgment in this area. Undoubtedly many attempted harmonizations of such passages strike one as most implausible. They read like acts of desperation. On the other hand, some supposed contradictions are so trivial as to be unworthy of consideration. Both the harmonizers and the contradiction finders are seeking to find support for their doctrine of Scripture.

Rather than seizing upon this or that 'contradiction', or coming up with a series of harmonizations of the various passages, we need to consider the whole phenomenon. The cases where the supposed contradictions occur between books give us a good starting point. Examples are differences in details between Kings and Chronicles, or between the various Gospels. If Kings and Chronicles were accounts of the history of Israel written independently of each other, then we could ascribe the differences to different sources and authors. However Chronicles is clearly dependent on Kings. Similarly, while there may be differences among students of the Gospels on the exact form of their mutual relationship, yet a certain degree of relationship and dependence is not denied by any.

Thus we have books clearly related to each other and yet showing differences here and there in the way things are narrated or even in what is narrated. Even more interesting is the lack of obvious attempts to harmonize divergencies or to present divergencies in a polemic form. Thus the author of the later book does not seem to see any need to explain his divergence from the earlier book.

Let us take an example. 1 Kings 15:9–24 describes the reign of Asa. We are told 'the heart of Asa was wholly devoted to the Lord all his days' (v.14). We are told of the treaty which he made with Ben-hadad the king of Aram without any criticism being expressed (v.18,19). We are also told of disease in his old age (v.23). 2 Chronicles 14–16 is also a description of Asa's reign. It is clearly based upon the account in Kings. It shares Kings' assessment of Asa as a good king (cf. 1 Kings 15:11 and 2 Chron. 14:2). Yet it records the criticism made by Hanani of Asa's treaty with Ben-Hadad (16:7–10). It also says that in the disease of his old age, Asa sought the help of physicians rather than of the Lord (16:12). Thus, Chronicles does not give nearly as favourable a picture of Asa as we derive from Kings. Yet Chronicles is clearly using Kings. It may well be that the source it refers to for the life of Asa in 16:11 is actually the Book of Kings.

Is Chronicles correcting Kings? There is no evidence of polemic against Kings. The overall assessment of Asa does not differ from Kings. Chronicles uses Kings and may well refer to it quite favourably as a source.

If the author of Chronicles saw his additional material as not in conflict with Kings, why did he make no obvious attempt to harmonize it with Kings? We can infer something of the Chronicler's regard for Kings from the use he makes of it. Even more significant is what he himself tells us about the authorship of the book he is using as his source. In a number of passages, but most clearly in 2 Chronicles 20:34 he tells us of the role of prophets in the composition of Kings. Given the Chronicler's regard for prophets it is most unlikely he would launch a polemic against a prophetic work. Yet this raises even more acutely the problem of his failure to attempt a harmonization between his material critical of Asa and the uniformly favourable portrayal of Kings.

The problem of lack of either polemic or harmonization is raised also by the supposed contradictions found between the various Gospels. Matthew, Mark, and Luke are clearly related though there is a variety of theories over which depended on the other. The relationship of John to the first three Gospels is not clear. Some think that it presupposes the readers' knowledge of the other Gospels. Others doubt this. If it does presuppose the other Gospels then the same point applies to any supposed contradiction between John and the others. Even if this is not the case, if the commonly accepted later dating of John is correct, then surely the other Gospels were in circulation by then. If none of this is true, if John is relatively early, and written independently of the other Gospels, it does not pose problems drastically different from those found between Kings and Chronicles or between various of the other Gospels. Additional material and different emphasis are part of the problem we are already considering.

If we hold that particular Biblical books are composites, put together from various sources, then the supposed conflicts between 'sources' manifest the same problem. They lack evidence of polemic against another's version or attempts on the part of the 'editor' to harmonize the various sources.

We thus have a phenomenon which needs explaining. What explanations are possible? One is that the authors or 'editors' were indifferent to contradictions. They calmly contradicted the source on which they relied. Another is that they did not see contradictions because to their mind what they were saying was a supplement and not a contradiction. A variant of the second explanation would be to say that the 'contradictions' are a figment of our own imaginations.

Can we find a way to choose between the various explanations? If the authors were not concerned with historical accuracy, why the reliance on sources and the way both Kings and Chronicles direct readers to further sources of information (e.g. 1 Kings 15:23 and 2 Chronicles 16:11)? Why the statement of historical method in Luke 1:1–4? Harmonizing statements are rare but they do occur. For example, the repetition of events in the lives of Abraham and Isaac has often been used to argue for different sources to Genesis which were confused as to whether the event in question happened to Abraham or to Isaac. However Genesis 26:1 makes clear that the famine Isaac experienced was not that experienced by Abraham.

Yet such statements are rare in Scripture. Generally speaking, the phenomenon which needs explanation is the lack of either polemic or harmonization. Let us say, for the sake of argument, that we cannot produce an explanation. Does that prove the accounts are contradictory? We do not know that the author of the second account saw them that way. Rather, the author of Chronicles would be most unlikely to quote Kings as an authority if he thought its account incorrect. If he thought it partly correct and partly incorrect, then he would surely be polemical against its 'errors'.

Some have tried to resolve the problem by saying that by the time the second work was written, the first had come to have canonical status. The author of Chronicles could not explicitly contradict his authoritative source. Hence his refutation, where he finds its position wrong, has to be indirect. Is that a convincing explanation of the problem? In this example the real issue is the portrayal of Asa. Chronicles gives a much more negative portrayal. Is the author 'correcting' Kings' positive portrayal? If he were doing that, he would hardly be likely to begin his treatment by repeating Kings' favourable summary of his reign (2 Chron. 14:2).

There is one obvious possibility to be considered. That is that the author of Chronicles saw himself as presenting a perspective on Asa which was complementary to that in Kings – using it as a foundation – and not contradictory. This is the explanation which best accords with the date. It explains the favourable use of Kings as a source and yet the willingness to present different information.

In this case it is possible to present some suggestions as to the differences in interest between Kings and Chronicles. Kings makes a positive or negative judgment on a ruler chiefly in terms of whether he suppressed or tolerated idolatry. Chronicles accepts that as a basis, but looks also at other characteristics of the reign. For that reason a good king may appear less favourably because his failures in other areas are treated. Such is the case with Asa. Conversely, bad kings, like Manasseh, may have something favourable reported (2 Chron. 33:10–17).

Is Kings wrong in making its general summary of a reign hinge on the question of idolatry? It all depends on what importance you attach to idolatry. Kings is certainly in agreement with the law and the prophets on the seriousness of the matter. Arguing with Kings on the point would be arguing against the importance of the first two commandments. Is it wrong for Chronicles to supplement that picture with other successes or failures from the monarch's life? It would be hard to argue that a fuller picture is wrong!

Are these two perspectives contradictory? Obviously not. Chronicles is even resolving questions which would naturally arise in the mind of a reader: was it right to make an alliance with Aram? Why was Asa sick?

The only objection which could be made would be against the author of Kings for not giving the extra detail himself. Yet the objection only really holds if one is arguing that the historian has to include everything. The extra detail would not change the fact that Asa did suppress idolatry. We come back to the question of the difference in standard of judgment between Biblical historian and secular historian.

It will not always be possible to suggest the perspective which the second writer is adding. One can note Matthew's far greater concern for recording events in Galilee and the greater part occupied by the Judean ministry in John. Yet this does not in itself explain the differences in content. It may well be part of the eventual explanation, but it is not the whole story.

Many other examples could be given of where we meet parallel accounts neither harmonized nor set against each other. Some can be explained. Some cannot presently be explained. Lack of ability to suggest an explanation does not mean the two Biblical books contradict each other. To argue that, we would need clear evidence of polemic. And that, as we have seen, is the thing lacking.

When the historian judges these differences of perspective as being contradictory, or as evidence of bias on the part of the Biblical writer, he shows the influence of secular views of history. There may be the implication that failure of the one author to give all the details, some of which are supplied by the other, indicates bias. Once again the idea that is dominant is that of exhaustive detail. Or there may be the implication that two perspectives on the same event or person cannot both be right. Once you grant that human knowledge is partial and incomplete, then it means that you can have two complementary pictures of the one event or person. Often the secular historian will grant that his picture is not exhaustive. However, he often draws two different conclusions from that fact, both of which are unacceptable. One will be that his selection of the data, based upon the primacy of political history, or the primacy of social history, is dealing more with the real heart of the matter. Giving primacy to political events reflects a seeing of the human leader as the moving and determining force in history. Giving primacy to social history is generally connected with seeing the human masses as the crucial influence. Both agree that man is the lord of history. Hence, the secular historian's view is shaped by his theological convictions. He is not less biased than the Biblical historian. Rather, his view reflects a different confession as to who is lord. Often the bias is concealed under cloaks, such as the claim to use 'modern' or 'scholarly' historiography. Nevertheless the issue is theological.

The second reaction of secular historians to the fact that their account is incomplete will be a retreat into relativism. They will claim that all accounts are incomplete and show bias. Hence one bias is as good as another. It cannot be said that any account gives the truth about what happened. This approach is an attack on Scripture. Behind it lies an attack on the Biblical view of man. For man, even though he is not God, may know truth. The non-Christian is caught by the logic of his desire to be as God. He claims that he can know the truth comprehensively as God knows it. When he is forced to acknowledge that he cannot know comprehensively, then he denies that truth may be known. The very fact that Scripture with its historical narratives is called the 'truth' refutes this view. This does not mean that any partial account can be called 'true'. Is an account shaped to complement Biblical truths or is it shaped to obscure them? Biblical history includes elements of human political and social history, but it does not use these to claim that man, not God, determines history.

CONFLICTS WITHIN BOOKS

The claim that Biblical historical narratives are contradictory is not restricted to conflicts between books. It is claimed that contradictions exist within books. Such claims are often used as part of an argument that Biblical books are composed of elements from various sources, often with contradictory approaches.

An example would be the account of David's meeting with Saul. In 1 Samuel 16:14–23 David comes to Saul as a musician. In the next chapter David appears as a young man unknown to Saul (see especially vv.55,56). Here is what seems a contradiction.

When we investigate the portrayal of Saul and David in 1 Samuel we see that the contrast between David and Saul is clearly presented. Saul's attempt to kill David (18:10,11) contrasts with David's refusal to kill Saul (26:6–12); David receives the Spirit but the Spirit departs from Saul (16:13,14); David's bravery and trust contrast with Saul's cowardice (chapter 17). It is part of that story that we see not only that there is a contrast between the two, but that David compensates for Saul's failures. Thus David is the man to soothe Saul by his music and the one to fight Goliath when Saul, Israel's natural champion, is afraid.

Thus the author in 16:14–23 follows through the story to show how Saul's need is met by David. Then he presents the story of Goliath's challenge to show how Saul's failure is met by

David. There is a sense in which chapters 16 and 17 complement each other just as do Kings and Chronicles. However here
the complement does not arise from taking different aspects of
the same reign. It arises from showing how different aspects of a
complex situation illustrate the same general truth. There is no
indication in the text that the events of chapter 17 occurred
later than all the events at the end of chapter 16. It may well
have been that the plan to call in David to soothe Saul was
formed before the events of chapter 17, but could not be put into
effect until after the battle. The author has presented the
material together in chapter 16, so the contrast between David
and Saul is made clear and supplements the contrast that
emerges out of the events of chapter 17.

In cases such as this, by studying the way in which the author
has presented his material and the truths he is illustrating, we
can solve what seem on superficial reading to be contradictions.
However we do not have solutions to all such problems because
we have not yet come to a full understanding of Scripture.
Sometimes we have failed to be careful and discerning enough
in our study of the way the text is presented. There is no
incentive to such careful study if we believe that the text has
been formed by joining together contradictory stories.

Once again we have to look at this problem in a larger
perspective. Those who believe that Biblical books were formed
out of contradictory elements believe that some person or
group of persons joined the elements into one book. If the
stories were contradictory, why could not these editors see that?
In the end you have to fall back on the explanation that the
editors were not concerned about contradictions. They brought
together diverse traditions without concern for coherence.

This view about the editors' role is contradicted by a study of
the text itself. As we have seen in the story of David and Saul,
events have been told in a way that brings into view the contrast
between the two men. Events were not selected or omitted at
random.

Another example we could use is the book of Genesis. The
repetitions of that book are often used as proof of its formation
from various and discordant sources. Yet the repetitions show
an obvious pattern and purpose, as is seen for example in the
lives of the three patriarchs, Abraham, Isaac, and Jacob. Each

has a barren wife; each is in danger of losing his wife(s); each faces conflict with the inhabitants of Canaan. These repetitions are all connected with the conflict between God's promise and the experiences of the patriarchs, experiences which seemed to contradict the promise of numerous offspring and a land of their own. They created the situation in which the patriarchs had to exercise faith. Thus the repetitions are part of the story, not the accidental result of combining different sources.

A superficial attention to these elements in the Biblical history – the contrasting of Saul and David; the repetitions of the trial of faith in Genesis – can easily lead to the wrong conclusion. The presence of such patterns can be ascribed to the invention of the author. Generally this is done where the assumption is that history is purposeless, and that it has no patterns, because there is no God who overrules and directs history. To criticize the Biblical author for finding such patterns is to charge that there were no such patterns in the original history. So we come back to the basic question. Is God active in history? Is he shaping it according to his purpose? Or is he the absent deity who leaves history to its purposelessness? Once again the issue comes down to a question vital to the truth of the gospel. For God is in charge of history. To attack the patterns presented by the Biblical author is to question the role of God in history.

꩜ I I ꩜

Words and Meanings Again

The previous chapter considered the claim of historical contradiction in Scripture. There will also be claims of doctrinal and ethical contradictions. Once more, differences between various Biblical authors will be alleged. Sometimes the claim is made that Biblical authors have failed to integrate completely their various lines of thought and their ethics, thereby causing internal contradictions.

Generally this claim of doctrinal and ethical contradictions comes last in a series of claims. First the relevance of Scripture to science or other areas of scholarship will be denied. Then it will be said that the Scripture is not inspired in matters of history. The claims go little challenged because of the conviction of many Christians that it matters little as long as areas of doctrine are not involved. However the earlier doubts as to the authority and consistency of the Bible lead logically to a weakening of confidence. If the Bible contains contradictions in one area, then why not in another? Finally comes the charge of contradictions in other areas. If there are contradictions, then a man is free to pick and choose which aspects of Biblical teaching he prefers.

Typical examples of such alleged contradictions include the following: Paul and James disagree on the rôle of works in salvation; Paul's denial to women of a teaching/ruling rôle in the church contradicts his general teaching that Christ has united male and female; the specific teaching on the government and discipline of the church in the Pastoral Epistles contradicts the freedom of the Spirit taught in the other letters. One could come up with many other examples. The essential issue here is very similar to that considered in Chapter 9. There we saw that Jesus and the apostles appeal both to the general sense of Scripture and to the specific phrasing of Scripture. They could make the appeal to the specific phrases because the phrases are not isolated from the general truth of Scripture. Under the control of God that truth comes to expression in specific statements. Thus a unity is found in Scripture.

Similarly within the thought of a particular author there is a unity. His concerns come to expression in firm statements which are part of the total fabric of his thought. This produces some startling results. We have to consider the context of thought within which a statement occurs, for statements in different contexts can mean different things.

Let us consider what is happening when a statement from one author is picked out as formally contradictory to a statement by another author, or when two statements from the one author are held up as showing an internal contradiction. The assumption is that they are discussing the same issue, or closely related issues, and coming to differing conclusions. Alternatively, in the discussion of unrelated issues, conclusions may result which contradict one another.

Given the fact that words and phrases have meanings closely related to the context it is very easy for formally similar statements to have different meanings, depending on their context. Formal contradiction, or even formal agreement, is not the end of the matter.

Scripture has a polemical character. Much of it is argument against error. Hence one must see statements which are part of an argument in the context of that argument.

The formal 'disagreement' between Paul and James is a good example of this problem. The context of Paul's statement 'that a man is justified by faith apart from works of the Law' (Rom. 3:28) is clear. It is an argument that the keeping of commandments, for example, the command to circumcise, is not essential for salvation. The example given to prove the point is that of Abraham who was pronounced righteous before he was circumcised (Rom. 4:1-11). Paul makes it clear that his teaching at this point does not mean that the Christian is free to sin (Rom. 6). He is emphatic that continuance in gross sin excludes a man from the kingdom of God (1 Cor. 6:9-11). One could well ask whether this last emphasis is a contradiction to his teaching on justification by faith. It is a contradiction only if we turn justification by faith into something quite different from what Paul meant. We find Paul, in arguing against legalism, teaching justification by faith, and yet guarding that teaching against an interpretation which opens the door to licentiousness.

When we look at James' statement that 'a man is justified by works, and not by faith alone' we see that the context is an argument. It is an argument that a faith unaccompanied by works is a dead faith. It is against a faith that shows no compassion to the needy (1:27; 2:15,16) nor evidence of the controlling power of grace (1:26). Thus James' attack on bare unproductive faith reminds one very much of Paul's concern that faith leads to holiness and is not a cover for sin. In that the two are agreed. The crucial question is whether they are agreed in seeing the favour of God as not merited by human goodness.

James makes an interesting statement in 2:12,13 where he refers to a 'law of liberty'. Since the normal rôle of law is to bind a man to obedience, one wonders what this law can be. He explains it by saying that 'judgment will be merciless to one who has shown no mercy'. This is an obvious reference to the teaching of Jesus expressed in parables such as that of the unmerciful slave (Matt. 18:23–35). The slave who has been released from this debt is under obligation to release his fellow slave. Thus it is a matter of liberty because there is a setting free of the slave from his debt. However, there is also law because this imposes upon the liberated a responsibility to show mercy also. This meaning of the phrase 'the law of liberty' fits its other usage in James 1:25 where the point is that the gospel does not leave a man unchanged, but makes a lasting impression upon him. James follows the treatment of this subject in 2:12,13 by moving on to the necessity to show mercy to one's brother (2:14–16) and from that to the more general point that works must accompany faith (2:17ff.). The crucial point, it must be emphasized, is what James sees as beginning this transformation. The teaching of Jesus, which he echoes, sees it as being the mercy of the Lord who freely forgives the debtor. In 1:18 he ascribes the new birth to the activity of God. Nowhere in James do we find a defence of the position of Jewish legalism which regarded law-keeping as that which placed a man in the right relationship to God.

Why does James put his emphasis on what must follow the initiation of faith, rather than on the beginning of faith? It is clearly because of the error he is countering which would give excuse to unmerciful lives. This emphasis is very similar to that of the First Letter of John (4:7–11). We know that Paul was being misconstrued as saying that one was free to sin (Rom. 3:8). Thus James and 1 John are a polemic against a misinterpretation of Paul's teaching. Of course we cannot know whether that strain of heresy was present in Judaism before Paul began preaching or whether it was a result of some people seeing his teaching as an excuse for sin. It could be that James was countering an element that had very little real contact with Paul. Or it could be a group who took their supposed authority from Paul (2 Peter 3:15,16).

Thus we find in James a strong emphasis on what we might call the 'other half' of Paul's doctrine. James forms a complement to Paul by bringing that other side of Paul into prominence. A good illustration of their different emphases is the treatment they each give to Abraham. Paul draws attention to the incident in the story of Abraham when he placed his trust in the promise of God and that trust was counted as righteousness (Rom. 4:3; Gen. 15:6). Here we have the formal acknowledgement of Abraham's faith. That faith grew until he was able even to offer up his son, confident in the power of God to give life to the dead (Rom. 4:19–22; Heb. 11:17–19). It is upon this fruit of faith that James concentrates (2:21–23).

Abraham exemplifies both justification by faith alone and the works of righteousness that follow from faith. Thus Paul's treatment and James' treatment raise questions similar to the different treatments of Asa that we considered in the previous chapter. Each is partial and yet each is true. To set Paul against James is to divide Abraham. The Abraham who believed the promise was not a different Abraham from the one who offered Isaac.

Formally the statements of Paul and James disagree. Yet their teachings do not disagree. If we take formal statements out of context we do not understand Scripture. On the other hand we cannot ignore the very words of Scripture. After all, it is written: 'he believed in the Lord; and He reckoned it to him as righteousness' (Gen. 15:6). It was that explicit verbal statement which enabled Paul to defend the gospel of grace against the attack of legalism.

Obviously the emphases of Paul and James (or we could say Paul and Paul) will play a rôle in the church depending upon the heresy which threatens the church. Whenever threatened by a system of righteousness based on works the church rightly responds with justification by faith alone. When the prevailing atmosphere is one of licentiousness, then the church must be thankful for the other half of Paul's teaching. This is very relevant to the charge that Paul's concern for order in the church contradicts his teaching on the freedom of the Spirit. The concern for order is based upon an awareness that licentiousness and lawlessness will find refuge in appeal to the freedom of the Spirit. Conversely the freedom of the Spirit must be taught against all the bondage of man-made tradition.

Behind these charges of contradiction in the Scripture there lies a failure to appreciate the full scope of Biblical doctrine. The greater the departure from Scripture, the more man and not God is made the lord of history and the agent of salvation, and the more we can expect men to lack an understanding of the message of Scripture.

12

The Human Element in Scripture

The orthodox view of Scripture is often attacked as placing too much emphasis upon the divine nature of Scripture and ignoring its human side. It is accused of treating Scripture as a book dropped from heaven rather than as a book written by men. Sometimes this attack is combined with the claim that we should not develop our doctrine of Scripture deductively from what Scripture says about itself. Instead we should develop it inductively from a study of the phenomena of Scripture. By this is meant that we should pay attention to the 'inaccuracies', imprecision, 'errors', and 'contradictions' of Scripture.

The problem with this whole approach is that it assumes what needs to be proved. Often what is claimed as error or contradiction is not necessarily so. In many of these cases we do not have the whole story. Indeed the more blatant the 'error' the more cautious we should be. This can be illustrated from two cases of what look like blatant error. In 2 Samuel 21:19 we are told that Elhanan killed Goliath the Gittite. Here is a clear conflict with the story of 1 Samuel 17 where David killed Goliath. As it stands the conflict is obvious. So obvious as to make us suspicious. The story of David and Goliath is so prominent, and forms so important a part of the story of David's rise to the throne, that it is very unlikely that two men could be claimed as having killed Goliath in the one book (1 and 2 Samuel were originally one book). There is a way around this that is adopted by some scholars who reject the truth of Scripture. They claim that, as part of the legend which grew up around David, the story of Goliath was transferred to David from the real original hero. This view is incompatible with the way the New Testament regards the historical

[70]

portions of the Old Testament. It still does not solve the basic problem. If the victory over Goliath was 'borrowed' for David, why was the 'original' version still included?

When we look to the parallel account in 1 Chronicles 20:5 we find that the man killed was the brother of Goliath. The simple explanation of the problem is that the words 'Lahmi the brother of' were lost at some later time from the text of 2 Samuel 21:19 by a copying error. The books of Samuel do seem to have suffered particularly amongst Biblical books from copying errors. Of course those who claim that the story of David's victory is a legend will claim that Chronicles has added 'the brother of' in order to try to deal with the obvious contradiction. However, if it was such a problem to the author of Chronicles, would it not be an equal problem to the author of Samuel? (Making Samuel a composite work based upon different sources does not solve the problem. The problem would then have confronted an editor.)

In this case the existence of a parallel text in Chronicles allows us to suggest the source of the problem. For most of the Bible we do not have parallel texts. The point I would stress is that if something strikes us as a blatant error, it is as likely to have struck an original author or editor that way. There must therefore be an explanation. However we may not always be able to suggest what it is.

Another example of the same sort of problem is the case quoted already in Chapter 6. In Matthew 27:9 a quotation from Zechariah is ascribed to Jeremiah. A possible explanation has been considered. Once again the blatant character of the 'error' makes it unlikely that it is an error. A Jewish author, immersed in the Old Testament as Matthew was, is not going to make that sort of 'error' and he was writing for an audience who would have picked it up immediately.

The charge of blatant error is really a denial of the intelligence of the Biblical authors. Whether one likes their theology or not, one cannot deny their intelligence. Nor can one deny the Scriptural knowledge of the people who first received such works as having canonical authority. The more obvious an 'error' the less likely it would remain undetected. Hence paradoxically, whether we can suggest a solution or not, the blatant problems are not of great concern.

When people make such things of great concern and when they use them to claim that the phenomena of Scripture prove its fallibility, they lose their perspective. There may be simple solutions to these problem texts though we do not now have all the answers. We find ourselves back with the point that has been repeatedly stressed. The knowledge of the historian is limited. To claim such things as errors is to assume there is no explanation possible, not even one yet unknown. Appeal to the so- called phenomena of Scripture is generally appeal to the incomplete state of our historical knowledge.

Are we to base our doctrine of the Bible on the incomplete state of our historical knowledge or are we to base it upon what the Bible says about itself? There is a good rule which says that we should try to base our understanding upon the clear texts and not the obscure. To base our doctrine of Scripture on all the problem texts, which seem to involve error or contradiction, is really basing a doctrine on obscure passages! Why do this when there are passages which speak very clearly?

When we turn to such passages we find something very interesting. They stress the divine rôle in the origin of Scripture. We have seen that holders of the orthodox doctrine are charged with stressing the divine element instead of the human one. If it is a valid charge against them, it is also a valid charge against the Bible writers.

In the well-known passage in 2 Timothy 3:16 Scripture is described as 'breathed out' by God. Paul did not write 'inspired' as our English translations have it. He wrote 'expired'. Here is a very clear reference to the divine rôle in the production of Scripture. Similarly 2 Peter 1:21 says that prophecy arose not from human volition but by men being borne along by the Spirit of God. Once more the divine rôle is prominent.

While Scripture does not deny the human rôle and frequently mentions the human authors, it does not see the human side as what needed to be stressed. When it would move us to trust Scripture, it emphasises the divine agency in Scripture production.

The reason for the stress is obvious. The human authorship of Scripture is clear. The personalities and characteristics of particular authors come through. What is more likely to be denied is the divine character of Scripture.

Behind this aversion to the divine character of Scripture lies a number of things. One we have already met is the view that God is not active in the world. If God is an absentee God then it must be the human side of Scripture we emphasise. There is no divine agency in any special sense in the production of Scripture. Looking at the supposed 'error' passages does nothing to challenge the common denial of God's working in His creation and hence in Scripture.

If God is inactive, then man cannot be changed by divine power. To be human, for believer and unbeliever, means the same thing. It means a condition of sin and fallibility. Hence error cannot be avoided. When people say we should stress more the 'human' side of Scripture they generally mean its fallibility. For them that is synonymous with being human. However in a world where God in his grace is active that is by no means true. Sin and error are not inevitable.

A passage which contrasts sharply with such denials of God's activity is the prayer of Jesus in John 17. Jesus revealed the Father to the disciples by revealing to them the words of the Father (vv.3–8). He prays that they may be sanctified by that word, for God's word is truth (v.17). Scripture itself, as the Word of God, is evidence that God is active. And his activity is a sanctifying one, leading men into truth. However, the process of the transmission of the Word of God did not stop when Jesus gave it to the disciples. They also pass on that Word to others that others may believe (vv.18–20). To stress only the human side of Scripture would be to ignore the whole point of this prayer, that the Word came originally from God. Hence its sanctifying power.

Let it be clearly realized that the demand to stress the human rather than the divine character of Scripture must include the words of Jesus. Naïvely, people think that such attacks will only affect passages they may find embarrassing in any case, like the creation account of Genesis. Yet it cannot stop there. The words of Jesus are also part of Scripture. That is why such arguments, though originally directed at Old Testament books, soon come to call in question the Gospels. For the writers of the Gospels were also human. If error is an inevitable part of the human condition, then the words of Jesus have been erroneously reported to us.

[73]

We cannot stop there. For Jesus was also a man. Hence the logic of this position is further developed. Jesus is soon also charged with error.

There is one other factor in the dislike of the divine rôle in Scripture formation. It is the fact that God makes use of man. In an age in which man and his autonomy is stressed, it is repugnant to many that man should be an instrument in the hand of God. Man's originality must be stressed. It is seen as an offence to human dignity for the divine message to come through man without man adding anything. This feeling is reflected in attacks on the orthodox doctrine as involving a 'mechanical' view of inspiration or as a 'dictation' theory.

When we look at what Scripture itself tells us we see a great variety. There are cases like the Gospel of Luke where we are told of the activity of investigation that went into the making of the Gospel (Luke 1:1–4). There is no question that there was much human initiative in the writing of this Gospel. Yet a passage from Luke is quoted as Scripture in 1 Timothy 5:18 (Luke 10:7). An Old Testament book like Psalms also shows a great deal of the human feeling and character of its authors. And they are quoted as the authoritative Word of God in the New Testament.

Yet these books of Scripture, where the rôle of the human author is prominent, are not the whole story. There are books or parts of books largely composed of the words delivered directly by God. Notice the preface to the law in Exodus 20:1: 'God spoke all these words.' How do we emphasise the 'human side' of the composition of this section of Scripture? Either we acknowledge that here we have dictation or else we say that the story of the speaking and writing of the ten commandments is false.

Where the objection is to any activity of God in the world, there will be objection to accepting the Biblical account of the giving of the ten commandments. Where the objection is to God working through man, then the Psalms will be just as much a problem. If we take what is said about the Old Testament seriously, then we have God working through man to transmit his message. Peter indicates that the prophets did not necessarily understand the import of the message they were delivering (1 Peter 1:10–12).

The doctrine of revelation is not treated in Scripture as in conflict with the doctrine of man, because Scripture does not have an autonomous view of man. He is not a sovereign, an autonomous, and free agent. He is a creature. He was made and his Maker may use him as He sees fit. Where the Biblical doctrine of revelation through men is an embarrassment, then Paul's words in Romans 9:20–24 will also cause deep offence. For Paul declares God's right to use man as the potter uses his clay for his own sovereign purposes. It is not accidental that attacks on the doctrine of election come from the same quarters as attacks on the doctrine of Scripture.

The Bible has no problem with presenting human activity in the composition of Scripture and also affirming that it is the unadulterated Word of God. For Scripture does not see man as an impediment to the achievement of the divine purpose. Even man's sin and blindness cannot prevent God from achieving his purpose. God in grace overrules and conquers that sin. Once more we come to a truth vital for the gospel. If God cannot sovereignly intervene in the affairs of men and overrule their sin, then we are all still dead in our trespasses and sins. If it is an impermissible infringement of human dignity for God to direct the thoughts of man to produce infallible Scripture, then it is likewise impermissible for God to direct the thoughts of man towards repentance and faith.

Note that neither in regeneration nor in inspiration does the Bible give details as to the mode of God's working in the heart and mind of man. That is a mystery. What is said quite clearly is that God does it.

Much has been said and written about the 'human side' of Scripture. But as long as we affirm, as Scripture itself does, that the Holy Spirit used human authors, we shall never satisfy those who cry for more emphasis on the 'human side' of Scripture. For them, that implies the exclusion of real divine activity in man.

৩০ 13 ৩০

Contextualization

The term 'contextualization' is used for a variety of things. Basically it means the making of Biblical doctrine relevant to a different cultural and historical context. That can be done in a variety of ways.

For example, to say that the tenth commandment might refer in a particular culture to not coveting llamas or yaks rather than oxen, could be called contextualization. A different example would be to say that the presentation of the work of Christ as a sacrifice to appease God's anger reflects a culture where sacrifice was an accepted institution. In a modern culture which does not think in terms of sacrifice that is meaningless. Hence the work of Christ has to be presented in different terms, say in terms of a peace negotiation or a civil dispute mediator.

The first example amounts to giving a fancy name to something Christians have been doing for centuries. The second example involves a total transformation of traditional Christian teaching. Since 'contextualization' is used for both, considerable confusion surrounds the use of the term.

Those who would advocate the second sort of contextualization are saying that the fundamental concepts, ideas, and themes of Scripture are shaped by the culture within which Scripture was given. Scripture is bound to that cultural and historical context. It cannot be meaningful in another cultural and historical context unless we translate it into the concepts of that other culture. The analogy of translation is often used. Just as we have to translate from one language to another, so we must translate from one cultural context to another.

The issues go further than just the doctrine of the atonement.

How do we translate from a culture which believes in powerful and angry deities to an atheistic culture? Can the idea of God be contextualized to a notion of socially agreed ideas? To put it another way: is there anything in Scriptural teaching which is not expressed in terms of a particular culture and hence represents something which should not be changed in the process of contextualization to a different culture? Often proponents of contextualizing pick out this or that element which they would like to contextualize without considering broader questions.

The answer to the questions just posed is already supplied by the basic assumption of the whole approach. If Scripture is shaped and its concepts supplied by the culture in which it arose, then it is all determined by that culture. Hence all of it, every idea and concept, must be changed to be relevant to another culture. We meet here the basic assumption of cultural relativism. That is, that there cannot be truths which are valid for all cultures. Each culture has its own set of norms which are true for it alone.

Scripture rejects this view simply because God is God. He is not bound and captive within history. Of course the exclusion of God and his revelation from the world lays the way open for such relativism. As we have already noted, such exclusion is rejected by Scripture. Similarly, the view that the message of God changes for every age is rejected; the gospel to be proclaimed on the eve of Christ's return is the same gospel as is proclaimed in the New Testament age: 'Fear God, and give Him glory' (Rev. 14:7); for, as Revelation 14:6 says, it is an eternal gospel.

Involved in cultural relativism is the belief that, although they may differ from one another, the concepts of cultures are neutral. We do not have to reject the ideas of a culture as contrary to Scripture. We can simply translate the ideas of Scripture into the ideas of a modern or a pagan culture. Actually the proponents of this extreme form of contextualization fail to do that, for each culture shows a clash of ideas. These contextualizers choose one set of the conflicting ideas as the 'Christian' set. The only way in which they could choose one side in the ideological conflict would be if there is some truth of Scripture which is not culturally determined and

[77]

allows us to choose right from wrong today.

An example of this is the choice of Marxism as the contextual form the gospel should take today. Generally this is defended by saying that Scripture shows that God is on the side of the poor. Hence we choose Marxism today in order to be on the side of the poor. If cultural relativism is true, then we cannot take the Scriptural teaching about the poor and make any use of it today, for the Scriptural teaching on the poor would be relevant to the culture alone in which Scripture was written. If cultural relativism is not correct then we have to look at all teachings of Scripture, not merely at one slogan plucked out of Scripture at random.

Actually the ideas of a culture are not neutral. They are much influenced by the culture's acceptance of, or rejection of, the truth of God. This was true in Biblical times. Much of Scripture is a polemic against the ideas of the time. If we may revert to the idea of sacrifice, the Scripture does not simply accept the ideas of the time. For contemporary ideas tended to see sacrifice as food for the god worshipped. Scripture, in rejecting this, is asserting a different view of God as the just, and hence the wrathful, God. If we change our view of sacrifice, and hence of the work of Christ, we must also change our view of God. There will no longer be a call to 'fear God and give Him glory' (Rev. 14:7) because his justice will no longer command awe. The fact is that such concepts as the justice of God cannot be relativized and 'contextualized' without destroying the gospel.

It may be objected that Scripture is very much in terms of the culture of its time. The tenth commandment refers to an ox or a donkey and not to a llama or a yak. Surely such passages of Scripture must be 'contextualized' in order to be applied today.

It all comes down to a crucial question: do we meet in Scripture a truth which transcends cultural barriers, even though it is applied to a particular culture, or do we meet a truth expressed in terms of the limited ideas of a particular culture? Let us explore the implications of each question.

If the truth is not culture-bound, yet is directed to a particular culture, then we can apply that same truth to different cultures and different situations. We have already considered ways of doing this in our second chapter. If we may revert again to the example of the tenth commandment, the commandment already provides the ground for including llamas and yaks by the fact that it includes 'anything that belongs to your neighbour' (Exod. 20:17).

In this sense Scripture is already 'contextualizing'. When Paul applies the command about muzzling oxen to the paying of evangelists he was 'contextualizing'. Paul did exactly the same thing when he modified the fifth commandment as he quoted it in Ephesians 6:2,3. He contextualized the command for the new situation into which God's people had been brought by the work of Christ. Whereas the original command referred specifically to Canaan the new form refers to the whole earth.

To apply this use of Scripture to new situations we must grasp the teachings and ideas involved in the specific applications we meet in Scripture. That is not simply a matter of slogans such as 'God is on the side of the poor' or 'Scripture teaches the right of private land ownership'. It is a matter of careful study of the whole teaching of Scripture. Such study is unpopular in a day which prefers easy slogans. It is condemned as 'casuistry'. Nevertheless, it is what we must do if we are to understand the Word of God and to know how to apply it.

If we accept the second alternative proposed above and say that Scripture is a compilation of culturally bound ideas, what follows? What follows must be the translation of those concepts into those of another culture. Yet that task is impossible according to the very premise that has been adopted at the beginning. We cannot extract any truth from Scripture to tell us what we should adopt as our new 'Christian' ideas. In any case, why should we bother? The missionary urge, the urge to bring thought and action captive to one God and his truth, is tied up with Biblical monotheism. Surely that also must be culturally determined. Hence we cannot take from Scripture the imperative to try to bring every thought captive in a pagan culture which has many gods or ideas and is indifferent to any claim of absolute truth.

All we see here is the basic truth about relativisms. Applied consistently they lead to impossible contradictions and hence total inaction. They work only when applied in a selective way. Those who charge that the teaching of Biblical authors was culturally bound generally make such selective use. They find something in Scripture which challenges contemporary ideas or institutions, and they try to find a way to set aside that element of Scripture. Relativism is a readily available idea in our culture. If there was some serious thinking through of the problems relativism poses, then this use would command more respect. Of course, such rigorous and consistent thought would lead to the conclusion that nothing can be learned from Scripture of relevance to our situation or to any other situation.

⚙ 14 ⚙

The Hermeneutical Circle

There are other relativisms besides cultural relativisms. One is psychological relativism, the belief that a person's psychological experience completely determines his comprehension of the truth. Whatever a person hears or reads he will interpret in terms of his own experience and ideas. This idea has entered into discussion of the interpretation of the Bible. Hence the term the 'hermeneutical circle'. It is held that a person will bring to the Scripture the ideas of his background and culture. He will naturally read those ideas into what he reads. Hence he sees those ideas as being confirmed by the Bible. He reads out of the Bible what he reads into it. Hence we have a circle of interpretation or a 'hermeneutical circle'.

This idea seems confirmed by observation. We see people trying to make the Bible say what they want it to say. Hence it seems plausible to accept this idea. The idea means that discussion of whether the Bible is the Word of God is rather pointless. In any case, it cannot say anything new to us. It means that the debate about the Bible is pointless. The various sides of the debate must be incapable of reading the Bible to see what it says for itself.

Firstly, it must be remembered that we are dealing with relativism, and relativisms cannot be applied consistently. If we applied psychological relativism consistently, then it would mean that the idea of the hermeneutical circle was completely determined by the experiences and background of the originators of the idea. Everybody else will interpret that idea in terms of his own concepts and ideas. When the proponents of psychological relativism try to defend or explain their position, they actually accept the truth of their opponents' position.

They believe that ideas can be communicated from one person to another.

It is true that certain people try to find in the Bible what it does not teach. However, we have to understand this tendency in the Bible's terms. Scripture attributes it to the influence of sin on man. Peter says that it is the untaught and the unstable who distort the Scriptures (2 Peter 3:16). Paul says that it is hardness of heart which prevents men seeing the truth of the old covenant (2 Cor. 3:14). Jesus said to those who would not receive his words that it was because of their affiliation with Satan (John 8:43–45).

Hence the crucial importance of the Holy Spirit. It is the Spirit who removes the veil of misunderstanding and enables a man to understand the Scriptures (2 Cor. 3:14–18). Often in Scripture this activity of the Spirit is so closely connected to the impact of Scripture that the cause of the effect is ascribed to Scripture itself: 'The unfolding of Thy words gives light; It gives understanding to the simple' (Ps. 119:130). The words which were given by the Spirit are also interpreted by the Spirit. Hence Paul's teaching in 1 Corinthians 2:6–16. The words the apostle speaks are taught him by the Spirit and the wisdom to understand them comes also from the Spirit.

When psychological relativism attributes man's ability to understand the Scriptures to the natural tendency of men's minds, it excuses their sin. It claims that it is not hardness of heart which makes them unwilling to receive the words of Jesus. It is the conditioning effect of their upbringing and experiences. The same excusing of sin is present when we are told that the modern world cannot accept this or that aspect of Biblical teaching. Prominent amongst the truths which the modern world supposedly cannot accept is that God is an active God. Yet the view that God is not active in the world is at least as old as New Testament times. Peter speaks specifically against that point of view in 2 Peter 3:3–10. He points out that the great proof that the world had not been left to go on its own merry way is the flood. Similarly God will intervene decisively once more to bring judgment.

The belief that modern man cannot understand Biblical concepts becomes a self-fulfilling prophecy. If we believe that men cannot accept such truths, then we will not preach and teach them. Hence they will not be received because faith comes by hearing the Word preached. Relativism paralyses the mission of the church to the unconverted.

Biblically, what is required of the church is not a capitulation to the hardness of men's hearts and their unbelief. Rather it is the bringing of every thought into captivity to the obedience of Christ (2 Cor. 10:5). And the desire of the church for every believer is that he should come to a fulness of understanding of the mystery of God's revelation. That is, to a fulness of understanding of the wonder of God's love as displayed in Christ (Eph. 3:8–19). The New Testament church sought to do that with pagans of the Graeco-Roman world to whom the concepts of Scripture were quite foreign. It is only because they attempted it that the grace of God has come to us Gentiles. We should not fail in taking that truth to other pagans.

If, as some hold, the basic intent of Scripture is inexpressible in words, or is actually contrary to the words of the Bible, then there could be no breaking of the hermeneutical circle. Men can assert that the Bible says this or that, even though the Bible never does so in words or actually contradicts it. Men are then at liberty to read anything they like into the Bible. And those who hold this belief often read in things quite contrary to the text! It is the expression of truth in words that breaks that circle. The reader has to reckon with a text which says things he would prefer not to believe.

What God says to Job, or Paul's arguments in his letter to the Colossians, or the express statements that Scripture comes from God: these are things that have to be faced if we would come to a proper understanding of the Scriptures. To ignore them and to continue with the positions and slogans which are refuted by these and other explicit statements is to be caught in the hermeneutical circle. It is to make the Bible say what we would prefer it to say. It is not our psychological preconditioning that will make us do that. It is our unwillingness to surrender our autonomous, sinful reason to the truth of God.

The debate over Scripture is sometimes dismissed as explicable in psychological terms. Defenders of the orthodox doctrine are dismissed as motivated by fear of change and new ideas. Of course, psychological relativism cuts both ways. If the defenders of orthodox doctrine can be psychologized, so too can their opponents. They can be said to be influenced by the fear of holding doctrines and positions unfashionable today. It is the explicit statements of Scripture which lift the debate above the level of psychological charge and counter-charge. The teaching of Scripture allows a test to be made as to who are motivated by conformity to God's revelation.

∾ 15 ∾

The Redemptive Focus of Scripture

In the light of what has already been said we can return to one
of the fundamental questions before us. Does the Bible have a
restriction to its authority imposed by its focus on salvation? Is
it irrelevant to other major subjects or areas of life?

This question is not asking whether the Bible speaks with
equal detail in all areas of life. It is asking whether we know
ahead of reading a particular passage that it cannot apply to
certain questions. As we have seen, the range of issues on
which the Bible cannot speak is variously defined. Some define
it more narrowly and some more broadly. What is common is a
determination that there are areas in which the Bible does not
speak, no matter what a particular text says. We are thus
looking at an issue where there is a claim being made as to the
basic intent and meaning of Scripture.

Does the Bible explicitly limit the range of its own authority?
There are no such limitations in Scripture. Certainly the whole
Scripture directs our attention to Christ and focuses on him
(John 5:39). Yet that focus is on Christ not only as Redeemer,
but also as Creator (John 1:1–3). It directs our attention to him
as Creator and Sustainer of the universe (Col. 1:15–17) as well
as Mediator and Reconciler (Col. 1:18–23). This emphasis on
Christ as Creator and Sustainer is of vital relevance to the
debate. For the crux of the debate is the relevance of Scripture
to areas of creation and history. Certainly there will be those
who also limit the ability of Scripture to speak on ethical and
doctrinal matters. But what is initially brought into question
will be the authority of Scripture in matters of creation and
providence. Simply to say that the Scripture centres on Christ
does not prove a limitation of the authority of Scripture. For

[85]

Christ is presented as Lord of creation and of the whole history of the world since creation.

The passages of Scripture which deal with its authority do not contain limiting clauses. They tend rather to be universal and comprehensive in their claims. For example 2 Timothy 3:17 says that Scripture prepares a man for '*every* good work'. There are no limitations on the wisdom and knowledge hidden in Christ. Rather in him 'are hidden all the treasures of wisdom and knowledge' (Col. 2:3). Therefore believers are urged to turn to the Christ revealed in the apostolic instruction and not to human philosophy or tradition (Col. 1:4–8).

Given that Christ has such cosmic rôles, given that Scripture speaks of creation and providence and the rôle of Christ in such things, given that Scripture is comprehensive in its claims rather than disposed to accept limitations on its authority, what right then have we ourselves to impose limits on that authority?

Sometimes the claim is made that it is the 'gospel' which is infallible, but that other elements of Scripture, depending on whether or not they relate to the gospel, are more or less fallible. This limitation is not found in Scripture itself. Rather, Jesus and the New Testament appeal to the Old Testament as authority without any such limitation.

One implication of this limitation of the authority of Scripture is that there are elements of human activity which are impervious to human sinfulness. Notice that Scripture is defined as equipping the man of God for 'every good work' (2 Tim. 3:17). Let us suppose that there are areas of human life to which Scripture says nothing. Will man's activity in those areas be free of sin? Let us suppose it is not. Then a Christian, having no guidance from Scripture, could be expected to sin in those areas. How then could he be equipped for every good work? Sins are not good works.

This somewhat theoretical discussion can be put in terms of a common example. It is often claimed that the scientist, as he investigates the creation, or the scholarly historian as he studies his history, is neutral. The prejudices and influences of sin, or the opposite influences of regeneration, do not affect his work. Sometimes the area of neutrality will be more narrowly defined. It will be acknowledged that sinful propensities to pride can

influence a scholar's judgments. His actual reasoning, however, and hence the presentation of his theories, will be declared
neutral. If this is the case, there is no necessity to bring
Scripture to bear to judge or correct such thinking. Obviously if
Scripture is needed to correct such reasonings, then we could
not claim they had been unaffected by sin.

Thus a limitation on the scope of Scripture naturally carries
with it a limitation on the scope and range of sin. This can be
put in another way in terms of the limitation of Scriptural
authority to matters of redemption. Any areas outside the scope
of Scripture must be areas without a need for the influence of
redemption. Hence they must be areas where sin has not had an
influence. We cannot limit the scope of Scripture without at
the same time limiting the scope of redemption. Calling
Scripture 'redemptive' simply emphasises this point.

Are there areas of human life impervious to the influence of
sin? Are the reasonings of the scholars neutral? Scripture
returns an emphatic negative answer to both questions. The
mind of man is not less depraved than the rest of him. Notice
the way Paul develops the doctrine of human sin in Romans.
Man's sinfulness is particularly revealed by his reaction to the
creation. He should have been led to acknowledge the true God
by his experience of the created world (Rom. 1:18–20). This
gives us an easy test as to whether human scientific activity is
unaffected by sin. Do all scientists acknowledge the Creator?
The answer is clearly 'No'. Hence we cannot claim that they
carry on their scientific work in a neutral and unbiased fashion.

People may be reluctant to acknowledge that the much
vaunted activities of human research and scholarship are
tainted by sin. However, when they refuse to accept this, their
argument is not just with the application of Scripture to areas of
science. It is with the Biblical teaching on the key doctrine of
sin.

Paul goes on to identify the state of mind connected with this
rejection of the Creator. It is a mind proud of its own wisdom
(Rom. 1:21–23). The consequence of such proud rebellion, in
the judgment of God, is the spread of other forms of depravity,
particularly degrading vices (vv.26–32). We see here that there
is no watertight division between man's view of the creation
and ethical issues. Rather they are interconnected. Refusal to

acknowledge God as Creator leads to sin in other respects.

Elsewhere Scripture includes the thoughts of man within the scope of sin's effects (Gen. 6:5; 8:21; Eph. 2:1–3). Since the thoughts of man are corrupt, then it logically follows that the renewal of the mind is part of the regenerating and sanctifying work of the Spirit (Rom. 12:1,2; Eph. 4:20–24; Col. 3:10).

Note that the issue in this discussion is not whether we declare the purpose of Scripture to be man's redemption. It is one of how much of human life needs to be redeemed. The moment you admit that all of it needs to be redeemed, then you can no longer limit the range of Scripture's authority.

We thus meet another case of a theological interconnection. If the range of Scripture's authority is limited, then man's sinfulness and consequent need for redemption are also limited. Thus the scope of the gospel's claim too is limited. To define infallibility as applying only to the 'gospel' and then to limit the scope of infallibility must necessarily also limit the gospel's claim. Its effects on man's life are also limited. Thus a defence of the full authority of Scripture in all areas of life is a defence of a broad and wide-ranging gospel.

This point needs to be emphasised because the impression is often given that those who defend the full authority of Scripture are indifferent to the central message of Scripture, namely, Christ's coming to redeem sinners. That is not at all the issue. The issue is whether the whole of man's life is covered by that redemption.

We have already seen other ways in which the arguments of those who want a reduced authority for Scripture threaten truths central to the gospel. The whole idea that God does not interfere in the affairs of the world is a good example. If God remains outside the world, then Christ was a man and not God, and his virgin birth, miracles, and bodily resurrection from the dead are myths. The believer also could not be renewed by the work of the Holy Spirit. As such ideas are often not consistently applied, the last of the problems raised is of particular significance.

Inconsistently, an exception will be made for Jesus. With respect to him the 'supernatural' element will be allowed or at least not explicitly denied, at least at first. What will be denied is any activity of God in the world apart from Jesus. Such a belief threatens not only the Old Testament miracles, the inspiration of Scripture and the Biblical doctrine of providence. It threatens also the Biblical teaching on the renewal of man by the Holy Spirit. Where the confidence is absent that the Holy Spirit will use the foolishness of the gospel preached to renew man, then resort has to be made to human methods of persuasion. If we must emphasise more the 'human' element of Scripture because God is shut out of the world, then for the same reason we must emphasise more the 'human' element in conversion. It is this theological interconnection which creates a tendency for the combination of a move away from Scripture with a modification of the gospel.

We saw the gospel also being threatened by the idea that man, who can change times and laws as his customs and beliefs change, is logically also his own saviour. If it is human culture which brings us into a new age where the old Biblical law is not valid, then it will be human culture that saves us. In all these instances, a reduction in the rôle to be played by God will flow from the area of authority and inscripturation to other areas. If God's rôle in the guidance of his people is limited, it will not stay the same in the redemption of his people.

The idea that all Scripture is bound up with culture must include the gospel. It too will be a product of a particular culture, needing change to fit another culture. Of course people who say that Scripture is culture bound often do not initially mean to include the central gospel message. In excluding the gospel from this relativism they are being inconsistent. That involves for them and their followers and students a choice. Do we resolve the inconsistency by rejecting the idea of cultural relativism or by including the gospel among the things which need to be contextualized? Sad to say, many will accept the second alternative.

Other examples could be given of the involvement of the gospel in the debate over Scripture. Criticism of the Scripture as not an 'objective' writing of history and hence not reliable history is really criticism of the centrality of Christ. For the selection of material is dominated by the theological themes of the plight of man and the redeeming power of God. This is not 'objective' history if the secularist's view of the world is correct. However it is really secularism which produces biased history.

Ultimately the issue is whether the Biblical God does or does not exist.

Thus the issue is whether the Scripture testifies to Jesus as Redeemer. However it is those who are limiting the testimony of Scripture who are ultimately calling in question that testimony. Scripture is comprehensive in its claims simply because the Redeemer is also the Creator and the Lord of the world ever since creation. Structures of thought which call in question his rôle as Creator and Governor must also call in question his rôle as the initiator and overseer of the work of salvation.

PART TWO

Points of Contention

๑๙ *Introduction* ๑๙

In moving from basic thesis to more detailed studies it is easy to lose sight of the main point at issue, namely, whether Scripture is a sufficient authority in every area of human life or whether its authority is more limited. That case has already been argued in its general principles. The debate over Scripture has tended to throw up some areas of particular concern. A more detailed study of these questions is needed.

As emphasised in the earlier chapter on 'The Bible and the Historian', our historical knowledge is limited, as is all our knowledge. To some of the issues thrown up in the debate we have only very tentative answers. Examples of questions which deserve a cautious answer would be: When and why did Pharisaic use of the Bible change? What was the role of women in New Testament times? Nevertheless an answer of some sort needs to be attempted to these questions. Otherwise the reader may feel that a difficult question has been avoided. Or he may be left convinced that something is true because some author has asserted dogmatically an erroneous or debatable view.

Yet not every area of detailed investigation is so uncertain. The attempt has been made in what follows to distinguish those issues on which certainty is possible, because Scripture is clear, from areas where we must acknowledge our ignorance.

The approach which we take to the Bible in the first part has ramifications for other issues or questions. One such issue would be the way we *prove* the Bible true to one who doubts it. Another is the approach to be taken when translating the Bible.

Thus this second part is of quite heterogeneous material. Some of it allows for certainty; some is tentative. It is important to point this out lest the tentativeness of these investigations be turned against the basic thesis. It is a familiar device in refuting a disliked argument, to pick upon a peripheral part of the thesis

[93]

and to direct criticism against it. That danger could be avoided by refusing to enter into areas where there is no certainty. Nevertheless such refusal would be a disservice to the reader who wonders about the relevance of the thesis of this book to some of the other issues thrown up in the debate.

꩜ 16 ꩜

The Creation Account

We have already seen that the issue of the authority of Scripture in matters of science is one of the major issues. Those who would limit the scope of scriptural authority have a general tendency to exclude matters of science from that authority. Thus the creation account in Genesis becomes a matter of debate. The debate centres particularly on whether we may take the narrative in Genesis as giving us an account of what actually happened. Some would say that it tells us *that* God created the world, not *how* he created it. Others say that it is poetry and hence not to be interpreted literally. Some claim that it is a polemic against idolatry. The truth to be learned is that we should not worship idols, not that God created the world in six days.

Obviously if Genesis says reliable things on how God created the world, then Scripture must be relevant to many scientific questions. We cannot say that Scripture is so narrow in its focus and concerns that it cannot be relevant to matters of science.

Various approaches are taken to the interpretation of the creation account. Those who reject the authority of Scripture tend to see it as a variant on a myth or myths of the ancient Near East. They also tend to see chapters 1 and 2 of Genesis as two different accounts of creation, contradictory in many respects.[1]

Among those who claim to accept the authority of the Bible there is a variety of positions. There are those who look to Genesis to teach nothing but 'religious' truth. Hence nothing it

[1]E.g. E. A. Speiser, *Genesis* (The Anchor Bible), Garden City, N.Y., Doubleday, 1964. For the allegation of a connection to myth see my 'Biblical Creation Accounts and Near Eastern Myths', *Biblical Creation*, 8 (1986), 35–57.

says can have any bearing upon the views of a scientist, a psychologist, or a historian. In the main this conclusion is reached not from a consideration of the text of Genesis, but via a dogmatic assertion about what the text may or may not teach. The whole attempt to limit the Scripture to 'religious' matters has already been considered. Since this view does not directly depend upon the interpretation of the creation account in Genesis, it will not be considered in this chapter.

Positions which make an attempt to reckon with the text themselves vary. There are those who argue that the text is not to be taken as historical narrative but to be interpreted as one might interpret poetry or a parable. Others argue for a literal interpretation but wish to keep open the possibility, or even argue a strong case, that the 'days' of Genesis chapter 1 are long periods of time. There are others who press for a literal interpretation, including of the 'days'. Within all three groups, that is the non-literalists, the day-age group, and the strict literalists, there are various approaches to the interaction with secular scholarship in matters of science, anthropology, etc. Generally speaking the non-literalists tend to think well of secular views. The day-age people include those who argue that if the 'days' are taken as long periods of time, there is close agreement between Genesis chapter 1 and scientific discovery. The strict literalists tend to be very critical of accepted science and in this they would be joined by some of the day-age people.[1]

THE SHADOW OF SECULAR SCIENCE

While some authors claim to be interpreting Genesis with never a thought about the views of dominant secular science, such claims are rather unconvincing. Obviously a conviction that

[1] Not considered in this list is the 'Ruin – Reconstruction' or 'Gap' theory. This holds that Genesis 1:1 describes a creation of the heaven and earth and all of its inhabitants. These were destroyed as a result of Satan's rebellion. Hence Genesis 1:2 is said to mean that 'The earth *became* waste and void.' What follows in Genesis 1 then is the description of a recreation in six days. This view depends on a grammatically impossible translation of 1:2. (To say 'become' Hebrew uses verb *plus* preposition. There is no preposition in 1:2.) It has been often refuted by others (e.g. J. C. Whitcomb, *The Early Earth*, London, Evangelical Press, 1972, ch. 5).

[96]

the majority of scientists cannot be wrong must lead to a disposition towards non-literal interpretations. Less obviously, a tendency to reject secular science and to develop an alternative creationist science can influence exegesis. We can interpret texts to conform with our alternative science just as we can interpret them to conform with evolutionary science.

Are there any general thoughts or convictions with which we should approach the Genesis text? Our answer is in the affirmative. We have already considered in Chapter 15 what Romans chapter 1 says about man's refusal to acknowledge the Creator. We have seen also that Scripture speaks of man's mind as changed by conversion and sanctification. Hence we should not be surprised if unbelieving humanity has a different view of origins from that of believers.

We can be guilty of a lack of proper historical perspective. Is it any more surprising that most scientists are evolutionists than it is that most philosophers of the Hellenistic world rejected Judaism and then Christianity? Or that most religious writers contemporary with the Old Testament were poly-theists? We are not the first age to have had problems with Genesis. From the first century AD, when the Jewish writer Philo lived and wrote, the tendency has been to accommodate Genesis to whatever the dominant philosophy was.[1] It was such an accommodation that allowed Aristotelian cosmology to be accepted by the late Medieval church and set the stage for the church's defence of Aristotle against Galileo.[2]

Holding to a minority position should not indicate to the Christian that his view is incorrect. Nevertheless the problem is not just one of being in the minority position. Anglo-Saxon

[1] '. . . from Philo (on) throughout Christian, Moslem and Jewish philosophy, there was a general tendency to disregard the literalness of the story of creation and to harmonize it with what each particular philosopher happened to believe with regard to the origin of the world.' (H. A. Wolfson, 'The Veracity of Scripture in Philo, Halevi, Maimonides and Spinoza' in *Alexander Marx Jubilee Volume*, English Section, New York Jewish Theol. Sem. of America, 1950, p. 608.)

[2] This does not mean we should be uncritical of Galileo, though he is often paraded as the hero in the conflict of pure science and theological prejudice. He had his own blindness when faced with inconvenient arguments. See P. Duhem, *To Save the Phenomena. An Essay on the Idea of Physical Theory from Plato to Galileo*, Chicago, University of Chicago, 1969, ch. 7.

thought, indeed all Western thought, has been much influenced by the philosophical tradition of empiricism. This is the tendency to think that man can appreciate the 'facts' of the world without any prejudice on his part. The facts, we might say, write this truth upon his mind without his having to do any interpretation and possible distortion. While this tradition is increasingly under challenge it determines many people's views of science. They might believe that the individual scientist, or the collective mass of scientists, show political prejudice, religious bias, or even disgraceful treatment of their family members. However they find it hard to believe that bias and preconception distort their interpretation of what they see through telescope or microscope. All that can be said for this belief is that it would create an area of human life less permeated by sin. For that belief there is no Scriptural warrant, rather the reverse.

There are people who hold such views who are part of academic communities and know the scholarly work of the people they hold to be neutral. One wonders whether they argue against their own experience of such men. In retrospect, so much of what is accepted as the only possible interpretation of the data in one age is seen by the next as the consequence of the prejudice with which the former age approached the data. Would an 'empirical' study of all scientists and scholars of the past lead to the conclusion that their work was without bias? A defence of the past generation against bias would be impossible to sustain. We so share the biases of our age that it is hard to see our own inconsistencies. Nevertheless there is no reason to regard ourselves as better than the past.

Having said this there is still a warning on the other side. We may honour the memory of the apologists of the early Christian centuries who carried on a lonely defence of Christianity against the weight of pagan philosophical criticism.

Yet we would not today want to endorse all the apologists' arguments. Similarly we must remember that Genesis was not primarily written to furnish arguments against evolution any more than it was written to provide refutations of Aristotle. In our zeal to develop such arguments we may miss what it is saying.

The reading of Scripture to ascertain what it really says means trying to allow the text to speak for itself against both secular science and 'Christian' science, against secular philosophy and 'Christian' philosophy.

THE RELATION OF GENESIS CHAPTERS 1 AND 2

The relationship between the supposed two accounts of creation is taken up first for a number of reasons. Investigating the relationship between the two accounts forces us to confront the basic thrust of the creation accounts. The difficulty, or otherwise, of reconciling the two accounts may give some indication of the extent to which we can see the accounts as intended to be interpreted literally.

How does the account in Genesis 2:4ff. differ, if at all, from that in Genesis 1:1–2:3? Several things are clear on the face of the text. Genesis 2:4ff. is integrated with the overall structure of Genesis. It consists of sections introduced with the title 'These are the generations of . . .'. A study of the use of that title shows that only one concept or translation will fit all the cases. That is 'generations' or 'things/people generated/begotten by . . .'. That is, it focuses on the progeny of the things/person named in the title.[1] Thus the focus of this section is on the things which come from the heavens and the earth, rather than the heavens and the earth themselves. In other words, the concentration is on vegetation, animals and man.

Genesis chapter 1 also deals, in brief, with vegetation, animals, and men. Hence some people have concluded that the two accounts come from different sources and were placed in the same book by a later editor.[2] The whole argument that there are two accounts depends upon assumptions about the way people write history. One assumption is that if there were one author he would integrate all the material into one account, rather than spread it over two accounts. Such an assumption fits well with the idea we have considered earlier that truth consists in possessing comprehensive, exhaustive knowledge.

[1] D. Kidner, *Genesis*, Downers Grove, Ill., I.V.P., 1967, pp. 23f.;59.
[2] This is the approach of the Documentary Hypothesis exemplified by Speiser, *op. cit.* For refutation of the hypothesis as a whole see O. T. Allis, *The Five Books of Moses*, 3rd ed., Philadelphia, Presbyterian and Reformed, 1964; E. J. Young, *An Introduction to the Old Testament*, London, Tyndale, 1964, chapter 8.

The modern historian tries to demonstrate his command of the truth by writing an exhaustive, integrated account. Hence the expectation that Biblical authors would write in the same way.

We have seen however that the Bible does not have that view of truth. Hence there is no reason why a Biblical author might not separate different aspects of a complex story to ensure clarity. That does not mean that he might not also integrate the materials in one story. It simply means that the biblical author has options.

There are other examples which might be explained in the same way. However the person holding to the thesis of different sources will simply explain them in terms of his thesis. Hence they do not prove the point. Such an example comes from a comparison of Genesis 8:15–22 with Genesis 9:1–17. There is a certain repetition of elements in the two passages, but also a more detailed elaboration of some in the second passage.

It comes down therefore to a question of approach. Do we commit the historical anachronism of expecting that a biblical author has to share the assumptions of a modern historian? Are we willing to learn the techniques of Biblical historical writing from the text itself, instead of imposing upon that text our own expectations?

When we look at the concerns of Genesis chapter 2 we find that vegetation is a major topic. The need of water for plants is raised first. There is no mention of provision of water for irrigation in chapter 1. Hence something must be provided for the plants God creates.

How would this fit into the structure of Genesis 1? We find an answer elsewhere in Scripture itself. Psalm 104 is a poetic commentary on Genesis 1. It follows the order of events of the creation days. In the earlier part of the psalm the emphasis is on creation as a display of God's glory and as his servant. The parallels are Day 1: v.2a; Day 2: vv.2b,3; Day 3: vv.5–18; Day 4: vv.19–23; Day 5: vv.24–26. Fresh water for the creation is a concern in verses 10–13. What is significant is the point at which it occurs in the psalm. It occurs in the account of the third day, between the emergence of the dry land and the mention of vegetation. Thus the author of Psalm 104 has integrated a major concern of Genesis 2 into his treatment of Genesis 1. The psalm thus gives important evidence as to the

translation question about Genesis 2:6. What does God cause
to go up from the ground?

Psalm 104:10 speaks of springs. This would accord with the
possible meaning of the Akkadian cognate[1] of the Hebrew word
which has traditionally been translated 'mist'. The mention of
a spring or stream in 2:6 could be connected to the river
mentioned in 2:10.

We see therefore that the author of Psalm 104 had no
difficulty in integrating a major concern of Genesis chapter 2
into his treatment of Genesis chapter 1. The psalm emphasizes
the way in which God has supplied the world with all the things
needed for his creatures. That is precisely the point that comes
through from the way the story is told in both Genesis 1 and
Genesis 2. God first creates the environment, then places the
creature into that environment. In chapter 1 the environment is
created on the first triad of days and then the creature on the
corresponding day in the second triad of days. Thus day one
corresponds to day four and so on. In chapter 2 that point is
made by telling us how God provides water for his creation and
how he prepared the garden for man. Thus the two accounts
are not contradictory but in complete accord in their concerns.

The second main subject of chapter 2 is the relationships
between the creatures. Just as God in chapter 1 gives names to
his creatures so man gives names to the animals. The parallel
to God's activity in chapter 1 shows that naming implies
overlordship. Further, man recognizes that there is no animal
fit to be a companion. Hence the creation of woman for the
man.

Thus authority and mutual relationship within the creation
is a major theme of chapter 2. These same themes are found in
chapter 1 also. God creates the sun and moon to rule (1:16). He
created man to have dominion (1:28).

Thus two major concerns emerge from the first two chapters.
They are the provision by God of the environment to meet the
needs of his creatures and the mutual relationship between
those creatures. Those themes must be understood or chapter 3
does not make sense. For the sin of man emerges clearly, from
that introduction, as ingratitude. In spite of all God had given

---

[1] It seems to be a Sumerian loanword in Akkadian.

him, he reacted with disobedience. Further, the mutual relationships of the creatures must be understood if we are to understand the temptation and its result.

Instead of the created order of authority of God, man (male, female), animal we have the animal setting the pace to be followed by the woman, who is then followed by the man, with God's Word being ignored. Hence the punishments of 3:14–19 have to do with the reassertion of the created order of command. Hence also the breakdown of the relationship between man and woman, and between man and God.

LITERAL OR NON-LITERAL?

The question about the creation account generally comes down to a simple choice. Do we interpret the account literally? Putting it this way seems to ignore the day-age view, but when pressed, that view generally turns into a variant of the literal or the non-literal view. Suppose we say that the 'days' are very long ages, ages of millions of years. We learn from the text that such ages have also mornings and evenings. Thus we would have an age of millions of years of light followed by millions of years of darkness, if we take every other part of the text literally. Since there is a definite tendency with holders of the day-age view to try to reconcile Genesis and secular science, such a view, with its scientific difficulties, is not appealing. Hence the tendency to slide towards the non-literal view.[1]

The non-literal view most commonly depends upon an appeal to the literary character of the text. The literal view depends upon an appeal to the way other passages of Scripture treat the creation account. The defender of the non-literary view may be happy to say that the 'days' are probably to be read as ordinary days, but that does not mean that creation

---

[1] There are many variations and gradations between these main views. One might cite, for example, the theory that the days are ordinary days which begin creative periods millions of years long (R. C. Newman & H. J. Eckelmann, *Genesis One and the Origin of the Earth*, Downers Grove, Ill., I.V.F., 1977). What tends to discredit such variants as this is the introduction of much that is not found in the Biblical text. They seem to affirm the literal meaning of the text but eventually produce something one would never have thought of just from the text.

actually took place in an ordinary week. For, he argues, the description in terms of days is only a literary 'framework' for presenting the narrative.

Defenders of this 'framework' view appeal to the obviously structured and carefully shaped account in Genesis 1. The clear parallelism between the first set of three days and the second set has already been mentioned. In the account, words or phrases tend to occur in multiples of 3, 7, or 10. Thus ten times 'God said'; ten times we find 'let there be'; ten times the verb to 'make' is used; three times God blessed the creature; 'and it was so' is used seven times, as is 'God saw that it was good'. Other similar statistics could be given.[1] The account uses anthropomorphisms[2] and, in the account of the creation of man in chapter 2, figures of speech and puns.[3]

Obviously in poetry we expect such concern about structure and the use of literary figures. Such concern in Genesis 1–3 has been used as a reason for calling the text semi-poetic[4] or akin to a parable. If we assume that the account is to be treated as a parable, we proceed to ask: what then does it teach?

We have other instances of parables in Scripture. We could take the parable of Jotham in Judges 9:7–20 or those of Jesus, e.g. Matthew 13. How do we interpret these parables? We interpret them from the information given in association with them. We know from the history and the interpretation that the bramble in Jotham's parable represents Abimelech and we have Jesus' own interpretation of his parables. Thus the parables occur in an interpretive context. What is the context which interprets Genesis 1–3 for us? There is not any. Hence interpretations amongst those who assume that the text is not to be taken literally differ considerably. Some would say we are taught little more than that God created the world, and that man is a creature now in rebellion and alienation from God.[5] Others would derive more from the details given in the text. For

[1]See for these statistics and the attempt to argue the framework view from them, H. Blocher, *Révélation des origines*, Lausanne, Presses Bibliques Universitaires, 1979, esp. pp. 25f.

[2]*Ibid.*, p. 44.

[3]*Ibid.*, pp. 92f.

[4]E.g. J. A. Thompson, 'Genesis 1–3. Science? History? Theology', *Theological Review*, 3(1966), 25.

[5]*Ibid.*, pp. 63ff.

example, Blocher finds in the clear separation of events and created things represented by the division of days a reflection of the New Testament teaching that God is not a God of disorder but of peace.[1]

These various interpretations may seem unobjectionable, but they do not confront a basic problem. What is the key to the interpretation of this so-called 'parable'? How do we know that we are not pressing a detail which is not meant to be interpreted but functions just as part of the story? Of course we may avoid this problem by reducing the amount we derive from the story to a bare minimum, but even then we might be making a mistake. Perhaps we are meant to derive more.

In Genesis 1–3 we face not just the problem of no context which interprets the 'parable'. Biblical symbolism relies heavily upon the preceding history. We have only to note the use of Old Testament types in the presentation of Christ to realize the importance of images derived from past history. Genesis 1–3 has no past history upon which to build. It has no store of persons and events to produce images. Its presence in Scripture is the beginning of the store from which future Biblical writers will draw.

Thus the only clues to the interpretation of the 'parable' must lie within itself. Perhaps we should see as significant those details which show repetition, or to which our attention is drawn by some part of the structure. Let us examine some such aspects of Genesis 1. 'After its kind' is one such repeated phrase. Surely the repetition, along with the clear allocation of separate creative events to different days, is meant to teach us something. The obvious thing it could teach is that living things were created to reproduce within prescribed limits. Thus the theory of evolution is excluded.

Many of the advocates of the framework hypothesis will not be happy with this conclusion for they want to avoid a quarrel with secular science on this issue.[2]

Another example is the parallelism of the first and second triad of days. Surely the obvious interpretation points to the preparation of the environment before the introduction of the

[1] *Op. cit.*, pp. 63ff.
[2] Blocher (*ibid.*, pp. 216ff.) and Thompson (*op. cit.*, p. 25) both argue for the compatibility of evolutionary theory with the Biblical account.

creature into it. Are we to take it from the account that God actually did engage in that work of preparation? If he did not, then what does the passage teach? The problem with this interpretation for holders of the framework theory is with days one and four. For then we would have the creation of the light before the creation of the light-bearers. Once again the concern of the proponents of the framework theory to avoid deviation from accepted scientific hypotheses gives them problems with this possibility. They will often say that the days are not meant to be taken in chronological order. However, if God in fact did not prepare the world for his creatures, what is the passage telling us? Perhaps we could say that it conveys the theological truth that man and his fellow creatures found the world perfectly shaped for them, but in physical reality that was not so. Does it make sense that something is theologically true but not physically true?

A final example would be the creation of woman. It has already been pointed out that the whole passage is much concerned with the mutual relationship between the creatures. The way in which woman was created becomes the basis for the statement of the doctrine of marriage in 2:24. What is the meaning of this part of the story? Let us suppose that the story is just a parable to illustrate the closeness of the marriage union. The problem with this suggestion is that we have no non-parable account of the closeness of the marriage union to be *illustrated* by this parable. On the contrary the closeness of the union is based on this account.

All this is but illustration of the fact that if this is poetry/parable it is poetry/parable with no context and basis of interpretation. Biblical stories like that of Jotham, or Nathan's story of the poor man and his lamb, or Jesus' parables, have figures in them that can be identified with historical people. The bramble is Abimelech, the poor man is Uriah the Hittite, the one who sows the good seed is the Son of Man, etc. Who is Adam? The answer is not given.

I would suggest that the reason this problem has not concerned the proponents of the non-literal view is that they have been concerned less with the problem of interpretation than with avoiding a literal reading of the text. Hence they have not meditated upon the situation, quite unusual for the Biblical text, of a parable without clues for its interpretation.

With this problem in mind we can go back to the arguments presented for a non-literal reading. Are they convincing? To begin with, does the use of anthropomorphism in the description of God, or the use of figurative description, indicate that a text is not meant to be taken historically or literally?

Biblical history in general describes the activities of God in human history in human terms. It is full of so-called 'anthropomorphisms'. This presents a problem if we develop our idea of God by philosophical means and describe God as a sort of 'Holy Other' who is indescribable because he has no characteristic in common with any creature. The Scripture does not do that. One can suggest a simple reason why it does not. Man was made in the image of God. There is a likeness between God and man. To use terms which might be applied to man in a description of God is therefore no problem for the biblical text. Certainly God does not have the limitations of a creature and certainly not the perversities of sinful man. However, likeness remains.

Later in Genesis we are able to look at the way in which God's activity is described. What is the difference between God making man in 2:7 and God shutting the door of the ark for Noah in 7:16? God walked in the garden (3:8). He appeared to Abraham in the form of three men (18:1,2). The creation of woman is told with the use of a play on words (2:23: Hebrew *ish* 'man' and *ishshah* 'woman'). The birth of Isaac is similarly prepared by a play on words (Isaac means 'he laughs'; note the mention of laughter in connection with his birth in 17:17; 18:12; and 21:6).

Of course those who do not believe in the divine authority of Scripture assign all such references to the activity of God to myth, and commonly regard the word-plays as part of the 'folk lore' character of the Bible. This course is not open to one who takes the Bible seriously. Yet if we use such arguments to prove that Genesis 1–3 is a non-literal account, they should prove that much of the rest of Genesis is a non-literal account.

Apart from 'anthropomorphisms', Genesis 1–3 does not use much in the way of literary figures, though the story is certainly told with literary and psychological artistry. However, that is true of Biblical history in general. One could compare for literary and psychological finesse the story of finding a wife for Isaac in Genesis 24.

The crucial case comes down to the careful construction of Genesis 1. Description of this text as 'poetry' is clearly inappropriate. It lacks the parallelism that characterizes Biblical poetry. To see the characteristics of a poetic account, we have only to look at Psalm 104. What that psalm does is to show how the work of creation contributes to the glory of God and the needs of the creatures. It thus spells out the significance of what is recorded more tersely in Genesis 1. Even granted that Psalm 104 is poetry, would we say that the events recorded did not happen? Biblical poetry commonly draws its material and its images from the past. That the record of God's victory over the nations in Psalm 135:8–12 is poetic does not mean that it did not happen. Certainly other cases take their images from past history and are not intended to be taken literally. When David says in Psalm 18:16 that God 'drew him out of many waters' he puns on the name of Moses (Exodus 2:10) and compares his deliverance to that of Moses. Yet David's experience was not literally the same as that of Moses.

In short, Biblical poetry may be referring to events which happened as told in the poem. Or it may employ images from past history to describe the significance of events which were not literally the same as the earlier events. 'Poetry' is not itself a clue to the literal historicity of the events mentioned. Thus a determination that Genesis 1 is 'poetry' does not contribute much to the question of whether it is to be interpreted literally.

However, as already pointed out, Genesis 1 is not poetry. It is very carefully constructed prose. What does that mean for our understanding of its historicity? Virtually nothing, because we have no similar passage with which to compare it. As already pointed out, parables have some accompanying narrative to give a clue to interpretation. Biblical poems refer back to earlier historical events. None of this is true in the case of Genesis 1.

The claim that careful structure in the composition means that the passage is not to be taken literally is nothing more than a claim. How do we know that structure and literalness are incompatible? We are thrust back upon the text itself. As already mentioned, were we to judge from the repetitions and emphasis of the text itself, we would come up with enough material to disturb at least some proponents of the framework hypothesis.

A different argument for the framework hypothesis has been proposed by M. G. Kline,[1] who has argued that the reasons given for the lack of vegetation in Genesis 2:5 presuppose the operation of normal providence during the creation period. It is presupposed that rain or irrigation supplied by humans is necessary, just as in the ordinary course of post-creation history. Now if normal providence was operating during the creation period, events would have taken longer than a day. Furthermore we would not have plants before the sun. Hence Kline argues the narrative of Genesis 1 must be a framework for explaining events and not an account of how things actually came to be.

Whether Kline's view is convincing depends on the way we see the information given in 2:5. We have already seen that one of the emphases of the narrative is that God prepares the environment for the creature. It is natural to see 2:5 as part of this emphasis. All that is needed for vegetation was not present. Hence God set about providing it. There is nothing which clearly indicates that normal providence was functioning during the creation period. Whereas rain is mentioned as the normal way in which vegetation is watered, in 2:6 the earth is watered by the going up of a mist. We cannot infer from 2:5 that there had been a long period prior to the situation reported in that verse during which the earth had become dry. Rather it fits into the framework of God first providing the environmental necessity (water) and then making the plants. Certainly springs do continue as one of the ways in which the earth has been watered since creation but the concern of the verse is the way it first began. The actual beginning does not assume the operation of normal providence.

REFERENCES ELSEWHERE IN SCRIPTURE TO THE CREATION ACCOUNT

We have seen that there is no antecedent history or accompanying narrative to explicate the supposed 'symbols' of

[1] 'Because It Had Not Rained', *Westminster Theological Journal*, 20 (1958), 146–57.

the creation account. There are, however, many references later in Scripture back to that narrative. An especially clear one is the reference in Romans 5:12–21. Here Adam is clearly treated as an individual in contrast to the one who came later in time, Jesus Christ. He is declared to be 'one man'. He is not a representative of every man's typical experience of rebellion against God, for we are told that those who came after did not sin in the way he had sinned (Rom. 5:14). Furthermore it was through his transgression that death came into the world. Of great significance for the interpretation of the creation account is the question of whether death is here understood in general, or whether it refers only to human death. If death came into the world only with Adam, then all evolutionary reconstructions of the development of animals would be excluded. Obviously without animal death there is no animal evolution. Furthermore the periods represented by fossils must occur after man's sin.

It is natural to connect Romans 5 with the statement in Romans 8:20,21 about the whole creation being subjected to futility. Paul's reference here is obviously to the curse placed upon the ground in consequence of man's sin. If we add this to the statement in Genesis 1:30 that the plants are given to every animal as food, then the natural inference is that animals were originally vegetarian and that animal death was also not present before sin.

There are some who will find this too much to prove from Romans 5, which is primarily concerned with human death. Hence let us restrict what we obtain from Romans 5 to the indisputable. Adam was an individual man. His sin brought at least human death into the world.

Even more significant, there is no attempt to explain the 'symbol' Adam. For Adam is introduced as a man, not a symbol. In other words, in regard to the sin of Adam, Paul treats it as a historical occurrence and not as a parable.[1] 1 Corinthians 15:21,22 confirms Paul's approach to the Genesis text as strictly historical.

In 1 Timothy 2:14 an argument is built upon the events of the narrative in Genesis 3. The detail of Eve rather than Adam being the one deceived by the serpent is the basis of the

[1] Many advocates of the framework hypothesis accept this, e.g. Thompson, *op. cit.*, p. 34; Blocher, *op. cit.*, pp. 16off.

argument. In the preceding verse a further argument is developed from the account. This time it turns upon the order of events: Adam was created first and then Eve. With this should be compared 1 Corinthians 11:8,9. Thus the details of the narrative of the creation of man and woman, as well as the subsequent events of the temptation, are treated as historical.

Those who do not want to take these events literally will sometimes object that Paul's use of these texts does not assume their historicity. However their own logic tells against them. Their basic argument is that it is not permissible to build arguments on the details of the text, including chronological ones, because it is a parable or an account full of literary symbols. But Paul does build arguments on details of the text, including chronological details. Hence either Paul is wrong or the account is not a parable.

In general we meet here another case in which Paul does not first interpret the 'symbols' of the narrative before using them in arguments. He treats the story as a story of people and events, rather than as a parable.

Another significant passage is Matthew 19:4–8. It is not only Paul who sees the events of the beginning as of lasting significance. The same form of argument is used by the Lord Jesus Christ also. Once again the reference is simply to what God has done, not to the interpretation of the symbols of the account.

Putting all these passages together, we find it very hard to avoid the conclusion that the New Testament authors, including the Lord Jesus Christ himself, were reading Genesis 2 and 3 as a historical narrative. It was treated as a very significant historical narrative because the original order was the standard for what should follow. Furthermore, it was also treated as a narrative of people and events from whose details one could argue conclusions.

Once one looks at the way the New Testament treats Genesis 2 and 3, certain very significant conclusions follow. The account of the creation of man and woman and their subsequent fall into sin is to be taken as a historical narrative. Thus human evolution is excluded as a possibility.

Since Scripture records factually an event of the greatest interest to science, namely, the origin of man, it is impossible to argue that Scripture does not in any way impinge upon science.

In this detail at least, one has to choose between Scripture and the common opinions of secular science. Further, human death occurs only following sin. All 'human' fossil forms must belong to a date later than Adam.[1] Further, it is not unreasonable to assume that there was also no animal death before the fall. Such an assumption would make it even more difficult to accommodate the Scripture to prevailing scientific views.

So far the treatment of references back to Genesis has been concerned only with Genesis 2 and 3. There are also references to Genesis 1. In considering this chapter we enter an area likely to be more controversial. Many people, realizing the consequences to the whole Biblical view of man of accepting an evolutionary origin for man, are happy to say that man did not evolve. However, they are disinclined to reject animal evolution. In effect they accept the framework of secular science but try to make man a special case. They feel that if they safeguard the case of man himself, then they can concede the rest to evolutionary theory. Hence they would be inclined to accept the historicity of Genesis 2 and 3 but argue that Genesis 1 is basically a symbolic account.

In 2 Peter 3:4–6 there occurs what is primarily a reference to the flood. Peter is arguing against a view that we have already considered on a number of occasions, the view that God does not intervene to change the history of the earth. Against this Peter asserts one crucial instance. It is the destruction of the world by the flood. Peter's whole argument would collapse if the flood had not occurred. In the course of his treatment Peter makes a reference to the construction of the earth (v.5). There is an obvious reason for this connection between the circumstances of the earth's creation and the flood. We have already seen that the earth was prepared for man. Part of that preparation involved the waters. The waters were placed above the firmament or withdrawn in the form of seas. Obviously any reversion to the original condition of the earth would mean a world in which man could not live. Hence such reversions are a means of judgment.[2] When the waters return as rain and the

---

[1]Let us not assume that everything called a 'human' fossil did come from a man. Some might be ape.

[2]Besides the return of the waters to cover the earth, other examples are the withdrawal of light and the withdrawal of water to irrigate the earth.

seas rise to cover the land, then the judgment sent by the Lord takes place.

How is Peter using the narrative in Genesis 1? He is taking it for granted that what the text reports about the earth being separated from the waters is to be accepted. No argument is built upon the narrative. Peter simply makes the connection between the circumstances of the world's creation and the circumstances of the following judgment. Since no argument is built upon details of the narrative we cannot press Peter's use. Yet it is another case in which the narrative is simply accepted as it stands rather than having its 'symbols' interpreted. The fact that the same entities, which are part of the creation account, reappear later in history as implements of judgment raises a question for the symbolic theory. Are they also symbols when they appear later? As already pointed out, Peter's argument would collapse if there was no actual flood to appeal to as the crucial example. The waters that cover the earth in the flood narrative are real waters. Is it not logical to expect that the waters which originally covered the earth are also real waters rather than symbol?

A far more crucial case of appeal to Genesis 1 is found in the fourth commandment in Exodus 20:8–11. There the reason for the pattern of six days of work and one of rest is the activity of God in creation. Man is to imitate the model set by God. The notion of the precedent-setting rôle of the creation reappears here again.

This passage provides a crucial problem for the framework theory. The non-literal approach argues that the six days are not to be taken literally but are merely a framework in terms of which the events are reported. Why is this framework used? Sometimes this is represented as another anthropomorphism. God's creative activity is described in terms of a human work-week. However the fourth commandment says the precise reverse. God's activity is not described in terms of man's. Rather man's work-week is shaped by God's activity.

What can we infer about the narrative in Genesis 1 from this reference? At the very least there has to be some sort of divine activity which man can imitate. Further than that, it has to be an activity that is adequately represented by a pattern of six days of work and one of rest. Here the framework theory is shown to be untenable. For it alleges that the seven days of Genesis 1 are only a framework to describe events. God's activity did not have that form. How then could man imitate God's activity in the weekly cycle if God's activity was not originally as described in Genesis 1?

One of the basic themes of Biblical theology is that piety for man consists in being like God. The fourth commandment is but an example of that basic theme.

Thus once again we encounter a case in which the account of creation is seen as a narrative to be taken at face value, not as a parable to be interpreted. Surely the accumulation of such interpretations by Scripture itself must make the point eventually! We have seen that there are no antecedent events or accompanying narrative to explain the 'symbols'. We have seen that the narrative is in prose and integrates into the historical narrative of the rest of Genesis. The references to it from elsewhere in Scripture take it as a narrative of events which occurred as described. What other evidence could one ask for as proof for treating the account as historical narrative and not poetic parable?

Those who favour a non-literal view of Genesis 1 fall back upon a number of other arguments. Essentially they argue that God's activity, while described in terms of our weekly cycle, is in terms of some other divine 'timetable'. The problem with this argument is that it introduces something not said in any Biblical text and certainly not expressed in this particular text. Surely what they are arguing for this text would hold for any other description of God's activity. That is, though expressed in terms comprehensible to man, it really means something else. God's activity is in some other realm and in terms of some other system.

We come thus to the basic question of how it is that the activity of God can be described in human words. We face two possibilities which will apply not merely to Genesis 1 but to every mention of divine activity. Either God can be described in human terms and comprehended by man because he created a world and particularly a man to reflect him, or all human description of God is basically misleading, for God is so different from man as to be indescribable in human terms. Certainly God is not limited by time and does not have a created consciousness of time. That is the whole point of 2 Peter 3:8. The question however, concerns God's action with respect to a world created time-bound. When God acts in the created world he does so at particular points of time. We need some specific indication from Scripture for treating Genesis 1 differently from any other passage describing God's work in the creation. Exodus 20:11 is the most relevant passage. Instead of indicating that God's 'week' is wholly other than a human week, it relates the two.

A way is sometimes found for making the Genesis week to be other than a normal week by an appeal to the seventh day. It is claimed that the seventh day is quite different from the weekly sabbath. Often the argument claims that the sabbath of God's rest is still in progress. While it is often asserted that God's seventh day is eternal, there is no positive Scriptural support for this idea. Blocher adduces John 5:17 as support for the idea of an eternal sabbath.[1] Jesus claims that in working on the sabbath he is following the precedent of his Father who 'is working until now, and I myself am working'. Blocher argues that Jesus' argument only has validity if God is working on *his* sabbath. If God is working on his sabbath, then Jesus may work on the sabbath. But there is another way of understanding the argument. The argument would have equal force if God was working on the regular weekly sabbath. In context, the work in question would not be primarily a work of creation or providence but the work of redemption and mercy.

One wonders whether the notion of God's eternal sabbath places a one-sided emphasis on the cessation of work on the seventh day of the creation week. The explanation of the sabbath commandment in Exodus 31:13–17 draws attention not just to the cessation from activity: 'on the seventh day He ceased and was refreshed' (v.17). Since God does not grow weary the refreshment is not a physical one. Rather it seems to point to a refreshment of delight in work fully accomplished. The divine recognition that the work of each day had been well done reached its climax in a sabbath of cessation and delight. The sabbath is not a sabbath of endless inactivity. It is rather a climax of satisfaction in work fully accomplished. Certainly God's character is not limited by time and hence his satisfac-

[1] *Op. cit.*, p. 48.

tion cannot be limited. Yet just as creative activity in a created world occurs in time, so the climax to that activity is in time.

There is no warrant within Scripture for making the seventh day of different duration from the other days. Neither is there any warrant for seeing it as of eternal length. Hebrews 4:4 is one other passage which alludes to it, but without any clear indication as to the duration of the day.

Hence our understanding of the seventh day must be determined by our understanding of the other days.

Thus we are forced by Exodus 20:11 to see the creation week as having real analogy to the human week. It will be argued by some that such analogy would still exist even if the days of the creation week were ages rather than normal days. That would certainly be true if we had some other indication in Scripture to take them as other than normal days. The sequence of seven days with morning and evening, night and day, darkness and light, fits easily into a normal day interpretation.[1] It fits poorly into an age. The darkness creates very great problems for the 'day-age' theory.

In the absence of any Biblical evidence to the contrary, and the presence of frequent references to the narrative as historical narrative, the obvious way to read the text of Genesis 1 is the *obvious* way. It is impossible for God to use a misleading form of description. Those who advocate a limited doctrine of scriptural authority sometimes claim that the Scripture has factual, scientific, and historical errors, but will not mislead the person who follows it. We can turn that very argument back on them. If Genesis 1 was not meant to be taken as a literal account, why was it written that way?

A final argument which needs to be considered rests upon a parallel between the Biblical description of the beginning and the end of history. It is claimed that Genesis 1–3 shares a highly symbolic, non-chronological interpretation of events with the Book of Revelation,[2] and that we should use special rules of interpretation for both books.

---

[1] Proponents of forms of the framework hypothesis are generally ready to acknowledge the obvious and say that the text is written in terms of normal days (e.g. Kidner, *op. cit.*, pp. 54ff.). They avoid the implications for science by making this just an explanatory framework.

[2] E.g. Thompson, *op. cit.*, p. 33.

There is no question that the Book of Revelation uses symbols. We know it because the Book tells us it is using symbols and they need to be interpreted (11:8; 12:1; 17:5–18, etc.). If Genesis had similar indications, then there would be no argument! Yet we can be guilty of making Revelation overly different from the rest of Scripture. The use of symbols drawn from the past history of the people of God is a common thing in prophecy. Blocher, who is not at all inclined to give weight to other Biblical references to Genesis 1–3, sees the references in Revelation 12:9 and 20:2 as particularly significant,[1] for there Satan is called the 'serpent of old' in obvious reference to the serpent of the temptation. Blocher rejects the normal interpretation that Satan used the serpent.

He argues that since the Book of Revelation says that Satan was the serpent, there could be no animal involved. One wonders why he does not also conclude that because Exodus 20:11 says that God worked for six days, it is a precise literal period.

Since this passage is one commonly used to prove myth and folk lore in the narrative of Genesis 3, it deserves careful consideration. We must remember that the basic concern of the text is the mutual authority-relationships. The order of authority is reversed by man's listening to an animal rather than to God. The order of authority is re-established when the serpent is sentenced back to its lowly position (Gen. 3:14,15). To argue that no animal is involved makes the text of Genesis 3 meaningless. Furthermore the text leaves Satan out of the picture, so that the basic point about authority relationships is not obscured. It is left to other passages to point to the ultimate source of the temptation (e.g. Revelation 12:9; 20:2; 2 Cor. 11:3).

The question was raised earlier whether the careful construction of Genesis 1 excluded a literal interpretation. We find no evidence of such thinking in the passages from the rest of Scripture which allude to it. Surely all indications point to the literal reading as the most natural, the most in harmony with the larger context, and the most supported by the rest of Scripture.

[1] *Op. cit.*, p. 147.

THE CREATION NARRATIVE AND SCIENCE

If we have here a narrative of the events of the early history of the cosmos, this must bring scripture in contact with, and maybe in conflict with, science. Certainly we can avoid letting Scripture speak for itself and declare it ahead of time to be 'religious'. Yet that is not being true to Scripture.

Nevertheless there is a danger that conflict with secular science will play too much of a rôle in our interpretation. One can readily grant that Hebrew uses 'day', as do most languages, in a metaphorical way. Yet context must determine the interpretation. The whole context of Genesis 1 is against an interpretation as 'age', as is Exodus 20:11.

Furthermore the day-age theory does not really achieve the object of removing conflicts with secular science. The order of events is still 'wrong'.

The same dangers threaten scientific theories developed by literalist or 'creationist' writers. We have already seen that water enters into the creation narrative as one way in which God prepared the world for his creatures. We are told in Genesis 2:5 that it had not rained. To take this as proof that there was no rain before the flood[1] makes the text say something outside its concern. There is the additional problem that Psalm 104:13, in the context of describing the third day, mentions rain.

Given that judgments are reversals of creation, it is fair to ask whether the waters of the flood are related to the waters of Genesis 1. The rain relates naturally to the waters above the firmament, and the 'fountains of the great deep' (Gen. 7:11) to the seas. The common creationist's interpretation that the 'fountains' are geysers of steam or subterranean water[2] probably depends on the impression created by the English translation. The Hebrew word refers to a basin of any size containing water.

In defence of a world-wide flood against the sceptics and in explanation of the massive growth of the so-called Carboniferous Era, it may be attractive to propound theories like the

---

[1] J. C. Whitcomb and H. M. Morris, *The Genesis Flood*, Phillipsburg, N.J., Presbyterian and Reformed, 1961, p. 241.

[2] *Ibid.*, p. 242, but note also p. 9 where oceans are included.

vapour canopy theory or the contribution of geysers to the waters of the flood. Yet we can go beyond the text or make the text say things it does not say in our zeal to produce a creationist science.

Where is the proper balance to be found? Perhaps the flood is a good example. It is very hard to escape the evidence of Genesis and 2 Peter 3 that the flood was world-wide. We are within the limits of Scripture when we argue such a case.[1] To say that the flood caused the fossils is something else. It is a possible view for one who holds to Scripture. Yet it is not taught by Scripture itself. Hence we should see it as a hypothesis to be tested by evidence, for all science, including creation science, is fallible. In our zeal to refute unbelievers we should never confuse our scientific theories with what we hold to be clear and certain because Scripture says it.

CONCLUSION

In spite of all that has been written to accommodate the creation narrative to secular science, the plain straightforward reading of the text is the one supported by Scripture itself. Certainly the text makes theological points. It shows God's merciful gift of a world to his creatures. Yet it does not mean that it did not happen just because it was done in mercy! It is certainly a legitimate conclusion from the narrative that we should not worship idols. However one cannot characterize the text as dominated by a polemic against idolatry.

We should see to it that our science is in accord with what the text tells us. Yet the text is not primarily concerned with giving us answers to the questions posed by unbelieving science. We may trust that such answers will come as we pursue our science on the foundations laid by the Biblical narrative. However, the text and its concerns must be the guide to our interpretation, not the questions posed by science.

[1] As Whitcomb and Morris have very ably done.

∞ 17 ∞

The Interpretation of Prophecy

We have seen in the previous chapter that the past history provides images and metaphors for describing the later experiences of the people of God. Thus, for example, David can describe God's deliverance of him from human enemies in terms of Moses' deliverance from the waters (Ps. 18:16). There is a pattern in the experience of God's people. It is not necessarily that events are literally repeated. What is repeated is the experience of the saving mercy and the righteous judgment of God. Just as God delivered Moses so he delivered David. David is thus a 'second' Moses.

We have seen also that this use of images from past history draws upon the whole range of history. It is prominent in the use of images from the creation account.

Is this use of images proof of a lack of interest in historicity in Scripture? It might seem so from David's talking about 'waters' which were not literally involved in his case. However a moment's reflection will reveal that it is evidence of a very definite interest in history. To interpret one's experience in terms of pictures drawn from the past shows a very strong concern for history.

The future acts of salvation and judgment that God promises are also described in terms of pictures derived from the past. That is to say, prophecy regularly uses metaphors from past history. The correct interpretation of prophecy therefore depends upon recognizing the use of these metaphors.

We can use a case of an already fulfilled prophecy to illustrate this process. Hosea foretold the punishment and captivity of Israel. He pictured it in terms of Israel's former captivity in Egypt. In 8:11–14 he says that they shall return to

Egypt. In 9:3 the prophecy of expulsion from the promised land and return to Egypt has an interesting parallel. It is captivity in Assyria. Finally in 11:5 we have the statement that they will not return to Egypt. Instead, they will be ruled over by Assyria.

We know from the history that Israel were not deported south to Egypt. They went north to various sites in the Assyrian kingdom (2 Kings 17:6). Yet the references to Egypt are quite explicable. Egypt is here the model for the place of bondage and captivity of God's people. Thus the prophet can both affirm a captivity in Egypt when he is using it in this figurative sense and make clear that the literal place of their captivity will be Assyria and not Egypt.

A second case we can use, where the prophecy has already been fulfilled, is Amos 9:11,12. Interpretation of this passage is complicated by a difference between the Massoretic text and the Septuagint translation into Greek. It is the Greek text which is quoted in Acts 15:16,17.

The Massoretic text of Amos 9:12a may be translated: 'In order that they may possess the remnant of Edom'.[1] The Septuagint implies that its translators were using a slightly different text or that they were interpreting in the process of translation (or both)! It reads: 'In order that the rest of men may seek the Lord'.

We do not know for certain which was the original text, nor do we know whether James had any thoughts on the relationship of the Hebrew and Greek versions. What we obviously have is a prophecy of the re-establishment of the Davidic kingdom and that the Gentiles were to be incorporated into it in some way. The terms and images are those of David's empire. Since Edom was part of that empire the mention of Edom would not be out of place in the original text. However if Edom stood in the original, the parallel makes it clear that Edom was standing only as an example. Edom is in parallel with 'all the nations who are called by My name'.

This prophecy is seen by James as fulfilled in the church and the incorporation of Gentiles into it. Hence the image is David's

[1]It could be that Edom was present in the text read by the Septuagint translators. However they caught the force of the passage and paraphrased it as a picture of Gentiles seeking the Lord and thus incorporated into Israel.

kingdom. The realization of the prophecy is the multi-racial church.

This case makes one thing explicit. The church with its incorporation of Gentiles was predicted in an Old Testament prophecy. James makes this very clear. The topic of debate at the Jerusalem Council was whether the Gentiles should be incorporated as full members of the church. James says (Acts 15:14,15) that Peter's rehearsal of the history of Gentile membership in the church is in agreement with this prophecy. Yet the original prophecy was in terms of an incorporation of Gentiles into a renewed Davidic kingdom.

The use of the metaphor of the Davidic kingdom for the church is not really difficult. The form which the kingdom of God took in the Old Testament is a picture for predicting its re-establishment in the church, which is the form of God's kingdom in the New Covenant age. If Edom stood in the original it is a perfectly understandable choice. What better picture than Edom, with its hatred of its brother Israel, to picture the reconciliation in one body of Jew and Gentile.

We have many other instances of this use of images from the past in prophecy. We could list many cases in which the Messiah is promised in the form of a prophecy of the coming of David. Jeremiah 30:9 is a very good example. God promises a future day of salvation in which Israel will seek God 'and David their king, whom I will raise up for them'. (See also Isaiah 55:3,4; Ezekiel 34:23.) Clearly in such passages David functions as a type of Christ. Another example is the use of Elijah as the type of a prophet in Malachi 4:5,6 (cf. Matt. 11:14). Once again, as we saw in the case of Hosea's prophecy of bondage in 'Egypt', there was a need to make clear that this prophecy was not to be taken 'literally' (John 1:21).

Another whole group of such prophecies are those in which the exodus from Egypt becomes the figure under which the future salvation is depicted. See for examples: Jeremiah 23:7,8; Isaiah 43:2–7; 16–21; 48:20,21; 51:9–11; 52:11,12. This theme is taken up by Jesus who on the mount of the transfiguration discusses with Moses and Elijah 'His "exodus"[1] which He was about to accomplish at Jerusalem' (Luke 9:31).

[1]The Greek reads, literally, *exodus*.

There would be few, if any, who would deny that in the passages considered above, David is a type of the Messiah. From opinions reported by Peter (Matt. 16:14) and the questions John the Baptist was asked (Jn 1:21), it seems that there was in New Testament times some expectation of the literal return of Old Testament prophets. Nevertheless Christian interpreters would want to understand the prophecies of the raising up of David as king as prophecies to be interpreted in accord with David's typical rôle.

It is strange, therefore, that the typical interpretation of prophecy is abandoned when it comes to prophecies in which Israel or some other nation appears. Since the nations of Old Testament times no longer exist as such, the nations occupying the same (or thought to be the same) geographical areas are substituted for them. Prophecies of Israel or other nations are therefore interpreted as referring to political or military events involving the modern state of Israel and surrounding nations.

This interpretation runs against the way figures from Israel's history are used in prophecy. In this context the use of Egypt in Hosea and the kingdom of David in Amos is particularly significant. These are cases where Scripture itself is our guide to interpretation. We have seen that Scripture sees them as types and hence does not interpret them as referring to modern-day states. Surely this should be our guide to the interpretation of other similar prophecies.

We see a similar use of things out of past history in the book of Revelation. An indisputable case is found in Revelation 11:8. The place where the two witnesses are to lie is 'spiritually called Sodom and Egypt, where also their Lord was crucified'. Here Sodom, Egypt, and the earthly Jerusalem have to be explored for their typical significance before we can interpret this passage. The two witnesses themselves are also presented in terms of types, since they are described in verses 5 and 6 in terms of Moses and Elijah and in verse 4 in terms of Joshua the high priest and Zerubbabel (Zech. 4). Thus prediction in terms of types is definitely characteristic of this chapter of Revelation.

It may, of course, be argued that all the other nations and places referred to in the Book of Revelation are to be interpreted in a literal, non-typical fashion, since we do not have statements that every name is a 'spiritual' name. However, this not only rejects the clues for interpretation which we have found in chapter 11. It is contrary to the context in the other passages as well. An example is the use of the figure of Babylon in chapter 17. Is Babylon here used typically or literally? Babylon is pictured as a woman sitting on a scarlet beast (v.3). She also sits on seven mountains (v.9), a clear allusion to Rome which was the dominant city when the book was written. She also sits on waters which represent 'peoples and multitudes and nations and tongues' (v.15). This variety of images points to a typical use of the name Babylon. While there are various schools which insist on the literal interpretation of prophecy, unless they interpret Babylon here as a restoration of the ancient city and the re-establishment of the ancient Babylonian empire based on that city, they are interpreting Babylon in a typical way. Once we have interpreted Babylon in a typical way in chapter 17, then that interpretation is seen to fit also the mention of Babylon in 16:19. Indeed chapters 17 and 18 are an elaboration of the judgment upon Babylon described at the end of chapter 16. That means we must take typical interpretation back into chapter 16 with its mention of armies from the east (cf. Genesis 14) and Har-Magedon (cf. 2 Chron. 35:22 and the general strategic importance of Megiddo).[1]

The point needs to be stressed that this interpretation of prophecy was reached by considering how Scripture itself interprets prophecy and uses images from the past. It is in accord with the way the psalmists and prophets describe their own contemporary experiences in terms of the past experiences of the people of God.

There is thus an interesting contrast between scriptural interpretation of the creation account and scriptural interpretation of prophecy. Scripture interprets the figures of the creation account literally and the figures of prophecy symbolically. We cannot come to Scripture insisting that all be interpreted symbolically or that all be interpreted literally. There is, as has already been pointed out, a simple reason why it would be hard to make the creation account symbolic. Prophecy was written after a history had taken place which

[1]For a more detailed treatment of the typical elements of the Book of Revelation see W. Hendriksen, *More than Conquerors*, Grand Rapids, Baker, 1940.

provided symbols suitable to be used as types. Creation, however, stands at the beginning of the Bible. It provided symbols and images for later writers of Scripture, but it has no earlier store from which to draw such symbols.

∞ 18 ∞

Women in Teaching/Ruling Offices in the Church

From the attention paid to the issue of women in church office one is entitled to wonder whether it is the primary issue and Scripture is the secondary one. The issue of women in office seems to be the more visible and controversial one. Nevertheless the arguments developed in this matter are best seen as particular cases of more general arguments. Some may be led to those more general arguments from concern over the women's issue, and some may move the other way, to the more particular case. Yet to understand the debate we must put it in the broader context of the discussion about Scripture.

The basic debate centres around particular statements in Scripture which bar teaching and ruling offices in the church to women. The argument for allowing such offices to women takes various forms. Common to these forms is the assertion that there are elements of Biblical theology which teach the equality of male and female. The natural consequence of these elements is that all church offices should be open to women. The Biblical passages which reject this are dealt with in various ways.

One way is to say that Paul was deliberately accommodating himself to the social expectations and prejudices of his time. To do this he had to engage in some rather far-fetched exegesis of the creation narratives.[1] A variant on this is to say that Paul, a man of his own time, was allowing the way of thinking of his age to control his thinking.[2]

[1] K. Giles, 'The Order of Creation and the Subordination of Women', *Interchange*, 23 (1978), 186ff.; P. Sherlock, 'Women and the Arguments from Creation', *ibid.*, 20 (1976), 247ff.
[2] R. Banks, 'Paul and Women's Liberation', *ibid.*, 18 (1976), 101.

Common to all these approaches is a belief in a conflict in Scripture between the basic principles of the gospel and the statements on women in the church. When this happens, then the specific prohibitions on women in office are set aside in favour of what is seen as the principle of the gospel.

Thus this debate raises many of the issues already considered. In effect we find appeals to the equality of man and woman in Christ turned against the details of Biblical teaching. One aspect of Scriptural teaching is being considered as more authoritative than another. We also find cultural relativism. The Scripture is seen as deliberately or unconsciously conformed to the customs and standards of its time. It is argued that the Scripture's conformity to its time may be set aside in order to allow the church of our day to conform to the standards of our own time. None of the advocates of this position seem to have wrestled with the problems created by their appeal to both the liberating effect of the gospel and to cultural relativism. Suppose our culture should change to a denial of the social equality of women. What then should prevail in the church? Should it be the social standards of our new age or the supposed liberating and equalizing implications of the gospel? One suspects that most people would argue for the latter. Yet the suggested new state of our culture would be nothing more than a return to the situation which is claimed to have prevailed in New Testament times. It poses the question: should not Paul have been consistent with the gospel?

Thus much of the argument about changing cultures is not central to the debate. The crux is a claim of an inconsistency in Paul and the right to choose which part of Paul's inconsistency is most appealing to us.

How do we know which part of Paul's 'inconsistency' is most compatible with the gospel? That question is not as easy to answer as some might claim. Paul's argument for the submission of the wife in marriage in Ephesians 5:22–33 is permeated with concepts derived from the redemptive work of Christ.

Paul sets out first (v.21) the general principle that submission within the Christian community is to be carried out in the fear of Christ. Then he outlines several cases of relationship which involve submission and reciprocal responsibilities on the part of the one placed in authority (5:22–6:9). We might find such teaching incompatible with our views of relationships but it is highly unlikely that Paul saw this teaching as contrary to the gospel. Surely Paul has as much claim to know what is more consistent with the gospel as we do. Maybe he has more! (1 Cor. 9:1).

As in any other case of a claimed inconsistency within Scriptures, the authority of Scripture is nullified. If we may choose which part of Scripture we want to follow, we are the real authority, not Scripture.

Yet the appeal to cultural relativism raises a series of other issues. As we have seen, the appeal to cultural relativism is not really essential to the attempt to set aside the teaching of Scripture on the rôle of women. Yet it is a convenient and plausible defence of what is being done. If Scripture is conformed to the culture of its times on this issue, then surely it must also be on others. If we may set aside one teaching of Scripture that is unpopular today, then surely we may set aside other teachings.

If the Scripture clearly says that a certain practice was to be adopted to avoid giving offence to unbelievers (e.g. 1 Cor. 10:27,28) then we know that the practice is not wrong in itself and may be indulged in when there is no fear of such offence. However the question of the woman's rôle is not treated in that way. It is treated by appeals to our relationship to Christ or to the original created order.

Once again we come to a question of the authority of Scripture. May its unpopular teachings be dismissed as a conformity to the culture of its day? Of course the consequence of such dismissal is that the church of our day is given warrant for conformity to the culture of its time. Thus paradoxically, the appeal to cultural relativism enforces cultural relativism.

THE CRUCIAL TEXTS

The debate largely centres on 1 Corinthians 11:1–16;14:34; and 1 Timothy 2:8–15. Since those who advocate positions of authority in the church for women often reject the Biblical teaching on the submission of the wife to the husband, Ephesians 5:22–33 and 1 Peter 3:1–7 are also brought into the debate.

[127]

When we consider such verses we meet what seems like a contradiction. Paul in 1 Corinthians 11:5 speaks of women praying or prophesying. Yet in 1 Corinthians 14:34,35 he says that women are to keep silent in the churches and he even includes asking questions in this prohibition. In 1 Timothy 2:11,12 he says that women are quietly to receive instruction and are not to teach. How can these prohibitions make sense if women are allowed to prophesy?

Firstly, it must be noticed that the apparent contradiction exists within 1 Corinthians and even in the same section of the letter, that is the section dealing with the meetings of the church. Thus expedients, like denying the Pauline authorship of 1 Timothy,[1] do not resolve the basic problem.

Generally, the problem within 1 Corinthians is resolved by making one or both of the passages refer to very particular circumstances. Thus the passages really have no relation to each other. 1 Corinthians 11 is often explained by reference to local customs dealing with veils or hair length and 1 Corinthians 14 by reference to chattering between husbands and wives.

However, there are obvious indications that the two passages belong together. In both cases prophesying is a major issue. In the immediate context Paul refers to the uniform practice of the churches in both passages (11:16 and 14:33). In 14:34 Paul appeals to 'the Law'. Yet he does not tell us what teaching of the Law he has in mind. It is quite unusual for Paul to make such a general appeal. Generally he tells us specifically what portion of the Old Testament supports his argument. We therefore naturally wonder whether there have been any indications in the preceding context of the passage he had in mind. The one place where he referred to the teaching of the Old Testament in connection with women is in 11:8,9.

Thus there are indications of connection between the two passages. Instead of harmonizing them by making each refer to some special and different situation we should put them together. In other words 14:34,35 is Paul's brief allusion back to what he has already argued in more detail in 1 Corinthians 11. Since it is a brief allusion back to a subject already considered

---

[1] *Ibid.*, pp. 96f.; Giles, *op. cit.*, pp. 188f.

in more detail earlier, Paul can refer to 'the Law', knowing his readers would know what he meant.

It follows that the two passages must be saying the same thing. We do not need to attempt artificial harmonizations which make them refer to special situations. After all, the language Paul uses, with its reference to 'every' man or woman, and its categoric condemnations ('improper', 14:35), point to a general teaching and not a special situation.

If they are saying the same thing, then we must be reading them the wrong way to see them as apparently in conflict. In the situation where there are pressures to conform to the demand for women in church office and also a strong reaction to such pressure, it is not easy to choose the way in which we attempt to resolve this problem. 1 Corinthians 11, as presently read, has been a strong proof text for those who favour women in office. And 1 Corinthians 14 has been equally well used by those who oppose it. Any choice for resolving the dilemma will be accused of bias.

In this situation we must have recourse to some basic rules of Scripture interpretation. The plain reading of 1 Corinthians 14:34,35 is supported by 1 Timothy 2:11–15. Surely that gives it some weight as our initial starting point. Further 1 Corinthians 14:34,35 is the plainer passage. We are not confused as to what Paul means by veils, authority, etc. Hence it makes sense to go back to 1 Corinthians 11 and to ask whether it is saying the same thing as 1 Corinthians 14. When we do that we find that a lot of things which were formerly enigmatic make sense.

Paul begins the discussion in chapter 11 by discussing authority relationships. Christ is the head or authority over man; man is over woman; and God is the head of Christ. Obviously Paul is not opening the discussion by referring to a local situation but to the most general and world-wide relationships. What follows amplifies and illustrates the point that has been made about the relation of man and woman. Since in the relationship amongst humans man is the head, he should not deny that headship. There is a contradiction between taking a headship position and hiding the literal head. If he leads or teaches the church in praying or prophesying, he is taking a rôle as head. There is something ludicrous about being the head or authority while one at the same time hides one's physical head.[1] It follows therefore that praying and prophesying are authoritative functions which call for an unveiled, unshrouded head. Hence any woman engaging in those activities must also be bare-headed. Consequently Paul turns to what such unveiling must mean for the woman. In contrast to the man, when she prays or prophesies, the unveiling of her head must be dishonourable to her.[2]

What does it mean for a woman to be *bare*-headed? As Paul says, it is equivalent to being shaved or having her hair shorn off. That of course is dishonouring for a woman. Hence she should not uncover her head. That is, she should not pray or prophesy.

Paul then turns to covering the same ground in another way. He argues in verse 7 that the man stands, due to his creation in the image of God, in a position of authority. Hence it is inappropriate for the man to cover his head. However the woman was created for the man. Her beauty and fitness reflects glory on the man for whose sake she was created.[3]

Whenever Paul speaks of the submission of the woman in marriage, he is careful to qualify this by stressing the responsibility of the husband to his wife. He is very conscious of the problem of male tyranny and pride. So also in this context he qualifies his appeal to the original relationship of man and women by stressing that there is also a dependence of man on woman.

In verse 13 Paul returns to the original subject. He appeals to their own sensibilities. It is unnatural for a woman to appear

---

[1]Simply observing the use of the head with an authoritative, decisive speaker and then trying to imagine the effect if that head was hidden by an enveloping shawl, will help one to visualize Paul's line of thought.

[2]Paul's point has been somewhat obscured by the way 11:5 has been translated. The common translation depends upon the grammatical structure called 'the dative of accompanying circumstances'. This is a very rare construction. No other case is found in the New Testament. A paraphrase will bring out the force of this structure: 'Every woman praying or prophesying, having her head uncovered as the accompanying circumstance, dishonours her head.' The much more common use of the dative is the 'dative of means'. If we assume this construction then we would paraphrase: 'Every woman praying or prophesying, by means of the uncovering of her head, dishonours her head.' See my 'Of Silence and Head Covering', *Westminster Theological Journal*, 35 (1973), 21–7.

[3]'because of the angels' in verse 10 is difficult. Perhaps it refers to the meeting of the angels with the church in worship (*cf.* Heb. 12:22). Thus it serves as an abbreviated reference to the fact that the church meeting is a very public event.

with her head uncovered. Her long hair is a most appropriate covering. For a man, on the contrary it is a dishonour.

Thus the whole passage makes sense and fits in very well with chapter 14. We can then take chapter 14 within its natural context. Paul has been dealing with the rules governing speaking in the assembly. He had stressed that each, in their varied way, could make a contribution without domination by individuals or by a particular gift. Hence a warning is necessary to make clear that this does not contradict what has previously been said. He refers in brief to the subjection of the women, which is equivalent to their being silent. For Paul, speaking is incompatible with the subjection of the woman. He faces the question of how far he will take this teaching. There were all sorts of thin-end-of-the-wedge possibilities. For example: 'If they do not understand, surely they can ask a question, and if they can speak in that way. . . '. He rejects the possibility by telling them to ask their husbands later at home.

In 14:36, as in 11:16, Paul attacks the Corinthian deviation from the uniform practice of the churches. What he is dealing with is not a local rule for the Corinthian situation. It is a universal rule in the churches.

It is important to notice that Paul makes a clear distinction between what is permissible in the church and what is permissible in the home. In her home, naturally, the wife may speak. Thus the assembly of the church is a special event, surrounded by special requirements. That may explain the appearance of prophetesses in Acts. In Acts 21:9 we are told that Philip had four virgin daughters who were prophetesses. The information is not connected to anything else. Nor are we told in what context they did their prophesying. If we follow the line of Paul's thought from 1 Corinthians 14:35, then it would seem that there would be no objection to their exercising this gift outside the church meeting.

It remains to deal with some of the rather artificial harmonizations which have been proposed. Often it is argued that Paul in 1 Corinthians 11 is requiring women to conform to the Oriental custom of wearing a veil. His teaching is thus asking women to conform to the normal standards of propriety in the culture. However Paul's appeal is not to community standards. It is to creation. Nowhere does Paul tell women to wear veils. Indeed nowhere does he even refer to the face. He is dealing throughout with the uncovering of the head which accompanies a leading function in the assembly. If it were considered improper for a woman to be unveiled then it would be improper whether she was prophesying or not.

It must be remembered that Corinth was a Greek city. It is highly doubtful that women in that city would have veiled their faces.[1] As will be discussed later, Jewish women did not normally veil their faces.

The common attempt to harmonize 1 Corinthians 14:35,36 suggests that Paul was trying to stop unseemly chatter by the women. This is sometimes based upon the claim that the word used for 'speak' in 14:34 means to 'chatter'. This, however, is the meaning of the word in classical Greek, a meaning it does not have in New Testament Greek.[2] Rather than importing meanings from classical Greek into this passage, we can learn what Paul meant by 'speak' simply from its usage in this chapter. Paul uses that verb in question twenty-two times in this chapter. It occurs in contexts like: 'For one who *speaks* in a tongue does not *speak* . . .' (v.2); 'however, in the church I desire to *speak* five words with my mind . . .' (v.19); 'let two or three prophets *speak* . . .' (v.29). In this context of repeated usage of the word for the various forms of speaking in the assembly, Paul's statement in verse 34 has to be understood as referring to the various forms of speaking previously mentioned.[3]

[1]When the Greek orator Dio Chrysostom (born *c.* 40 AD) describes Tarsus he singles it out as a peculiarity of the city that the women veiled their faces (*Oration* 33§48). This seems to indicate that the custom was not common in Greece.

[2]'Moreover, the primary meaning of *lalein*, to utter one's self, enables us easily to understand its very frequent use in the sacred writers to denote the utterances by which God indicates or gives proof of his mind and will. . . . (Perhaps this use may account in part for the fact that, though in classic Greek *lalein* is the term for light and familiar speech, and so assumes readily a disparaging notion, in biblical Greek it is nearly if not quite free from any such suggestion)' (J. H. Thayer, *A Greek – English Lexicon of the New Testament*, 4th ed., Edinburgh, T. & T. Clark, 1901, p. 368a).

[3]The same problems face any thesis which restricts the prohibition to a specific form of speaking (e.g. not participating in the judging of the prophets; see J. B. Hurley, 'Did Paul Require Veils or the Silence of Women? A consideration of 1 Cor. 11:2–16 and 1 Cor. 14:33b–36', *Westminster Theological Journal*, 35 (1973), 216ff.). If Paul wanted to prohibit only a very special form of speaking, why did he use such general terms?

The suggestion that Paul's aim was merely to stop unseemly chatter is sometimes elaborated by the claim that men and women sat separately, as in the synagogue. Hence it is suggested women were shouting questions to their husbands across the aisle! As a matter of fact we are not sure that the church attempted to imitate the synagogue. Even more to the point, we are not sure women sat separate from the men in early synagogues.[1] Even if they did, Paul's prohibitions are general, not directed to such a specific problem.

In defence of the idea that Paul was appealing just to popular customs, some have cited his discussion about long hair in 11:14[2]. He refers there to 'nature'. A consideration of the use of 'nature' in Paul will show that it does not mean custom (e.g. Rom. 1:26; 2:14,27; 11:21,24; Gal. 4:8). It is a reference to the constituent or inherent character of a thing or person. Thus uncircumcision is a 'natural' condition; idols are by 'nature' not gods. When Paul says in Romans 2:14 that the 'Gentiles . . . do by nature the things of the law', he obviously refers to some remaining inherent sense of what is right and wrong. This usage comes close to that in 1 Corinthians 11:14. Paul appeals to an inherent sense that long hair is appropriate for women, but not for men.

The other major passage on the subject, 1 Timothy 2:8–15, is much more straightforward. There Paul singles out the 'males' as those who should pray (v.8). As he is drawing a contrast between men and women he does not use the normal word for 'man' which means men in general, including females. He uses instead a word which means specifically 'male'. In contrast to

---

[1]There was a definite attempt to design the later synagogues in such a way as to replace the temple, once the temple had been destroyed. One part of this attempt may have been the construction of the women's galleries on analogy with the court of the women. Whether we can argue from these later synagogues to the synagogues before the destruction of the temple is doubtful. Both literary and archaeological evidence, though sparse, are against the idea that first-century synagogues had a separate place for women to sit. See B. J. Brooten, *Inscriptional Evidence for Women as Leaders in the Ancient Synagogue*, Ph.D. Dissertation, Harvard University, 1982; pp. 186ff.

[2]The long hair of the artists' Jesus seems to go back to the attempts of Renaissance artists to depict him as a Greek hero. It is thus based on the attempts to synthesize Christianity and paganism. For the Biblical standard see Ezek. 44:20.

this women are to learn in silence. Obviously making 1 Corinthians 11 teach that women may pray or prophesy in public brings that passage into outright conflict with 1 Timothy 2. Why would Paul single out males as the ones to pray if praying was permitted to women?

Another way of resolving the difficulties of these passages, or for some their unwelcome teaching, is to say that they concern what is done in the home, not what is done in the church. Thus many have tried to deal with the problem of the conflict of 1 Corinthians 11 and 14 by saying that chapter 11 concerns non-church gatherings. Once we see the obvious connection between chapters 11 and 14 there is no need to solve the problem this way. Further, the context is very strongly against it. Chapter 11 consists of two sections. Paul begins the first in verses 1 and 2 by praising them for adhering to the traditions he had taught them. He begins the second in verse 17 by refusing to praise them. Thus it is natural that we take both halves as referring to essentially the same topic. Paul has begun a new section of the letter at the beginning of chapter 11. The second part of chapter 11 as well as chapters 12 to 14 shows us that the concern of this whole section is corporate worship. Hence the first part of chapter 11 naturally fits in as also concerned with the church meeting. In verse 2 he refers to 'traditions'. Traditions are things which Paul does not originate but simply transmits. What is the nature of these traditions? We learn from 11:23 why Paul refers to traditions. He is passing on what he received from the Lord. It is a tradition which has its origins in the Lord's own practice. Verse 23 also shows clearly that what Paul is passing on is a tradition about worship. Hence it is natural to take 11:2 as also a reference to traditions concerning worship.

The contextual indications in 1 Timothy 2 are not as clear. However we must remember that Paul is instructing Timothy how to perform his functions as a leader of the church. It is natural therefore to take the prayers referred to at the beginning of chapter 2 as prayers in a church context. That leads naturally to the reminder that it is the males who should lead this praying.

If we take 1 Timothy 2:8–15 as dealing with what happens outside the church meeting, then we bring this passage into conflict with 1 Corinthians 14:35. For in 1 Corinthians Paul permits women to discuss things with their husbands at home. Yet in 1 Timothy 2:12 he tells women to be quiet. Taking all these passages as referring to the church meeting we have a consistent and mutually supportive line of teaching.

Why does Paul set a standard for the church that is not set for the home? There is a similarity in that submission of the wife is taught in both contexts (Eph. 5:22–24 and 1 Tim. 2:11,12). Yet silence is enjoined upon the wife only in the church. We may speculate as to the reasons for the difference. The Biblical text is not specific as to the reasons. That raises a further question. Should we follow a Biblical command whose rationale we do not completely understand? Where human reason is made the real authority, then failure to understand all the ramifications of a command will be used as a reason for ignoring it. Where our concern is to subject ourselves to God's will, then we obey, even if we do not understand in full. It is not only women who need to learn subjection!

The texts we have considered consistently appeal to the early chapters of Genesis. That in itself should rule out the idea that Paul was merely attempting to avoid giving offence to community standards. To argue the case that the matter was merely one of custom or convention, one has to make some judgments about Paul's strategy. One can say that Paul realized that Christian liberty was bringing offence to the watching community and hence he tried to suppress it with the one thing the church would respect: biblical arguments. Or one can say that Paul, a man of his time, shared the prejudices against women of his time. All such approaches are rejections of the authority of Scripture. When we argue that way we set ourselves in judgment on Scripture. For it follows from these arguments that we need not be bound to follow Scripture on the rôle of women in the church when women leading is no longer an offence to our contemporaries. We accuse an author of Scripture of biased or deceitful argumentation. It is the road one must take to set aside the teaching of Scripture on women in church office which makes it such a significant question. Suppose Paul had merely given command to women to be silent and given no argument. Then one might argue that Paul was dealing in terms of a problem for *that* time, which might not apply for our time. Such an argument would be weak, but it might be attempted. When Paul grounds his argument on creation, we face a different situation. For then to set it aside as irrelevant for our times, we must say that Paul was wrong in appealing to the created order. Once one has accused Paul of error on one point, there is no logical reason to refrain from searching for errors at other points, and the principle has been established that Scriptural arguments may be rejected.

Those who criticize Paul's argument often claim that he is misreading Genesis. Paul makes two different but related arguments from Genesis 2 and 3. In 1 Corinthians 11:8,9 he argues from the order and purpose of the woman's creation. In 1 Timothy 2:13,14 he adds the point that it was the woman who was deceived by the tempter, not the man. Those who reject the historicity of these chapters of Genesis will of course reject any argument from them. But if we take seriously the authority of Scripture we will argue the other way. As outlined earlier in chapter 17, we will see Paul's argument as evidence for the historical reliability of these chapters.

Is Paul's argument from Genesis 2 and 3 invalid? That really comes down to a question of whether the passage means to teach an order of authority as between man and woman. As argued earlier in chapter 17 the passage is very much concerned with relationships. Man is given dominion (1:26). He names the animals (2:20;cf.1:5,8,10). Yet he yields to the voice of an animal and disobeys God (3:1–6). Hence God's work of restoration involves subduing the animal and his mentor once more (3:14,15). Given this evidence it is plain that the dominion of man over the animals is a crucial issue in these chapters. Surely the parallels point to an authority of man also over the woman. The restoration asserts man's authority over the woman (3:6). Man names the woman (3:20). In the act of sin it was the woman who led the man, just as the serpent had deceived the woman (3:6). In that context we should then consider the account of woman's creation. She was formed subsequent to the man to be a helper for him (2:20–22). All of this points to an authority relationship also between man and woman. Unless that building of the story around authority relationships is understood, details become inexplicable. Hence Paul is not wrong in seeing the order of creation of the man and the woman, or the order of the temptation, as significant. Paul may just cite a particular event, but he has caught the significance of the event within its context.

RÔLE, AUTHORITY, AND WORTH

In the debate over women in church office, the esteem with which particular women were held by Jesus or the church is frequently raised. There is no doubt that women do play a prominent rôle as examples of faith, love, and service. It is the conviction of many that such esteem would be incompatible with those women being excluded from teaching and ruling rôles in the church. Yet once more we ask whether we are to be governed by our logic or by the logic of Scripture. For Scripture sets before us that esteem and yet also the command that women be silent in the assembly. Rather than rejecting one part of Scripture teaching as incompatible with another, we should amend our own thinking.

If a woman is denied a ruling rôle, is she thereby treated as inferior? Suppose we say that to be of worth she must be allowed to have a ruling rôle. Let us then explore the logic of this conviction. We are saying that esteem and worth is inextricably connected with positions of authority. If a person is denied such a position, then his or her worth as a human being is denied. Expressed another way, this is saying that those in authority have more worth and value than those who do not possess authority. To rule is to be worth something.

Is what we have reached a Biblical conclusion? Of course not! It is the delusion of human kings and governors which is repeatedly ridiculed in Scripture. The whole Scriptural concern for the poor and the powerless is against it. The admonition of Christ that we should not seek power but service points in a totally different direction (Matthew 20:25–28).

Those who advocate a ruling rôle for women in the church are inclined to dismiss such arguments as excuses for the preservation of male prerogatives. How then do they explain the clear evidence of the New Testament? The same Paul whose letters forbid teaching/ruling office for women greets women warmly and testifies to their devotion and service (e.g. Romans 16:1–4,6,12). Attention has often been drawn to that fact that in references to Priscilla and Aquila, the name of the wife often comes first (Acts 18:26; Romans 16:3; but cf. 1 Corinthians 16:19). This is used as evidence that Priscilla was the leading figure in the marriage and perhaps took the lead in instructing Apollos (Acts 18:26). Even if this rather tenuous line of argument is correct, there is another fact to be kept in mind. They were members of the church at Corinth and it was to that church that Paul gave very clear instructions on the rôle of women. The New Testament combines high esteem for women with prohibition of the teaching/ruling office to them. Those who claim that that esteem must mean a position of leadership are arguing against the Word of God.

The same is true of those who try to use the unity of male and female in Christ (Gal. 3:28) against the Biblical teaching on their church rôles. To say that Paul did not carry his principles far enough is to say that he made errors in refusing to grant authority to women.

THE SOCIAL POSITION OF WOMEN

It is common to represent women of Biblical times as a suppressed group, oppressed, belittled, and despised. The attitude of Jesus to women is placed in contrast to this and then used as evidence that he was a social reformer intending to change the position of women.[1]

While one might like to see Jesus as such an enlightened reformer, a note of caution needs to be sounded. Much that is said about the status of women in New Testament times is exaggerated and some is plain wrong. There are several reasons why the errors in such treatments need to be considered. One is so that a proper appraisal of the rôle of women in New Testament times can be made. Another reason is that this particular instance can serve as an illustration of a wider problem. Along with cultural relativism has come an emphasis on interpreting the Bible 'against its historical/social/cultural background' or 'in terms of the ideas of the time'. This is often presented as the method which will resolve the misconceptions and misinterpretations of those who work from the Bible alone.

[1] K. Giles, 'Jesus and Women', *Interchange*, 19 (1976), 131–6.

While any information from Bible times is welcome, we can exaggerate the amount we know about the times. Often information from other times is brought in to fill the gap and sometimes it is filled by sheer speculation.

One of the most influential works on the rôle of women in New Testament times is that of J. Jeremias.[1] In reading Jeremias' work one would think that there is a multiplicity of sources for Judaism in New Testament times. As a matter of fact this is not the case and to reconstruct the Judaism of the time is difficult. Our main source for Palestinian Judaism is the Talmud.[2] The Talmud consists of two parts. The Mishnah is a compilation of teachings and discussions of Pharisaic teachers written down some time in the second century AD. The traditions incorporated reach back into the first century AD and perhaps earlier. Our problem in using this work stems partly from the cryptic nature of its contents and partly from the problems of whether the traditions have been preserved accurately. It is important to remember that between the time of Jesus or Paul and the codification of the Mishnah lie the traumatic events of the First and Second Jewish rebellions. Paradoxically, people like Jeremias who are very happy to assume the unreliability of the traditions of the New Testament accept the reliability of the traditions of the Mishnah, and even later Jewish traditions, without a murmur.

The Mishnah was commented upon by subsequent generations of students. These comments were codified in the fifth century. This is called the Gemara. Mishnah and Gemara together are called the Talmud. There are differences between the Talmud produced in Palestine and that produced in Babylonia.

Outside the Talmud were a large number of other traditions, which were committed to writing over a long span reaching down into Medieval times. Amongst these were traditions of Biblical exposition which are referred to by the term Midrash (pl. Midrashim). Thus the writing down of many of these traditions took place after the Islamic conquest of the Middle East.

[1] *Jerusalem in the Time of Jesus*, London, S.C.M., 1969, esp. ch. 18, 'The Social Position of Women'.

[2] For an introduction to the Talmud see H. L. Strack, *Introduction to the Talmud and Midrash*, New York, Meridian, 1931.

Thus the Jewish sources from Palestine stretch over many hundreds of years. Our best source was written down a hundred years after New Testament times. Attitudes to these Jewish sources vary from those who, on grounds similar to those used against the New Testament, see them as having very little worth. At the other extreme are those who use them quite uncritically. Perhaps a reasonable position would be to take the Mishnah seriously where it quotes rabbis of New Testament times. The later sources should be considered but not accepted unless there is good evidence for seeing them as reflecting accurately New Testament times.

There is another problem to be considered in using the Talmud. It is the product of a movement. Within that movement were strong differences. Thus one commonly finds that quite opposing opinions are expressed. In this situation it is wrong to quote one opinion as representative. One must also remember that what is preserved is often part of an argument or discussion. We have to be careful not to quote out of the context of a debate. Finally the Talmud is the work of one party, the Pharisees. While an important party, they were not the only party in Judaism.

Let us consider some of the main claims made by Jeremias. He claims that 'When the Jewess of Jerusalem left her house, her face was hidden by an arrangement of two head veils . . .'.[1] His main authority for this statement is the compilation of passages from Talmud and Midrashim by H. Strack and P. Billerbeck.[2] Yet Strack and Billerbeck, while conceding that there are passages in the Gemara which might just possibly be interpreted that way, conclude that the evidence is that Jewish women were not normally veiled! The crucial evidence is in Mishnah Shabbath Ch. VI which lists the things that are permissible for a woman to carry outside on the sabbath: 'Arabian women may go forth veiled and Median women may go forth with their cloaks thrown over their shoulders.'[3] Strack

[1] *Op. cit.*, p. 359.
[2] *Kommentar zum Neuen Testament aus Talmud und Midrasch*, Vol. 3, Munich, C. H. Beck, 1926, pp. 427f.
[3] 65a. All quotations of the Babylonian Talmud, unless otherwise indicated, are taken from *The Babylonian Talmud*, translation ed. by I. Epstein, London, Soncino, 1936.

and Billerbeck conclude that this indicates that at this time the custom of veiling the face was confined to women of Arabian background.

Jeremias then quotes in support of this position an anecdote from *Pesiqta rabbati*. What he does not tell us is that this is a ninth century work![1] Since it is after the Islamic conquest it may be influenced by Arab views of female modesty.

The best evidence that women would cover their heads comes from Mishnah Kethuboth 72a. In listing women who were to be divorced without receiving their dowry it includes those who offended against Jewish practices. One of these was 'going out with uncovered head'. However there is a question whether the offence in question is the uncovering of the head or having the hair loose or unbound.[2]

Thus the weight of the evidence points to Jewish women not covering their face. The head may have been covered or they may merely have had the hair bound in some way.

Jeremias claims that a woman 'was expected to remain unobserved in public'.[3] His evidence for this is the saying ascribed to an early teacher, 'Talk not much with womankind'. Let us quote the whole section of the Mishnah in question: 'Jose b. Johanan of Jerusalem used to say: "Let thy house be wide open, and let the poor be members of thy household; engage not in too much conversation with women". They said this with regard to one's own wife, how much more with regard to another man's wife. Hence have the sages said: "As long as a man engages in too much conversation with women, he causes evil to himself [for] he goes idle from [the study of] the words of the Torah, so that his end will be that he will inherit Gehinnom."[4]

There is no evidence in this whole section that the warning against talk with women was motivated by a feeling that women should be unobtrusive in public. We do not know what was in the mind of Jose b. Johanan. The thought of the sages is clear: talking with women is a pleasant pastime that diverts a

[1]Strack, *Introduction to the Talmud and Midrash*, p. 213.

[2]Obviously both could be included, depending on the way the woman's hair was normally arranged or covered. The same problem has confronted the translators of Num. 5:18.

[3]*Op. cit.*, p. 360.

[4]Mishnah Aboth I,5.

man from study! Surely this whole passage is evidence against the whole idea that the women were not expected to speak to men. It should be noticed that the sages' emphasis on study is a Pharisaic trait. It would be dangerous to generalize from this to general attitudes.

There is evidence that a woman who talked very freely and indiscriminately with men was regarded as being immoral. Thus amongst the transgressions of Jewish practice which could lead to divorce without return of dowry we find 'conversing with every man'.[1] Yet this is clearly not saying that women were not expected to talk to men. It is saying that it was considered improper and suspect for a woman to strike up conversation with any and every man.

One of the teachings of the Mishnah that is often quoted to show the despised position of women is the supposed teaching that women were not to be taught the Scripture. Thus Jeremias says: 'R. Eliezer (c. AD 90), tireless upholder of the old tradition, says impressively, "If a man gives his daughter a knowledge of the Law it is as though he taught her lechery." '[2] The question here is not whether Eliezer is so quoted in the Mishnah. It is what he meant and whether he represents any sort of a majority opinion. Once again it is important to look at the context. The subject is the belief that 'merit' postpones the action of the water of bitterness in the test for adultery (Num. 5:11–31). Since knowledge of the Torah was considered a 'merit' this created a problem. The whole passage reads: 'Therefore Ben Azzai said a man ought to give his daughter a knowledge of Torah, so that if she must drink the bitter water she may know that the acquired merit will suspend her punishment. R. Eliezer said; If any man gives his daughter a knowledge of Torah it is as though he taught her lewdness.'[3]

Thus we see that the opinion of R. Eliezer was contested. R. Eliezer's logic would seem to be that the woman would then be free to commit adultery, knowing the water of bitterness

[1]Mishnah Kethuboth 72a.

[2]*Op. cit.*, p. 373. For some reservations on the view that Eliezer was a conservative, see J. Neusner, *The Rabbinic Traditions about the Pharisees before 70*, Vol. 3, Leiden, Brill, 1971, p. 354.

[3]Mishnah Sotah iii, 4 (E. J. Lipman, *The Mishnah*, New York, Schocken, 1970, p. 181).

would have no influence. It is difficult to know whether R. Eliezer represents a majority, the older tradition, or something else. He was excommunicated from the Rabbinic circle for refusal to accept the majority decision in another issue.[1] One often has the impression that he represented Rabbi Eliezer! The possibility exists that R. Eliezer's opinion was a shot in the debate over the rôle of 'merit' in postponing the action of the water. Thus it ridicules the whole idea by pointing out that its consequence is that teaching the law inclines one to sin. It must also be kept in mind that such debates took place in a historical context. That context was the destruction of the temple and the dispersal of the Palestinian Jewish community. One wonders whether behind the idea of merit suspending the action of the water was an attempt to rationalize the discontinuation of a practice which was very much dependent upon the sacrificial system. Hence the comment by R. Eliezer is by no means as straightforward as a quotation out of context would indicate.

We do have other evidence that women were taught the Scripture. Mishnah Nedarim 35b regulates the relations between two men when the first man has taken an oath not to benefit from the second: 'He may teach him Midrash, Halakoth and Haggadoth but not Scripture. Yet he may teach Scripture to his sons and daughters.'

Much of the case that women had no rights rests on their relationship to their father or to their husband. In considering the relationship to the father we must remember that sons were similarly supposed to obey and take care of their parents.[2] The basis of the teaching was not necessarily that girls were under particular obligations. Similar very restrictive obligations were imposed upon sons.

The distinguishing factor in the case of girls was the father's right to give her in marriage. If we were to follow the practice of quoting material without regard to date, then we might quote the Gemara to Qiddushin 41a: 'For Rab Judah said in Rab's name: One may not give his daughter in betrothal when a minor, (but must wait) until she grows up and says, "I want so-and-so".' The authorities mentioned in this quotation

[1]L. Finkelstein, *Akiba*, Cleveland, Meridan, 1936, pp. 122–4.
[2]See G. Blidstein, *Honor Thy Father and Mother. Filial Responsibility in Jewish Law and Ethics*, New York, Ktav, 1976.

belong to the third century AD. How common that opinion was earlier is difficult to say. The existence of such a teaching attests that fathers did have the right to make early betrothals. We do not know how commonly it was done.

It has been argued from Mishnah Qiddushin ch. 1 that the woman was considered as property. This is because we read: 'A woman is acquired in three ways. . . . She is acquired by money, by deed or by intercourse.' This is compared by Jeremias with the purchase of a Gentile slave.[1] He further says: 'There is therefore a negative answer to this question: "Is there any difference between the acquisition of a wife and the acquisition of a slave?" '[2]

There are two very important points to note here. The first concerns the meaning of the passage which gives the various ways in which a woman could be acquired for marriage. What Jeremias ignores is that the main concern of the Mishnah quoted is to settle the legal question of what constitutes a valid marriage. The payment had become a mere formality to ensure a legally valid ceremony.[3] It also must be remembered that this 'bride price' was the main constituency of the bride's dowry. Most families would not have ready cash to give to a daughter as a dowry. They depended on the bride price for this. Though little money might actually change hands, the theoretical payment was written into the marriage contract to provide security to the wife in the event of widowhood or divorce. Thus 'bride price', however strange it may be to our thinking was a means of providing financially for the wife. One has to ask honestly whether this is all that inferior to our modern system under which widows or deserted wives are dependent upon inadequate state pensions because of the inability or unwillingness of modern society or the modern state to enforce maintenance orders against delinquent husbands.[4] This is not to hold

[1] *Op. cit.*, p. 367.
[2] *Ibid.*
[3] For a discussion of Jewish marriage law throughout this period see Z. W. Falk, *Jewish Matrimonial Law in the Middle Ages*, Oxford, O.U.P., 1966, esp. p. 39.
[4] Easy divorce creates impoverished widows as well as deserted wives because, due to divorce and remarriage, a husband may leave several widows. There is often not enough in his estate for both of them and wills rarely divide it equally anyway.

up the system of bride price and dowry as an answer to our modern problems. Neither dowry nor alimony will solve the basic problem created by a system in which husbands are free to divorce their wives.

In saying that the purchase of the wife was considered the same as the purchase of a slave, Jeremias refers to two passages of the Palestinian Talmud. He is referring to discussion in the Gemara and so once again we have a problem whether such attitudes were found in New Testament times.[1] The discussions in question are not directly on the equivalence of slave and wife. Rather they are about legal questions and use the argument that something permitted or forbidden with respect to a slave would be equally permitted or forbidden in respect to a wife. In at least one case it is explicit that the argument was an *a fortiori* one. That is, if something was permitted to a slave then there is much more reason for permitting it to the wife. In the other case the logic of arguing from slave to wife is not made clear. What we can say is that in the *legal* argument of the Gemara, payment of bride price was seen as valid and as settled a transaction as payment for a slave. Hence arguments were made from one case to the other. To say that this means that they thought a wife was no better than a slave takes the discussion quite out of its legal context and ignores completely the use of an *a fortiori* argument.

Perhaps it may be as well, in order to counter the picture that Jeremias tries to give of the menial rôle of the wife, to quote another Gemara – this time from the Babylonian Talmud – 'R. Huma stated in the name of Rab: A woman is entitled to say to her husband "I do not wish either to be maintained by you or to work for you".'[2] Reading this by itself could give the wrong impression. The context indicates that it is a case of a woman of independent means. The logic of this section both of the Mishnah[3] and the Gemara is clear. A wife's work for a husband is a fair exchange for the maintenance he provides. If she provides her own maintenance or is rich enough to have maids

[1]The passages in question are Kethuboth v.4 and Shebiith viii.8. A translation of the Palestinian Talmud (into French) may be found in M. Schwab, *Le Talmud de Jérusalem*, Paris, Maisonneuve et Larose, 1871–90.
[2]Kethuboth 58b.
[3]See particularly Mishnah Kethuboth 59b.

to do the work, then naturally she does not have to work. That is not the way one thinks about a slave!

Yet it must be said that it is a very *legal* way of viewing the marriage relationship. Did the average Jew really think in these terms? One doubts it. And then we are back with the whole problem of the use of late, technical, legal discussion to try to recreate *personal attitudes* to women. It creates an absolutely distorted view of the question. One would also receive a distorted view if he tried to use our formal statute criminal law and the legal commentaries connected to it to create a picture of attitudes.

Works like the work of Jeremias in consideration here 'know' what the answer to the question of the status of women is going to be before they consider the data. Instead of presenting the complexity of the data, the clash of rabbinic opinions, the difficulty in distilling attitudes from legal commentary, they choose the material to obtain the required image of women. When this is used in turn to 'interpret' the New Testament then we are in a scholar's make-believe world.

The point has been well made that Jesus was criticized for associating with women of dubious reputations, but not for associating with women as such.[1] The closest we find is the disciples' amazement that Jesus spoke with the Samaritan woman (John 4:27). Perhaps we may deduce from this that one would not carry on conversation with a woman, especially a strange or a Samaritan woman. That may not necessarily indicate the rôle of women within the family circle or the circle of acquaintances. Aside from this comment there is no evidence that Jesus' attitudes to women were considered exceptional. What is stressed is his attitude to the poor and to sinners.

There is no teaching of Jesus which could be singled out as attacking discrimination against women. If the despising of women was so prominent and the attitude of Jesus as radically different as some would claim, then the lack of actual teaching on the subject is all the more remarkable.

Acts gives some interesting incidental details on the rôle of women. In Antioch of Pisidia there were 'devout women of prominence' as well as 'leading men' (13:50); at Philippi there

---

[1] J. Pryor, 'Jesus and Women: A Reply', *Interchange*, 24 (1978), 247–54.

was a merchant woman, Lydia, who gave hospitality to Paul (16:14,15). Other prominent women are mentioned at Thessalonica (17:4) and Berea (17:12). How do we reconcile the existence of these prominent women with the supposed despised status of women in New Testament times?

Those who argue that the New Testament was merely accommodating the view of women in its time are entangled in a number of contradictions. If women were so despised and suppressed as a sex, how does one explain the existence of such leading women? Generally the New Testament warnings against women teaching and leading are explained as directed against women who have been inspired by their freedom and equality in Christ. Paul is then portrayed as being less consistent than these women were. But Acts shows us that there were women who held prominent positions in society before the gospel came to them. Is it not possible that they expected to carry such leading positions into the church and that caused the problem? If the problem was one of misinterpretation of gospel liberty, why did Paul never respond to it in those terms?

What was the social position of women in New Testament times? To answer that question we must rid ourselves of the perspectives of modern times. Modern Western societies have sought to eliminate all social distinctions. They have then been confronted with the distinctions which go deeper than the 'accidents' of birth, wealth, and social class, that is, the question of racial and sexual divisions. Modern societies are characterized by debate and division along racial and sexual lines. We must not project such divisions back into Biblical times. Premodern times tend to be characterized by divisions along lines of wealth and position in society rather than racial or sexual lines. Hence a woman, if she belonged to a wealthy family, could play a prominent rôle in society. To say that *all* women were despised is to import our division of society along sexual lines into societies in which the main division was on another basis.

Scripture persistently attacks the notion that worth in the true sense is connected to one's position in society. Thus its heroes are often those not in leading positions: the poor, the young and women. (Eccl. 9:13–16; 1 Sam. 17:41–49; Judges 5:24–7). The New Testament here is at one with the Old Testament (James 2:1–7; 1 Tim. 4:12; Matt. 26:13). To say that Scripture has accommodated itself to the social views of its time is a slur on Scripture and a denial of its witness against false views. Nevertheless, the same Bible insists on the proper relation of authority and respect between old and young and between man and woman.

There were of course racist and sexist sentiments expressed in antiquity. But even there we must place such remarks in their unique context. Racist doctrines today tend to be biological. They see intrinsic inferiority in certain races. Racist comments in the Ancient Near East tend to be more cultural. They despise the lack of culture of certain groups but place no barrier to those groups joining their culture and coming to high position in it.[1] Sexist comments today tend to ascribe emotional or intellectual inferiority to women. The Scripture does not express itself that way. It sees a difference in created rôles. Even the much-quoted, but late, synagogue prayer in which a man thanks God he was not made a woman, has its own context. That is the theology of Pharisaism which sees religious status as being dependent upon keeping commandments. Women were exempted from keeping certain commandments. Hence the joy of the man who had to keep all the commandments!

We must not read the rationale for modern sexism into those Biblical texts which discriminate between men and women. Neither may we read the modern view of society, divided primarily on sexual lines, into ancient societies. There women of prominent families had status and women of lowly families shared the low estate of their fathers and husbands. Of course modern equalitarian sentiments were not expressed and women's rôles tended to be traditionally defined, but business women who contradict conventional sterotypes did exist. Thus the whole attempt to explain away the New Testament doctrine as a concession to its times is really based upon simplistic views of ancient societies.

[1]Thus one can contrast the remarks made against Nubians by Sesostris III (J. H. Breasted, *Ancient Records of Egypt*, Vol. 1, Chicago, Univ. of Chicago, 1906, p. 296) with the coming of Nubians to important positions in Egypt (B. G. Trigger, *Nubia under the Pharaohs*, London, Thames & Hudson, 1976, p. 138) or the derogatory remarks made against Amorites (G. Buccellati, *The Amorites of the Ur III Period*, Naples, Instituto Orientale di Napoli, 1966, pp. 330ff.) who nevertheless came to rule many Old Babylonian cities (G. Roux, *Ancient Iraq*, Harmondsworth, Penguin, 1980, pp. 169ff.).

There is another intriguing line of evidence that should be considered. We have inscriptions in which women are listed as holding synagogue office. Thus women are attested as 'president of the synagogue' (the Greek word is the same as used for Jairus in Luke 8:49), leader, elder, and mother of a synagogue. There are several problems with the use of this data. Like most of our data on the synagogue it is later than the New Testament period. The earliest such inscription is second century AD. The inscriptions are brief and give no real evidence on the functions of the people named. That means it is possible to suggest that these were honorary titles held because the woman in question was married to a synagogue officer or maybe in recognition of donations for the building of the synagogue.[1] If these titles are functional and if this practice went back into the first century then there is another way of understanding Paul's admonitions against women teaching or ruling. Paul was warning against taking over a practice which had become common in the synagogue. Due to the image that has been created of women in Judaism this suggestion may come as a shock, but there is nothing in what we know in general about the rôle of women in the time which would contradict the possibility. What it does show is that the whole popular explanation of Paul's admonition may rest on poor historical research. It is commonly argued that Paul was conforming consciously or unconsciously to the low status of women. If women functioned as synagogue rulers, then the whole argument collapses. Our data is not sufficient to prove that they did. It is sufficient to open the possibility.

This instance illustrates again the superficiality of glib claims of interpreting Scripture in terms of its historical background. Our understanding of that background can be distorted by our prejudiced and poorly informed views of the past. Appeals to historical background have to be consonant with the indications of the text itself. Scripture does not tell us what was creating the pressure for women in office. It tells us only the reason against it. The reason against never turns upon the contemporary estimation of women. It always goes back to the created order.

[1] Brooten, *op. cit.*

Really to defend women in the teaching and ruling offices of the church one must say that Paul was wrong to appeal to the creation account and/or that the creation account itself is wrong. Once that inevitable logical step is taken it is clear that the authority of Scripture has been rejected.

ᥰ 19 ᥰ

Slavery

In the discussion on Scripture one often encounters references to slavery. Generally the argument can be summarized into a few simple steps. (1) Scripture approves slavery. (2) We now know slavery is wrong. (3) In this regard we have gone beyond/corrected/modernized Scripture. (4) Hence in other regards we may/should go beyond/correct/modernize Scripture.

This argument seeks to place before those who believe in the authority of Scripture a difficult dilemma. If they really think Scripture is fully authoritative, should they not also approve slavery?

This dilemma, and the whole argument presenting it, depends upon seeing slavery as a simple phenomenon. That is, it does not distinguish between various kinds of slavery. Further, it does not bother to consider the complexity of Old Testament legislation regarding slavery, nor the differences between Old Testament and New Testament on the matter. When we consider the issue in greater depth, the dilemma as posed is not there. That does not mean there are not other difficult questions.

In looking at Old Testament legislation we have to take into account several factors. There is an element in Old Testament legislation which is normative for us as well as the Old Testament saints (see chapter 7). There are elements which are valid only for the time before Christ's coming. Finally there are cases in which the Old Testament legislation, because of the hardness of men's hearts, sought to regulate an abuse rather than to eliminate the crime. This last is a particularly difficult issue. The one clear case has to do with the Old Testament's

[151]

failure to enforce enduring monogamous marriage (Matt. 19:3–9). It would be quite illegitimate to label every 'inconvenient' Old Testament law a case of a concession to the hardness of men's hearts. Nevertheless, at particular points this may be relevant to slavery legislation.

The Old Testament touches on several possible causes of slavery. They are slavery because of debt, prisoner-of-war slavery, kidnapping, and the purchase of somebody already a slave. It does not treat them in the same way. Further it makes a distinction between the treatment of a fellow Israelite and that of a foreigner.

It is assumed that the cause for enslaving a fellow Israelite will be slavery for debt (Ex. 21:2–11; Lev. 25:39–43; Deut. 15:12–18). The law concerning Israelite slaves made a distinction between men and women. A woman would be purchased with a view to marriage. Hence to release her would be divorce. We see here one of the many instances in Biblical law where the law in a specific situation is shaped by the need to do justice to several principles. The woman was not to be released. However that made the woman vulnerable to exploitation. She might be sold to another when the master no longer wanted her. Or she might suffer in comparison to another wife. The woman was given some protection from such abuse by being given her freedom.

Obviously we are dealing here with law designed to regulate and control the problems which inevitably arise in polygamous situations. Obviously the tightening of the law in the New Testament makes such provisions no longer relevant. Can we dismiss the whole slavery law as law designed to control something which would better be suppressed totally? That is too easy and simplistic an answer. Other things are involved in these laws. The release of the male slave reflected the sabbatical institution. He was to be released in the seventh year, or in the year of jubilee if that came sooner.

The sabbath becomes in the Old Testament the type of release from labour. Just as God rested on the sabbath from his creation work and man rests from his daily work, so there is to be a culminating rest from the tedious labour of a world beset by sin and its consequences. Redemption and sabbath are brought together (Deut. 5:12–15; Is. 61:1,2; Heb. 4). The time of service for debt slavery is set by this sabbath symbolism.

[152]

Since that symbolism reaches its fulfilment in Christ's work of redemption, can we say that debt slavery was purely a type of man's bondage to sin and release through Christ? There may be another factor. The Scripture is insistent that debts be repaid (Ex. 22:14). Obviously labour is the only way in which a completely impoverished man can repay a debt.

Thus there is a complexity in the Biblical law relating to precisely this one sort of slavery. Certain aspects of the legislation can be seen as designed to regulate abuses in a practice which was not itself right, namely, that of polygamy. We see also that debt slavery was made an illustration of redemption, that is, it served a typical function. Finally we may also see a moral concern about payment of debt.

In the world around Israel many slaves were prisoners of war. There is little reflection of this in the Biblical text. That is because the main battle Israel fought was against the Canaanites and they were commanded to put them all to death. However there was provision made for when they fought against a more distant enemy. If that enemy refused to surrender, they were to kill the males and enslave the women and children (Deut. 20:10–18).

The moral problem created by this is connected with the moral problem of the extermination of the Canaanites. There is a series of basic issues which have to be resolved. The most basic one is whether God, as judge, has the right to take away life. Nobody can deny that he has the right without attacking the whole Biblical teaching about God. Does God have the right to delegate others to carry out that judgment for him? Once again to deny that right is to attack the Biblical view of God's sovereignty. However, if we concede these rights, we can make no objection to God's delegation of that responsibility to Israel in the case of the Canaanites.

God's judgment is in terms of the way he has created man. That is, having created man to live in families, he judges families. With the Canaanites, all experienced the judgment. However, with those who are not in the land of Canaan, there was to be gradation in judgment. The men were to be put to death and the women and children enslaved. The problem of fitting this enslaving into the whole Biblical teaching is no different from the question of the judgment of the Canaanites.

To fight against the people of God was to oppose their God. Hence God had the right to enforce a punishment. In this case the punishment on the men was more severe than that upon the women and children. Yet even in this case there was a problem for the Biblical doctrine of marriage and there were provisions to give freedom to a captive wife, rather than to sell her (Deut. 21:10–14).

Thus prisoner-of-war slavery cannot be understood apart from the delegation of a judicial responsibility to Israel. That makes it very difficult to justify prisoner slavery in any other context. God restricts to himself the right to enforce a punishment upon a whole population. Despite specific exceptions like that of the Canaanites the general Biblical teaching was that the principle of family solidarity was not to be used in punishing crime: 'Fathers shall not be put to death for their sons, nor shall sons be put to death for their fathers' (Deut. 24:16). Hence in an extra-Biblical situation nobody would have warrant for enslaving a population, even when their leaders could be judged offenders in a just war. That still leaves open the possibility that a male aggressor in an unjust attack might be enslaved in punishment. There is really little Biblical data on this possibility. If we approve the execution of those responsible for war crimes in World War II, we can hardly object to the lesser punishment of slavery.

We can be brief on the matter of kidnapping as a means of obtaining slaves. 'He who kidnaps a man, whether he sells him or he is found in his possession, shall surely be put to death' (Exod. 21:16). Most of the slavery we have known in the modern world obtained its slaves by kidnapping.[1] Thus the Scripture is very clear on its condemnation of this sort of slavery.

Finally, another way Israel could obtain slaves was by purchasing them (Lev. 25:44–46). They were allowed to purchase foreigners as slaves and to make slaves of their children. This seems like an endorsement and acceptance of the systems of slavery around Israel. However the law also says that an escaped slave was not to be returned to his master (Deut. 23:15,16). Thus Israel was to serve as a refuge for slaves. This hardly seems endorsement of the slavery systems around Israel.

[1]Slaves acquired as a result of an unjust war are really no different from those kidnapped and forced into slavery.

The acceptance of slavery in this form is rather similar to the New Testament's acceptance of the slavery of the Graeco-Roman world. Hence it can be conveniently considered in connection with that topic.

It is the opinion of some that slavery in any form is morally indefensible. They hold it against the Scripture for tolerating what to them is totally wrong. Certainly some of this feeling arises from reading back into the Scripture the situation of modern slavery. As has already been pointed out, Scripture condemns the seizing of men for slavery. However, it is often defended on the more philosophical ground that it is wrong to treat a human being as property. Obviously if slavery is totally morally indefensible the Old Testament and the New Testament are at fault for approving it.

Let us first consider debt slavery. How is indebtedness to be resolved as a socio-economic problem? There are basically three solutions. One is debt slavery. As we have seen, the length of the period of service is determined in the Old Testament by sabbatical symbolism but outside of that context would be nothing against making the period of service proportional to the debt. Another way is distraint. That is the seizure or holding of goods or, more often, the person or a relative of the debtor, until the debt is paid. The old debtors' prisons were a version of distraint. Obviously to imprison a man who has no assets and cannot work to pay off the debt, is unproductive. The only form of debtors' prisons now in operation are those in which are placed debtors to the state. That is, those in which are placed people who fail to pay taxes or fines to the state. It is part of the peculiar moral hypocrisy of our age that debt slavery is scorned as immoral and yet debt imprisonment to the state is tolerated. Yet imprisonment is far worse than slavery. A slave has his wife and family and his contacts with normal society. The prisoner is cut off from his family in a morally degrading and dangerous society. Finally there is bankruptcy. That relieves the debtor but not the creditor. Certainly Biblical teaching urges the creditor not to exact payment from the poor, but it also urges the responsibility of repaying debts.

Why is state debt prison and bankruptcy (which are the solutions of our day) moral whereas debt slavery is immoral?

All the arguments against treating a person as a thing should apply equally to imprisonment for debts to the state. Further, imprisonment is far less productive than slavery. It may be objected that the state could not survive if it had no way to enforce payment of its dues. But such arguments from practical security cannot excuse a practice if it is really immoral in itself. The survival of the state is not an excuse for evil.

The main point of this argument is not a plea for the return of debt slavery. It is merely to point out that we find it easy to criticize the solutions to complex problems offered by other societies but do not see the vital problem of our own societies. To require a man to work for a certain period as a slave to pay off a debt cannot be called evil in itself. Moral questions come when the period is too long, the conditions of service inhumane, or when future generations also enslaved.

The difficulty of the question of prisoner-of-war slavery has been already mentioned. Undoubtedly many of the slaves outside of Israel in both Old Testament and New Testament times were enslaved as a result of war. Further, many of these wars were wars of naked aggression which could not be in any way condoned. While slavery may not always be wrong, in such cases it has to be called contrary to God's teaching (cf. Amos 1:6,9).

The problem created for the church by slaves from such wars, or the descendants of such slaves, is complex. We may compare it with the problem of Europeans who several generations ago unjustly appropriated other lands, as in Australia, North America, or Africa. How does one reverse the injustices of long ago? Another comparison would be with the problem of polygamy faced by the church in many situations. We may infer from the qualification for eldership given in 1 Timothy 3:2 that there were men in the New Testament congregations with more than one wife. Thus the New Testament church did not force the dissolution of polygamous marriages. Where missionaries have tried to do this they have brought great suffering to the wives cast off. Reforms of evil social situations have to be carried out with care. Thus to require the release of all slaves would not necessarily be in the best interests of those slaves. Where would they find alternative employment, accommodation, and other necessities of life?

The problem can be summarized as follows: it is not a scriptural position to claim that slavery is always and inevitably wrong. That is because other methods for dealing with the problem of debt have their own difficulties. Given that fact we would not expect a blanket Biblical condemnation of slavery. Certainly there is an awareness of the evils of slavery. Hence the Biblical laws regulating slavery and the refuge to escaped slaves. The New Testament deals with the problem not by releasing slaves to follow their own devices, but by putting the onus on Christian masters to be fair and kind to their slaves.

Are these Biblical approaches to be seen as something obviously wrong which we have now rejected? Certainly not! The crusade against the trade in African slaves had good Biblical warrant in Exodus 21:16. Further there is every reason to seek ways in which men may work off their debts, particularly debts to the state. In our treatment of this fundamental problem we in the modern world have still not caught up with the ancient world. Certainly some form of restriction might be required to make men work off their debts, but that is far preferable to imprisonment. The damage to the family that results from imprisonment should be of major concern to the Christian.

Further it must be asked whether the Biblical approach to the correction of a past injustice or sin is itself wrong. Perhaps the example of past injustice to native peoples can be used as an example once more. Obviously there must be an end to the injustices that have resulted from European appropriation of native lands. Yet a too sudden casting of deprived people upon their own devices, or an attempt to return them forcibly to a lifestyle they have now forgotten, is neither justice nor mercy. First must come a true concern for these victims of injustice as people. The New Testament demanded that slaves be treated as men and women deserving of justice and, when also believers, as beloved in the Lord. That is where any correction of long standing and now institutionalized injustice must begin.

∞ 20 ∞

The Worship and Government of the Church

One of the practical consequences of the view that the Bible is limited to its own day is that the approach to the operation of the church set forth in Scripture will also be seen as purely limited to its time. Hence there are many calls to change the church to make it 'relevant' to our time. Of course many of those calls are thoroughly legitimate. Often the call is to jettison traditional baggage with which the church has been burdened over the years. The call is to abandon antiquated practices which have no Biblical warrant.

However sometimes the call is to abandon practices that were found in the New Testament churches or to add new practices which have no other defence than that they are likely to be popular in our day. Thus the whole question is one of whether the organization and practice of the New Testament church is the authoritative model for the church in later times.

The best place to start an investigation of the question is with Paul's treatment of the problems of church order in 1 Corinthians. Chapters 11–14 are concerned with the worship of the church. Essentially Paul uses two different sorts of argument. One is an appeal to general principles. The other is an appeal to the 'traditions' as he had passed them on to the Corinthians.

Paul's expectation and demand is that there will be uniformity in practice throughout the churches. Thus he says, 'But if one is inclined to be contentious, we have no other practice, nor have the churches of God' (11:16). The very idea of uniformity throughout the churches shows that this is not a matter of indifference. If there were no authoritative position then there could be no appeal to the uniform practice of the

[158]

churches. An appeal to the common practice of the churches shows that there was one standard throughout. Paul is criticizing the Corinthians for thinking they could begin a new practice formerly unknown in the church. He returns to this note of criticism for innovation in 14:33,36.

Why is uniform practice of some concern to Paul? It is because the practice he has passed on to the Corinthians has its origin in Christ. Deviation from that practice is deviation from Christ. This note is sounded already in the passage which forms the transition between the previous topic and this one: 'Be imitators of me, just as I also am of Christ' (11:1). Paul saw himself not as the innovator but as a link in the chain of tradition. The ultimate source of that tradition, as he points out in 11:23–25, is Christ. It is his practice which sets the pattern which the church is to follow.

A list of the elements of New Testament worship would include teaching (Acts 11:26), prophesying (Acts 11:28), singing (1 Cor. 14:15), prayer (1 Tim. 2:8), and the Lord's Supper (1 Cor. 11:17–26). Each of these can be related to the example set by Christ: teaching (Matt. 4:23), prophesying (Luke 24:19), singing (Matt. 26:30), prayer (John 17), and the Lord's Supper (Matt. 26:26–29).

Hence one can see the reason for Paul's concern about innovation. It is the Lord Jesus who sets the pattern for worship. To remove an element or to add some previously unknown element is to assume a prerogative which belongs to Christ alone.

However, details of the way the worship is to be conducted within these limits, raise questions that were not settled by an appeal to the example of Jesus. For instance, when Jesus was speaking, no other person could speak at the same time. However what of two ordinary prophets? Could both speak at the same time? This issue Paul resolved by appeal to a general principle, the character of God (1 Cor. 14:27–33). Other examples of this appeal to general principles are found in the issue of the woman's rôle in worship (1 Cor. 11:2–16) and the treatment of the poor in the assembly (1 Cor. 11:22; James 2:1–9).

Hence the worship of the church is not subject to free variation. It is fixed by the example of Jesus and general

Christian principles. That means that the practice of the New Testament church must be normative for later ages. For in it we see the application of the example of Jesus and general Biblical principles.

We do not have a discussion of church government comparable with the discussion of worship in 1 Corinthians 11–14. Rather what we find is a uniform practice in the New Testament period. The government of the church is committed to councils of elders or bishops. The terms 'elder' and 'bishop' refer to the same office as can be seen by comparing Acts 20:17 with 20:28 and Titus 1:5 with 1:7. It is clear from Paul's address to the elders of the church at Ephesus in Acts 20:17–35 that he saw them as being responsible for the pastoring and discipline of the church. The work which Titus was left to complete on Crete involved appointing elders (Tit. 1:5). Peter addresses the elders as a fellow elder and exhorts them to follow the example of Jesus the Chief Shepherd (1 Peter 5:1–4). Paul in writing to the Philippians includes the bishops (overseers) and deacons in the salutation (Phil. 1:1). The elders joined with the apostles in the decision made regarding Gentiles and the ceremonial law (Acts 15:22). As well as the task of the elder mentioned in Acts 20 and 1 Peter 5 we have information on qualifications in 1 Timothy 3 and Titus 1.

Can all this be set aside to set up a new way of administering and governing the church? This is not a new question for it is something that has been frequently done.

First of all, there is no indication within Scripture that this system of rule by elders was of limited duration only. The incorporation of passages like 1 Timothy 3 within Scripture would make one naturally expect that it was to be enduring. Those who want to depart from the church organization of the Scripture will argue that there is nowhere a specific teaching that that organization was to continue after the New Testament period. This argument singles out the Biblical teaching on the church and expects a special commandment with respect to it. There are many other teachings of the New Testament where we have no specific declarations that their validity is to continue after the New Testament period. Can we say that all such teachings are limited to the New Testament era? Of course it is the minority of Biblical teachings which are specifically marked as being enduring. With most it is simply assumed.

Sometimes the attempt is made to class instructions such as those to Timothy and Titus on church government as pragmatic rather than theological, or organizational rather than spiritual. Such distinctions are foreign to Scripture. The Scriptural view is that all gifts to edify the church are 'spiritual' (1 Cor. 12). Undoubtedly the proper exercise of these offices is a practical necessity for the church (Acts 20:28–31). However that task is understood not as a pure technical and unspiritual exercise. It is compared to Christ's care for the church (1 Peter 5:1–4). The elders are the under-shepherds of the Chief Shepherd. Once again the model is Christ. To do away with the New Testament structure is to remove that element where Christ's rôle as shepherd is reflected in the organizational structure of the church itself.

One of the common directions in which people move when they abandon the New Testament structure of rule by a council of elders is to dominance of the church by one man. They thus ignore the very thing the Scripture repeatedly stresses. The great danger to New Testament church structure is pride and the desire for a following (Acts 20:30). The New Testament structure clearly does not commit control to one man, for there are dangers in that. The church has again and again experienced those dangers and yet is sadly reluctant to follow the better way of Scripture.

It seems fairly obvious that the seven chosen in Acts 6 are deacons. The term is not used for them but their function corresponds to the meaning of the Greek word. That men should be set apart to care for believers in need is once again a reflection of Christ in the organizational structure of the church. To set aside Paul's instructions to Timothy in 1 Timothy 3:8ff., and to ignore the reference to the bishops and deacons at Philippi (Phil. 1:1) is to ignore the way the New Testament church structure reflected Christ's concern for the poor.

Put simply, the New Testament church organization with its bishops and deacons showed the impact of Christ upon the church. It showed a structure in which Christ's spiritual and physical concern for people was continued. There is thus a theological logic to the New Testament church government just as there is to New Testament worship. That logical structure has Christ as its key. When we abandon that structure we move away from a close integration of our doctrine and our practice around the person of Christ.

THE ARGUMENT FOR NON-BIBLICAL PRACTICES

The most common argument for a departure from Biblical structures is that those structures are not given in exhaustive detail. Hence they are not authoritative.

We see here the same assumption that has already been considered, namely, that an authoritative source has to have exhaustive detail. As said previously, that assumption has no Biblical warrant and is contradicted by the fact that the traditions delivered by Paul, while not exhaustive, are author-itative because they go back to Jesus. Actually Paul's teaching in 1 Corinthians (11–14), with its pattern of specifics and appeal to general principles, fits very well into the whole pattern of Biblical teaching.

Another common argument is that we are able to devise new elements of worship which may have no authority from Christ, but which are appropriate for Christian worship.

To consider this argument we have to go back to Colos-sians 2. As we have already seen, Paul's argument in this chapter is designed to counter an appeal to human wisdom as an authoritative source in contrast to the apostolic message about Christ. We must remember, however, that that wisdom was employed in devising ways to worship God. These ways of worship embodied Old Testament ordinances (2:16) but were not restricted to Old Testament ordinances. The objection to Old Testament ordinances was not that they were man-made. The objection was that they had been superseded by Christ (v.17). This worship included man-made elements (2:23). How are these treated? This question is treated in verses 20 to 23. They also are a departure from Christ and of no real spiritual value. Certainly these ordinances were of a particular type that included severe treatment of the body. But the argument against them is not dependent upon their particular character. The argument fits into the thrust of the whole chapter. Man-made ordinances, like human philosophy, may have an appearance of wisdom, but the appearance is rejected for the reality in Christ.

The overriding concern of Paul is that worship be centred in Christ. How is this Christ known? How do we know what is appropriate for Christ-centred worship? It is not by the wisdom of man. It is through the apostolic teaching.

Thus the basic point of 1 Corinthians 11–14 and of Colossians 2 is the same. Worship which is acceptable to God is worship derived from the historical Christ, not from human imagination.

A variant on these arguments draws a contrast between Old and New Testaments. It is conceded that under Old Testament law the worship of Israel was regulated in minute detail. Moses was told to construct the tabernacle according to the plan God showed him (Ex. 25:40). The lack of a similar detailed plan for New Testament worship is used as an argument that God has left New Testament worship free to be modelled according to the wisdom of man.

The fallacy of the argument is obvious. It ignores the fact that there is a model and a pattern: Jesus. The real relationship of Old Testament and New Testament is one of fulfilment of the old by the new. Jesus is the living pattern which fulfils the Old Testament type.

A further refutation of the whole argument has already been considered. As a matter of fact New Testament worship was not left free. Paul passed on binding traditions.

A final argument can be seen as a reverse image of the argument from lack of detail. It is that, at some point, all churches, no matter how Biblical they claim to be, introduce things in worship which are not mentioned in the Bible. Hence it is impossible to have a totally Biblical worship. Hence we should not even try.

This argument tells against any attempt to obey the Scriptures on any subject. For once again it must be stressed that it denies authority to what is not exhaustive. Actually it is easily countered. For it ignores the fact that our lives are regulated by the general principles of Scripture as well as the specific commands. Those general principles cover the incidentals we introduce. Let us take a trivial example. Suppose a teacher in the assembly takes a drink of water while speaking.[1] Has he no Biblical warrant? Certainly, the Scripture does regulate the way we eat and drink with the overriding concern that we eat and drink to the glory of God (1 Cor. 10:31). Any attempt to say that the speaker, having no Biblical warrant for drinking during New Testament worship, must endure a dry throat, is easily confuted. For it ignores mercy, which is a very clear and overriding Biblical concern.

Of course such trivialities are also covered by Paul's instruction that everything be done in an orderly manner (1 Cor. 14:26–33). They are not the introduction of significant new elements and ceremonies which have no warrant from Christ.

CHURCH ORDER WITHOUT SCRIPTURE

As has already been discussed, the sufficiency and authority of Scripture have been rejected by many. In turn that will have consequences for their approach to the church. These consequences are not always purely logical, theological inferences from the abandonment of Scripture. Some are psychological consequences. One of the things that is happening is that God is seen as a distant God. He has no close contact with the world. He did not intervene directly to create or to inspire Scripture. That belief must influence a man's personal relationship to God. There cannot be a personal closeness to a God who is distant and will not act directly in answer to prayer.

One of the things that happens is a growth of traditionalism. This is paradoxical because one of the reasons Scripture has been rejected has been because of a growth in historical relativism. If Scripture is dated and irrelevant, then so should be the former ages of the church.

What seems to happen is that people feel a need for a model somewhere to follow. They have rejected Scripture as that

---

[1] While trivial, this example was actually raised in a famous Reformation debate, that of John Knox with John Winram (John Knox, *History of the Reformation in Scotland*, London, Thomas Nelson, 1949, Vol. I, p. 89). Actually there are few really new issues in this debate. The argument from lack of detail was employed against the Reformation use of Scripture to reform the church.

model. Scripture with its absolute claims is too threatening. Church history is not so threatening. Hence ceremonies, forms, tunes, garments, etc. are dug up from the past to give the worship of the church some foundation. Often the forms are borrowed at the same time that the theology of those who devised them is ignored or denigrated.

If there is no clear, authoritative word from God, then preaching and teaching become very difficult. A substitute has to be found. Dialogue, rôle-play, and drama are attractive substitutes because they present human opinions on the present scene. Obviously all that Paul says in 1 Corinthians 11–14 and Colossians 2 could be said against these expressions of human wisdom. However if Scripture is not really authoritative and certain, then we cannot know the pattern which Jesus set. Paul's whole position on worship depended on his own faithfulness in passing on the traditions about Jesus.

Public prayer is a difficult thing for anybody whose God is distant, indistinct, and impotent. There is not the living reality of personal communion with God. Hence men desire forms and set prayers lest the nakedness of their personal communion with God be exposed before the congregation. This joins with the tendency to traditionalism already mentioned.

Indeed the whole pastoral task is daunting for such men. They are expected to speak things to people which they themselves have never experienced. Hence a flight from the real face-to-face, personal contact with people. The Biblical elder/bishop/shepherd cannot escape such contact. It is part of his basic ministry. Hence a move from the basic teaching, pastoral ministry to other jobs. Here the New Testament church order poses a problem. It has no spots for those who wish to avoid self-revealing contacts with people. Such spots have to be created. They are generally created by developing a centralized, bureaucratic administration. Church (and non-Church) agencies and boards are set up to be a refuge for those who lack the conviction and reality of Christian experience demanded of the pastor.

Hence the church has a tendency to become traditional, formalized, bureaucratic. One has only to look at the churches which have rejected Scripture to see those things in them. Yet in their own rhetoric they would depict themselves as free and non-traditional. While the odd 'experimental' worship service may give the impression of freedom and chaos, the more common structures are as described.

In reality Scripture is not a binding and stultifying form. For Scripture directs us to Christ. Where there is reflection of the Christ of the apostolic tradition in our churches, there is life. Without that Christ the church must ossify.

Certainly many churches which pride themselves on their orthodoxy carry the dead weight of unbiblical tradition and have ignored parts of the New Testament pattern. But the way is always open to go back to that pattern and to Christ, the life of the church.

೮ 21 ೮

The Scripture and 'Advances' in Psychology

We have seen that a major point in the debate about Scripture is the question of whether scriptural commands are valid today. Sometimes it is claimed that the writers of Scripture did not have the advantage of the knowledge of our day. For example there are various things which Scripture clearly condemns, which would today be defended on the ground of greater psychological insight.

Two examples will make the point clearer. Scripture condemns homosexual acts. Since Scripture also teaches that it is wrong to desire evil, this prohibition is generally understood to extend to the desire for homosexual acts. There are some who will argue that people are not morally responsible for their homosexuality. It is wrong to apply the condemnations of Scripture to them.

Another example is divorce. Scripture holds the person guilty who breaks a marriage. Certainly it allows divorce in the case of marital unfaithfulness on the part of the other party, but prohibits anybody taking the initiative in divorcing an innocent party. There are some who would claim that there are such things as psychological incompatibility or irretrievable breakdown of the marriage relationship.

One could add other examples of other acts or conditions which are condemned by Scripture but are defended today. They all raise the same point: can we set aside the commandment of God on the basis of greater 'knowledge' in our day? In both cases the commandments being set aside are New Testament commandments. Hence there is no question of these being Old Testament commandments superseded in the New Testament age.

The technique of arguing against the Biblical command is fairly uniform. It is to say that there are two forms of homosexuality or two forms of divorce. One is a wilful, sinful act. The other is something for which the person is not responsible. The Biblical prohibition is then seen as being against the wilful form only. Those who cannot help themselves are not being condemned by Scripture.

HOMOSEXUALITY

The position commonly taken is that certain homosexuals, because of an inborn tendency or experiences during their childhood, are unable to experience sexuality except as homosexuality.[1] This distinction between those who are responsible for their sinfulness and those who break the same law but are not held responsible is, of course, not made by Scripture. It is the distinction we make in order to allow, in some cases, what Scripture condemns. Is this distinction a legitimate one, or is it simply an attempt to set aside the law of God in favour of human wisdom?

There is of course a very large debate amongst non-Christian psychologists as to whether the distinction is a valid one.[2] Yet that debate is really not the crucial issue. At the moment there is no organic difference detectable between the sex hormones of homosexuals and heterosexuals, or any other detectable difference. Yet let us say that there was such an organic difference. Let us say that homosexuals have very high levels of hormone X. Would that decide the issue? It would not, because we would have no way of knowing whether the high levels of hormone X caused a homosexual disposition or whether some brain – body connection in those who dwell on homosexual thoughts caused the high hormone levels.

Similarly there are those who argue that homosexuality is the

[1] E.g. 'As a human being his entire person experiences the natural drive and need for sexual completeness, but due to conditions to a large extent, if not entirely beyond his responsibility, he cannot relate to a member of the opposite sex in sexual fulfilment, and in fact feels drawn to members of his own sex' (Report 42, *Acts of Synod of the Christian Reformed Church*, 1973, p. 630).

[2] See for discussion G. L. Bahnsen, *Homosexuality: A Biblical View*, Grand Rapids, Baker, 1978, pp. 74ff.

consequence of a certain home environment. Boys with weak fathers and domineering mothers are more likely to become homosexuals. Once again the scientific basis of this claim is disputed.[1] Yet let us say for argument's sake what nobody has been able to prove by any sort of rigorous statistical survey: that there is a high correlation between a homosexual and parents where the father is weak and the mother is domineering. Would that make homosexuality unique? It is already well known that there is a correlation between home background and sin. For example, children raised in state institutions had significantly higher crime rate than the rest of the population raised in normal home environments. Detribalized peoples have high crime rates, high alcoholism, etc. In other words there is a statistical correlation between social circumstances and behaviour. The family has a powerful influence in restraining sinful tendencies.

If the claimed correlation between homosexuality and family background sets aside Biblical law relating to homosexuality, then surely there are other laws which should be set aside as well. That is, of course, the argument of many moral relativists. They claim that people are shaped by their environment and hence cannot be held responsible for their actions.

Let us explore this logic further. If homosexual behaviour can be traced to home background, then surely the same is true of heterosexual sin and of people who engage in both homo- and hetero-sexual promiscuity. Generally the argument is that the true 'dispositional' homosexual has to be exonerated as compared with the person who just 'chooses' to engage in homosexuality or the person who engages in heterosexual sin. Why the distinction? It is quite likely that there is a correlation of some sort between bad home environment and heterosexual promiscuity or mixed heterosexual and homosexual promiscuity.

Really we come back to something that is particularly mentioned in the Book of Proverbs. Parents who train their children in the law of God and set them a godly example do a good thing for their children. However, what of the others who have not been so trained? Are they free of any responsibility and

[1] *Ibid.*, pp. 74ff.

guilt? Clearly Scripture does not hold them free of guilt. It does teach that those privileged with better instruction are more culpable if they sin, but the others are not exonerated (Luke 12:47,48). If this creates a problem for us, then we have not understood the logic of Paul's argument in the early chapters of Romans. Paul's point is that all men do show some knowledge of God's truth; hence all are guilty when they act contrary to the truth they know. This does not mean that all have an equal knowledge of the truth. It means that all know some truth.

This discussion has taken us off the narrow subject of homosexuality, but the whole point is that the argument used to exonerate homosexuals is not applicable to homosexuals alone. It is a form of environmental determinism, arguing that people are shaped by their environment and therefore without guilt for their sin. Scripture is well aware of the importance of home influences, but it never opens the door to environmental determinism.

Environmental determinism is also a very dangerous doctrine as far as the state is concerned. If crime is caused by environment, what right is there to punish criminals?

As a matter of fact the correlation between home and crime is statistical, not absolute. We are speaking of percentages and proportions, not of all the people who experience a certain upbringing. If environmental determinism is correct, why do all the people from the same background not act in the same way? The determinist will say that the exceptions are to be explained by small variations in the environment which we cannot measure or identify. There is also another explanation. It is that people, as responsible individuals, show different reactions to the same environment.

Hence there are two possible explanations for the correlation between background and sin. The determinist says that people who begin life morally neutral are shaped a certain way by their environment whether they want it or not. The second explanation is that man's inherent depravity will be restrained by family discipline or possibly come to expression in the particular way he reacts to his discipline or the lack of it.

Which understanding is consistent with Scripture? It is clear that the first denies the reality of human guilt for sin. Sometimes people attempt to incorporate determinism into a

Biblical world-view by making sin the same as sickness as a result of the curse upon the earth. A man is not personally responsible for sickness as he is for sin. Sickness is a consequence of living in a fallen world. The attempt will be made to picture homosexuality as a sickness. Hence the homosexual is not responsible.[1]

Thus the issue raised by this defence of homosexuality is wider than just homosexuality. It concerns the theory of environmental determinism. If we accept the theory in this case, then we have no reason for rejecting it in any other case. Conversely, if environmental determinism is incorrect, then the whole argument for homosexuality collapses.

As a matter of fact we have to reject environmental determinism because God holds man responsible for sin. Thus the issue of homosexuality is not settled merely by saying that we know more about it than the Biblical authors.

There are other ways we could approach the question of homosexuality. Let us put the argument for it in its common form. It is that human scholarship (psychology) has now discovered that homosexuality is not a sin. We are then confronted with the Biblical condemnation (Lev. 18:22;20:13) and with Paul's description of homosexuality as contrary to 'nature' (Rom. 1:26,27). Paul calls heterosexual relations natural and homosexual ones contrary to nature. We have already touched upon his use of nature in chapter 19. He is obviously influenced by the creation account. Heterosexuality is part of the original nature of creation. Homosexuality is contrary to it.

So we have a secular scholar saying homosexuality is permissible. And we have Biblical teaching, going back to the creation account, saying that it is a contradiction of God's plan and hence an abomination to him. Who has the better understanding of creation? Obviously we have to go back to the argument in Colossians 2 already considered. The whole point of that argument is that the one who created has the best understanding of creation. The Old Testament law was a revelation of God. Who knows best the nature of the world, the one who made it all or the one who looks at part of it in a biased way? The answer is obvious. Of course one can avoid this

[1]Note in the report cited in note 1 (p. 168) the description of the homosexual as one who 'bears the disorder of our broken world in his person' (p.626).

argument, either by denying that God created man or by denying that Scripture is the Word of God. When this is done, it is clear that the issue is not merely homosexuality.

One cannot create an argument for setting aside a Biblical command and leaving the rest of the Biblical doctrine untouched. The doctrine of sin, of creation, and of Scripture are all attacked.

Further, the gospel comes into question. If the homosexual is no more able to help himself than a man born blind, or blinded in an accident, then we cannot say that the gospel offers hope of liberation to the homosexual. We cannot tell him to trust in the power of Christ to enable him to overcome his sinful tendencies.[1] Thus the gospel hope is denied to such a person. What does the Scripture say? 'Do not be deceived; neither fornicators, nor idolators, nor adulterers, nor effeminate, nor homosexuals . . . shall inherit the kingdom of God. And such were some of you; but you were washed, but you were sanctified, but you were justified in the name of the Lord Jesus Christ, and in the Spirit of our God' (1 cor. 6:9–11).

It may seem kind to say that a person is not responsible for his sin. But it has the harsh and cruel consequence that sin is therefore outside the scope of the sanctifying work of the Spirit. The homosexual is doomed to live with the misery of sin. Make no mistake. Sin and misery go together. When we deny the homosexual the gospel we tell him to expect a continuance of his misery. The point is often made that the church should show compassion to the homosexual. So it should. The first item of that compassion is telling him how escape is possible. Why should he seek the church that tells him that nothing can be done for him? He may like such a church to ease the burden of his guilty conscience, but such a church has nothing to offer him.

We cannot stop here. For we have already seen that environmental determinism will excuse many other sins besides homosexuality. It must follow that those sins also are beyond the sanctifying work of the Spirit. That is, that the gospel cannot hold out to a man the hope of freedom from the

[1]'Many Christians who are sexually inverted know that their problem is not removed by prayer, any more than Paul's thorn in the flesh was removed in answer to his prayers . . . to expect the means of grace and prayer to redirect a firmly fixed homosexual is to expect a miracle' (*ibid.*, p. 627).

misery of sin. When we follow a belief that leads to this conclusion, we do more than deny the clear Biblical teaching on the gospel and the work of the Holy Spirit. We show a callous indifference to the misery of sinners.

DIVORCE

Divorce raises many of the same questions as those raised by homosexuality. There is the argument that we now realize that people may enter marriage psychologically unprepared for it, or find themselves married to a person with whom they are incompatible. It is argued that in such cases the Biblical prohibition on divorce cannot apply.

There is another approach formally akin to the comparison of homosexuality with a disease. This is to say that divorce is a great evil, but in our broken and sinful world, an unavoidable evil; also that while the church should counsel against divorce and try to help couples in difficulties, where such measures have not succeeded, divorce is to be allowed.

There is one respect where the situation is different with divorce. With homosexuality the crucial question is whether it is absolutely wrong. There is not a debate over the forms of homosexuality permitted by Scripture.[1] Scripture, however, has several passages which, on the face of them, seem to permit divorce in certain circumstances. The church is then faced with deciding whether a certain case of divorce is a case permitted under Scriptural rules or not. This is often scorned as casuistry. It is asserted that the attempt to determine whether a certain divorce is legitimate smacks of Pharisaic legalism. Under the gospel there should be no legal hair-splitting. In consequence of such ideas the practical result is that all divorces are treated as legitimate.

This approach often leads to a form of finding a basic teaching more ultimate than the words of Scripture. It is

---

[1]It is of course true that some try to make distinctions between a 'permitted' homosexuality (generally monogamous homosexuality for true homosexuals) and 'forbidden' homosexuality (promiscuous and/or practised by elective homosexuals). However no ground can be found in Scripture for these exceptions. They are attempts to soften and avoid the blanket condemnations in Scripture.

asserted that Christ came to bring liberty from legal rules. This freedom, seen as a consequence of the gospel, is regarded as more important than Jesus' actual words on divorce.

THE GOSPEL AND LEGAL PROHIBITIONS

Is it true that the message of Jesus is incompatible with all rules and prohibitions? That was not the view of Jesus himself. The Sermon on the Mount is full of prohibitions. Indeed in many points Jesus strengthened the prohibitions of the Old Testament law. The section which introduces the clarifications and reinforcements of Old Testament laws is prefaced by a strong statement on law-keeping: 'Whoever then annuls one of the least of these commandments, and so teaches others, shall be called least in the kingdom of heaven; but whoever keeps and teaches them, he shall be called great in the kingdom of heaven' (Matt. 5:19).

Those who ignore the very words of Jesus to create a Jesus who is indifferent to rules show their contempt for the real Jesus of the Scriptures. They have created a Christ to suit themselves rather than brought themselves into obedience to the real Christ.

DIVORCE: THE FORBIDDEN AND THE PERMITTED

Jesus' teaching on divorce comes in the section of the Sermon on the Mount in which the Old Testament law is intensified and clarified. It begins with an allusion to the Old Testament teaching on the subject (Matt. 5:31). It is important to note that it is an allusion and a rather garbled one at that. Jesus in this section is referring to things that the people have heard taught. The teaching they had heard had a link with the Old Testament law but often represented a simplification or a distortion of that law.

Hence it is important to go back to the law in question – Deuteronomy 24:1–4. This law, like many of the Old Testament laws, is a case law. It describes a situation and gives the rule valid for that situation. Thus part of it is descriptive, setting the scene as it were. The other part of it is normative. The two sections correspond to the sections beginning with 'if' and 'then' in English translation. To understand the law it is crucial to know where the 'then' clause begins. What goes before is descriptive of a situation, not a command. There is no doubt on the basis of the Hebrew that the 'then' clause begins at the beginning of verse 4. What goes before is descriptive of the situation, not a command. Thus the law does not say, 'IF a man divorces his wife, THEN he must give her a bill of divorce'. All that is commanded is that the original husband may not remarry the wife.

Hence what Jesus quotes as being taught is a misquotation of the law. This misquotation gives a certain legitimacy to divorce, while the original law says nothing on the question of the rightness or wrongness of divorce.

Jesus counters this by saying that divorce is not permitted. There has been much discussion of the verbs in verse 32 which describe the consequences of divorce for the wife. Why does Jesus say 'makes her commit adultery'? Does he contemplate a subsequent marriage on the part of the divorced wife? The simplest explanation is that the teaching to which Jesus reacted implied that all the husband needed to do was to give his wife a certificate of divorce and she was thus freed. Hence Jesus stresses that the woman is not set free in this way. The particular way in which this is expressed may also be designed to point to the responsibility of the divorcing husband in making an adulteress of his wife.

Of course, if the wife was already guilty of sexual misconduct, then the husband cannot be responsible for making her an adulteress. The term translated 'unchastity' or 'fornication' is a wider term than adultery and refers to sexual misconduct in general.

The treatment of divorce in Matthew 19:3–9 has many similarities to Matthew 5:31,32. Jesus was presented with a trap. If he answered that it was legitimate to divorce, he would be seen as contradicting his earlier teaching. If he denied divorce the Pharisees could say that he was ignoring Deuteronomy 24:1–4. Jesus anticipated the trap that Moses would be quoted at him by quoting Moses to them. He takes them to the original created order. That was the order set by God and should not be violated.

It is important to stress that this is Jesus' answer to the

question on divorce. Implied in the answer is the fact that men and women entering into marriage enter into that original ordinance. The becoming of one flesh means that they have the same God-given unity as the first pair.

The Pharisees respond with the question about Deuteronomy 24:1–4. Jesus answers that Moses tolerated an abuse which could not be completely stamped out because of the hardness of the heart of Israel. As we have seen, the answer of Jesus does justice to the actual wording of the law. There is nothing in it which commands any action of divorce. It merely describes such actions and seeks to curb one of the consequences of such actions.

Jesus then repeats in his teaching that divorce does not make a person innocent of the sin of adultery. This time the emphasis is on the action of the man. If he divorces and remarries, then he commits adultery.

How can such plain teaching be set aside or evaded? One way is to say that divorce is totally wrong, but once it has happened, we should extend forgiveness and an opportunity for a new beginning to those involved.[1]

Of course, when the church takes this approach it tells people by its actions that divorce is permitted. There is another way of dealing with marital breakdown, which we see when considering Paul's teaching.

Paul's consideration of divorce flows out of a much broader discussion of male-female relations. At the end of 1 Corinthians 6 he deals with Christians resorting to harlots. He answers this problem by developing the Biblical teaching on the body. The Christian's body is a temple and temples must be kept pure from any defilement. For a Christian to join his body to that of a harlot is to defile the temple of the Holy Spirit.

From this subject Paul turns in chapter 7 to consider the marriage relationship. His initial concern is that the sexual

[1]This is essentially the approach of B. W. Powers ('Divorce and the Bible', *Interchange*, 23 (1978), 149–174). In order to make the prohibition total he attempts to do away with the exception clause in 19:9 ('except for immorality'). Even if his rather strained grammatical argument could succeed here, if would not overturn the differently worded, but identical in meaning, clause in 5:32. If the Biblical relief is not allowed to those facing a spouse's unfaithfulness then it is easier to imply that the biblical ban on divorce is harsh and unworkable.

needs of each partner be met and that temptations be avoided.

In chapter 7 verses 10 and 11 he comes to the question of divorce. He knows that there is a commandment of the Lord on the subject. So he quotes that. The wife is not to leave her husband. Paul could be quoting from any one of the several teachings of Jesus on the subject. I suspect that he is quoting from Matthew 19 or the parallel passage, Mark 10. That is because of an interesting parallel between these gospel passages and the order of treatment in 1 Corinthians 7. Both Matthew 19 and Mark 10 record in succession: Jesus' teaching about divorce; his receiving of children; the rich young ruler with the warning about entrapment in possessions and family. Paul in 1 Corinthians 7 deals with divorce with specific allusion to our Lord's teaching. Later in the chapter the argument depends upon the special status of the children of a believer (v.14).[1] Then he considers the dangers of too much attachment to the possessions and relationships of this life (vv.29–31). Thus the topics of the Gospel reappear in 1 Corinthians 7. In the Gospel they are unrelated incidents. Paul has woven them into a coherent argument.[2]

Whether or not a Gospel passage and 1 Corinthians 7 are related in the way suggested, Paul explicitly refers to our Lord's teaching on divorce. That teaching is summarized as being that the wife should not leave the husband. However, what happens if the teaching of our Lord has not been followed? What happens if marital breakdown has occurred? This is an important question because of the argument of those who

[1]Professor E. Clowney's explanation of this passage is simple and convincing. Paul had argued at the end of chapter 6 that sexual union with an unbelieving harlot must be defiling. Surely the same defilement would arise in the case of an unbelieving marriage partner. Paul says it does not. Instead of the believer receiving defilement, the unbeliever is sanctified in the sexual union. Paul has thus made a claim that in marriage, the holiness of the believer counteracts the physical defilment of an unbeliever. What evidence can be produced to support that claim? Well, obviously if the sexual union of the marriage was a defiling one, then the products of that union, the children, would be defiled. However they are holy. Hence the physical union cannot be a defiling one. Paul's beliefs about the children of a believer can be supported in turn by the attitude of Jesus to children.

[2]This suggestion has obvious implications for the history of the writing of the Gospel. It implies that either Matthew or Mark (or both) existed with the stories gathered in their present order at the time Paul wrote 1 Corinthians.

would approve divorce in the Christian community. They say that the couple should be free to remarry.

Scripture does not ignore this situation. It speaks directly to it in 1 Corinthians 7:11. If the wife has left her husband she is not to remarry. She is to remain unmarried or to seek reconciliation with her husband. Clearly Paul is seeking to prevent the breakdown becoming worse or leading to further sin. If there is to be a change in the situation once separation has occurred, then it is to be in the direction of reconstituting the marriage. It is not to be a marriage to another party.[1]

Paul does not mention any responsibility or task of the church in dealing with such separated couples. However, given that the separation is declared to be contrary to Christ's teaching, the natural task of the church would be to urge both parties to a reconciliation. However this assumes that both parties are believers. What happens if the deserting party is an unbeliever? Paul turns to this problem. He encourages the believing party to continue in the marriage and he answers their fears of defilement through the sexual relationship. But what if the unbeliever leaves? Paul acknowledges that the question of a mixed marriage between believer and unbeliever was not one addressed by Jesus. Hence the answer given is on the basis of Paul's authority as an apostle. If, however, the unbelieving partner wants to break the marriage, then he or she ought to be allowed to do so. There has been much discussion of what Paul means by saying that the believer is 'not under bondage in such cases'. Does it mean just not under bondage to continue the marriage at all costs? Or does it mean free from marriage and thus free to remarry? A strong case can be put for arguing that it implies freedom to remarry.[2] If that is the case, it adds another legitimate ground for divorce and remarriage, namely the desertion of an unbelieving spouse. However this is not as common an occurrence, or as problematic for the church, as the cases which have already been considered.

[1] Powers (*op. cit.*) argues that because Paul speaks of these women as remaining 'unmarried' and elsewhere he speaks of the 'unmarried' marrying (7:8), he means that these divorcees are free to marry. But that is in total contradiction to what Paul says in 7:11.

[2] See J. Murray, *Divorce*, Philadelphia, Presbyterian and Reformed, 1961, pp. 62ff.

Thus the Biblical teaching may be summarized as follows. Marriage, which is in the pattern established by God, is not to be broken. If one partner breaks the marriage by sexual unfaithfulness, the other then can divorce and remarry. (This is not the same as saying he must always divorce. Forgiveness and reconciliation are also possible.) If a separation has taken place, the parties are not to enter into another marriage but to seek reconciliation with the original spouse. Desertion by an unbeliever forms a special case.

The Biblical teaching is clear and is not really problematic. It clearly condemns divorce except in certain defined situations.

CASUISTRY?

That means that the church may be faced by people desiring to divorce or desiring to remarry after a divorce. Should the church attempt to judge the legitimacy or otherwise of the divorce? How can it do anything else? Let us say that it is a case of wilful and persistent, unrepentant adultery. Is the church to refuse to the innocent partner the relief that Christ allows? Suppose on the other hand that there is no basis for the divorce. Shall the church, charged to teach, admonish, and discipline believers, accept such a divorce? If it does, then it acts and teaches contrary to Christ.

Certainly there are cases which are much more difficult to decide than these two. Extreme cases are chosen to prove that the church must make judgments. If it does not make judgments and teach and act accordingly, then it is unfaithful to Christ. Certainly in difficult cases the church should respond with due thought, prayer, and consideration. However the crucial problem facing the church today is not the problem of complex and difficult cases. It is rather the teaching of those who say that while the church should teach in general against divorce, it should not act to deal with members who divorce and remarry with no Biblical ground. Thus the church is faced with approving what Christ very explicitly condemns. It is a question of whether the church is for Christ's teaching or against it.

Often the church which responsibly tries to make judgments

and to counsel accordingly, is accused of hair-splitting, Phar-isaic action. That charge is irresponsible and slanderous. Rather the situation is exactly the reverse. It is those who will not make such judgments, and who indiscriminately approve divorce who are acting like the Pharisees. The Pharisees are criticized by Jesus, not only for adding unnecessary rules and regulations (Matt. 23:4). They are also criticized for setting aside the commandments of God (Matt. 15:3–6). Any human system of tradition will be used to add to God's Word and to take away from God's Word. To set aside the clear command-ment of God on divorce is to act like the Pharisees in putting human wisdom above the Word of God.

Sometimes the charge is made that those who will not approve indiscriminate divorce are being harsh and judg-mental. We meet once again an attempt to make the gospel of love a message beyond the actual words. Of course it is an open question who is being unloving. Any system of indiscrimin-ate divorce on average hurts women and children. It is the woman who is generally left to cope with the raising of the children without male support. The man generally has greater earning power and the means to change his location.

Those who think that the church should not oppose divorce and remarriage in cases of marital breakdown would probably claim they are not approving indiscriminate divorce. For they teach against divorce and try to repair damaged marriages. It is only when this has failed that they approve divorce and remarriage. However this is a case of saying one thing and doing another. How can the church say that God hates divorce (Mal. 2:16) and then say that it will approve the divorce and remarriage that has taken place? Our actions will speak louder than our hollow words and everybody will know that we approve what the Lord rejects.

MARRIAGE BREAKDOWN AND PSYCHOLOGICAL INCOMPATIBILITY

Thus the Scriptural teaching on divorce is clear. However, those who want to approve divorce turn to the discoveries of psychology. They talk of incompatible personality types; of people who are too immature for the responsibilities of marriage and are better released from it. Often they will deny the idea of legitimate divorce, saying that there can be no 'innocent' party – both parties contribute to marital break-down.

Even if we had no answer to all these arguments we could not approve indiscriminate divorce. For God does not approve it. To use such arguments to overturn the teaching of Jesus is to place human reason above the teaching of God's Son. It is a rejection of Christ's wisdom and authority.

However, we are not without answers to these points. What characterizes this position is the premise that a certain psychological state makes a man no longer responsible for his actions. In effect it is saying that a man is no longer responsible for sin. It is not a conflict of personality types which wrecks a marriage. We all know of happy marriages between very diverse people. It is the unwillingness to love and respect the partner; it is sinful selfishness that ruins marriages. Often what is referred to as 'incompatible' or 'difficult' personality is simply sin. It is a lack of love and concern for the spouse. People who are too 'immature' for the responsibilities of marriage are really people who are too self-centred and selfish.

How are these problems to be dealt with in Christians? They are to be dealt with by repentance and change through the work of the Word and the Spirit. When these problems are given up as hopeless cases, then once again the power of the gospel is being denied. Once again, as soon as we take away a man's responsibility, we deny the power of the gospel to help him.

In many cases both partners may be jointly responsible for the problems. To say that this is always the case is to slander many fine believers. Let us take some extreme cases to make this point. One is that of the believer whose unbelieving partner rejects the believer out of hatred for the Lord. Is the believer equally guilty for the marriage breakdown? Or we may take the wife whose husband turns to the 'pleasures of sin for a season' with another woman. Many adulterous husbands will attempt to blame their wives for what is their own sin. Should we accept that every adulterous husband is driven to it by his wife? We cannot do so because of the Biblical teaching on sin. We are not caused to sin by the actions of others, especially not when that other is a sincere Christian. We are led astray and enticed by our own lusts. Once again we meet the tendency to want to excuse a man from responsibility for his sin. Of course, that is what the unbeliever is always trying to do. The church must not follow the unbeliever in this offence.

Practically the great need is not for more marriage counselling and pre-marital counselling. Practically the great problem is a failure of nerve in the church. There are people whose relationships to others, including to their spouses, fall far short of what Christ expects. That may be notorious in the congregation and the general community. Yet the church fails to act in terms of admonition and teaching, and, if necessary, in censure and discipline. When a marriage breaks down, the church is partly paralysed by its own guilt in not acting sooner.

If we believe that people are not responsible for their actions and that people cannot be changed, then we will not have any real incentive for trying to help such cases. If we believe that God does not act in this world, then we will believe that people cannot be changed. As we have seen, behind the doubts about Scripture as expressed today lies a belief that God is a distant God, not active in the world. That same belief must take away any hope that the Holy Spirit will work to change lives significantly. If there is no hope for such change, then there is no hope for marriages in difficulty or for homosexuals. Thus it follows that doubt as to God's activity in giving the Scripture will have practical consequences in the church's approach to these ethical questions.

22

'Rabbinic' Exegesis in the New Testament

The argument for the authority of Scripture has always depended heavily upon the attitude to Scripture of Jesus and the New Testament writers. Further, in developing our own approach to interpreting Scripture, we have attempted to imitate the divinely appointed founders of the church. It is therefore important to consider the claim that the use of Scripture by Jesus and the apostles is just a reflection of the views of their day. They are held to be reflecting exegetical practices common in their time. Or they were using the arguments which they knew would have weight with their hearers.

This claim can be extended or amplified in various ways. For example we have seen that Paul always bases his teaching about the exclusion of women from ruling in the church on creation. Some would say that Paul's real reason was a pragmatic one of conformity to social expectations. He used a Biblical argument only because that was expected in the rabbinic circles in which he was trained. There a man conventionally defended, by appeal to Scripture, conclusions reached on other grounds.

Several things follow from this argument. One is that we are not bound to treat Scripture or regard Scripture as they did. They were merely reflecting the views of their times. We can feel free to reject the teachings they based on Scripture. Thus we might conclude that Paul's teachings about women, being 'really' based on pragmatism and not on Scripture, are to be ignored.

RELATIVISM ONCE MORE

While the argument applies specifically to the use of Scripture, it is but a variant of the argument we have encountered many times before. That is that the Biblical writers are conformed to the ideas and practices of their time. Those ideas and practices cannot be authoritative for us.

It should be noted that in this form of the argument, Jesus is not excluded from such conformity. Sometimes the attempt is made to soften the implied criticism of Jesus. It is said that he consciously adapted himself to his hearers. Or it is claimed that he was merely defeating his opponents by using their own arguments against them, although he did not necessarily accept their attitude to Scripture.

These claims are flatly contrary to what the text says. Rather than Jesus using Pharisaic methods of exegesis for the sake of the argument, he claims that they ignore Scripture! Matthew 15:1–9 is a good example. The Pharisees chide the disciples for ignoring the traditions of the elders. Jesus responds that they have transgressed the Scripture in following their own traditions. Certainly he is aware that they do derive teachings from Scripture, but even when showing this awareness, he suggests that they do not really understand that Scripture. For example, he asks why the scribes say the Christ is David's son when David himself calls him 'Lord' in Psalm 110 (Mark 12:35–7).

Thus one could not conceivably say that Jesus was unconsciously conformed to the approach to Scripture of his opponents. One could not say that he deliberately portrayed himself as accepting their view only for the sake of the argument. He consistently presents his own approach to Scripture as more faithful, consistent, and informed.

We come back therefore to the full and direct charge that in his use of Scripture Jesus was simply a man of his age. Why stop with Jesus' view of Scripture? Surely if historical relativism is true, then it must be true not just of Jesus' view of Scripture, but of all his other views as well. Thus we see historical relativism as an attack on the authority and divinity of Jesus.

JEWISH USE OF SCRIPTURE

The argument that we cannot follow the exegesis of the New Testament generally hides these anti-Christian assumptions. It is generally built upon two main points. One is that New

Testament exegesis bears a close relationship to Jewish exegesis. The other is that there are certain New Testament examples of exegesis which are embarrassing to us. We would not exegete in this 'false' way. This embarrassment can be avoided by saying that the New Testament writers were simply following the canons of their day and that we are not bound by them.

Hence it is important to know what were the methods of Biblical interpretation current amongst Jews in New Testament times. We come back therefore to the problem that concerned us in chapter 18. We have material about Scripture usage from two groups. One is about the Pharisees, preserved in the Talmud and other traditions of the same circle. The other is from the Qumran community. The matter of the relationship between the Qumran community and early Christianity is a subject of dispute. Hence it will be taken up in the second place.

We know Jesus clashed with Pharisees. We know that Paul was a Pharisee. Hence the exegetical approaches of the Pharisees are of importance. The usual approach to this question is well illustrated by the work of Longenecker.[1] He selects various instances of Rabbinic or Pharisaic exegesis which he feels are comparable with New Testament exegesis. He recognizes that there is a problem in that most of our sources for Pharisaic beliefs come from a later period, but he says 'we are dealing with a religious mentality that took great pride in the preservation of the traditional; and while changes due to development or different circumstances cannot be denied, this desire to preserve the traditional – barring other considerations – minimizes the severity of the problem.'[2]

As a matter of fact this appeal to the traditionalism of Judaism is quite misplaced. In the matter of appeal to Scripture and the use of Scripture, major changes took place in Judaism in the first two centuries AD. Scripture comes to be used in a new way. It may be used to support existing traditions, but the mode of use is quite different and was recognized as different at the time.

There is another way of approach to this question. That is to

[1] R. Longenecker, *Biblical Exegesis in the Apostolic Period*, Grand Rapids, Eerdmans, 1975, esp. pp. 28 ff.

[2] *Ibid.*, pp. 24 f.

take what we know of the Pharisees of New Testament times and to see how they actually used Scripture. Here we face the problem that our sources consist of what the later rabbis remembered about the first-century Pharisees. This material has been gathered by Jacob Neusner.[1] In the interpretation of this material Neusner attempts to imitate the method of New Testament form criticism. That is, he attempts to distinguish the original traditions about the Pharisees from the additions made by later ages. Knowing how much subjectivity is involved in New Testament form criticism we may be sceptical about the results when applied to Jewish traditions. Nevertheless Neusner has done us the great service of collecting together all that the later rabbis remembered about the Pharisees. Most of the material concerns Hillel and Shammai and their respective 'houses' (i.e. schools of disciples). The dating of Hillel and Shammai is uncertain, but the period of Jesus' ministry and Paul's training would probably be the period in which Pharisaism was divided between these two schools. We also have some other traditions, such as those about Gamaliel, Paul's teacher. The traditions are largely concerned with questions of Jewish law. There are some references in the Midrashim to the Pharisees. These are works corresponding more to our Bible commentaries and hence we know what was remembered of the views of various Pharisees on a few verses.

When one works through all this material, there is one overwhelming impression. The Pharisees *very rarely appealed to Scripture* to support their opinions. This lack of appeal to Scripture is well recognized by Jewish scholars.[2] Neusner believes that the exegetical material which occurs in the traditions was added by later generations and was not part of the original tradition from the first century.[3]

Appeal has been made to the fact that Hillel proposed a number of rules of Biblical interpretation.[4] These rules are

[1] *The Rabbinic Traditions about the Pharisees before 70*, 3 vols., Leiden, Brill, 1971.

[2] E.g. A. Guttmann (*Rabbinic Judaism in the Making*, Detroit, Wayne State Univ., 1970, pp. 85 ff.) quotes an opinion that less than ten percent of the controversies between the houses of Hillel and Shammai involved exegetical arguments. He then goes on to argue that the actual number is even less.

[3] *Op. cit.*, Vol. II, p. 36.

[4] Longenecker, *op. cit.*, p. 34.

fairly basic rules of argument and inference.[1] Yet we rarely find
Hillel using Scripture at all, let alone making use of these rules.[2]
The one tradition in which he makes greatest use of the rules
tells us that his view was accepted ultimately not because of his
exegesis but because he could cite the authority of his teachers![3]

Thus, from the traditions we receive the impression that the
Pharisees appealed to authority and tradition rather than to
Scripture. Is this a false impression caused by the imperfect
nature of our sources? The striking thing is the fact that it is the
very same picture as the one we receive from the Gospels! The
claim that the New Testament had taken over the views of its
time as far as Scripture was concerned is false. For what set
Jesus apart from his opponents was appeal to Scripture, rather
than tradition.

If Jesus was asserting against his opponents the authority of
Scripture, it is hardly likely that he was taking over their way of
interpreting Scripture. A concrete proof of this point is difficult,
given the little use of Scripture in the Pharisaic traditions. An
example of the difficulty is that both Hillel and Jesus argue
from a minor to a major. For example in defending what his
disciples did on the sabbath in eating in his presence, Jesus
points to the priests in the temple (Matt. 12:5,6). If it was
legitimate for the priests to eat the shewbread in the temple,
then surely it was legitimate for Jesus' disciples to eat in the
presence of one greater than the temple. Thus the argument
goes from the minor case of the temple to the major case of
Jesus. If eating is permitted in the temple on the sabbath, then
it must be permitted in Jesus' presence.

Argument from a minor to a major was one of Hillel's
exegetical rules. It could be that Jesus learned this form of
argument from the school of Hillel. Yet it is just as likely that
both are adopting what is an obvious logical argument. There
need be no dependence. Certainly the traditions we have of

[1]See Neusner, *op. cit.*, Vol. I, pp. 240 ff. Neusner believes that the later
tradition has attached a set of well-known rules to the famous name of Hillel.

[2]See Guttmann, *op. cit.*, p. 98.

[3]Neusner, *op. cit.*, Vol. I, pp. 246 ff. Neusner proposes a complex history for
the tradition. Yet the connection of Hillel to his teachers is prominent at all
the stages of the tradition that he proposes. If his scepticism about the
reliability of the tradition is justified, then we have even less to support the
picture of Hillel the 'exegete'.

Hillel's use of such argument, in which he explicitly identifies the logical basis of the argument as one from minor to major,[1] differ from the way Jesus uses such arguments. With Hillel there is a tendency to focus on the logical basis of the argument. With Jesus the emphasis is on the Biblical content, while the logical structure is not given prominence.

It is of particular interest that we have traditions about Paul's teacher, Gamaliel.[2] They conform to the pattern that has already been discussed. That is, there are a few traditions where Gamaliel's opinion on a verse are given. These opinions are very simple and not based upon any explicit exegesis. When it comes to legal matters Gamaliel's decisions are not supported by any proof texts, let alone detailed exegesis. If we did not have Acts 22:3, we would have nothing to connect Paul to Gamaliel out of this material. To ascribe Paul's use of Scripture to his Rabbinic training is to go against the little material we have.

Why have some people conveyed the impression that Pharisaic Judaism in New Testament times indulged in detailed, and perhaps fanciful, exegesis of Scripture? The reason is that they have read back the innovations of Akiba into the earlier period. There are uncertainties about the life of Akiba.[3] He was probably born around AD 40. He entered the Rabbinic academy that moved to Jabneh after the destruction of Jerusalem in AD 70. Hence his involvement in the Pharisaic movement dates to the late first century, too late to be an appreciable influence on the New Testament.

The innovation of Akiba was to find exegetical bases for positions which had earlier been held on the authority of tradition. He did this by insisting there was no superfluous word in Scripture. Even grammatical particles have to have some function which could be turned into an argument for some tradition. This use of Scripture was recognized both by its supporters and its opponents as an innovation.[4]

We cannot take Akiba's rules for exegesis, or their impact on Judaism, and treat them as New Testament background.

[1] *Ibid.*, p. 247.
[2] *Ibid.*, pp. 341–73.
[3] There is a biography: L. Finkelstein, *Akiba*, Cleveland, Meridan, 1936. Note also Neusner's critique of this work (*op. cit.*, Vol. III, p. 341).
[4] Finkelstein, *op. cit.*, pp. 157 ff., 171 ff., 308 ff.

Akiba is simply too late. Further there is no resemblance between his exegetical techniques and those we see in the New Testament.

There was one group within the Judaism of the first century who did make much more use of Scripture than the Pharisees. The Qumran community which produced the Dead Sea Scrolls made an extensive use of Scripture to interpret their own situation and to defend their position. That use has many points of contact with the New Testament, most notably in that they saw themselves as the community to which the prophecies about the end time pointed. There is thus a parallel with the way that the New Testament sees Jesus and his work as a fulfilment of prophecy. They collected together Biblical passages which they saw as referring to those events, e.g. Messianic prophecies.

Given the fact that the Talmud is primarily a legal work, the Qumran texts strike us as much more like the New Testament with its concern with the fulfilment of prophecy. Hence there has been a tendency to see the Jewish background of the Gospels in the Qumran community.[1] Paul still tends to be seen more in terms of Rabbinic Judaism. The apparent closeness of Paul to the Rabbinic side of Judaism, rather than Qumran, may merely be due to the fact that Paul deals more with the problems of conduct facing the infant church. The mere fact that Paul discusses 'legal' questions may produce similarities to Rabbinic discussion of legal questions.

Similarly we have to ask whether the similarity of the Gospels and the Qumran texts is due to both being concerned for the fulfilment of prophecy. That raises the question of whether there is a direct connection between Qumran and the early Christian community, or whether we have two independent developments from the Old Testament. Of course there are some scholars who would make Qumran the origin of Christianity.[2] Yet the theories of direct dependence flounder on the lack of direct reference in the literature of one movement to the other movement, and the obvious differences between the

[1] Longenecker, *op. cit.*, pp. 70 ff.
[2] For a survey of the way the connection between Qumran and the New Testament has been seen, see G. Vermes, *Jesus and the World of Judaism*, Philadelphia, Fortress, 1983, chs. 9, 10.

two movements.

We are really left with two possibilities. One is that the Qumran texts are a witness to a form of first-century Judaism which is little attested in the main-stream Rabbinic literature. Christianity was strongly influenced by that same form of Judaism. The other is that Qumran and New Testament are independent developments from an Old Testament base.

If we knew more about the early history of the Qumran community, we would be in a better position to choose between these possibilities. The hints as to the sect's history in the Qumran texts seem to point to a connection at some point to the temple and 'official Judaism'.[1] Yet Yadin has pointed out the clear relationship between the beliefs of the Qumran sect and the views *against which* Hebrews was written.[2] Further there is an affinity of some sort between the views against which Hebrews was written and the views against which Colossians was written, and perhaps also, what Stephen was arguing against in Acts 7.[3]

These relationships to the 'Hebrews heresy' and the 'Colossian heresy' seem to point to a contact with Judaism outside Palestine.[4] Thus the story of Qumran is probably far more complex than we presently appreciate. The suggestion of a connection between Qumran and the 'Hebrews heresy' tends to refute the suggestion that Qumran and the New Testament are part of one movement. Here is evidence of actual conflict between them. However the conflict appears when Christianity comes in contact with Hellenistic forms of Judaism.

Given the uncertainties about the history of the Qumran community and the problem of its position in the broader world

[1] For a consideration of possibilities see *ibid.*, ch. 10.

[2] Y. Yadin, 'The Dead Sea Scrolls and the Epistle to the Hebrews' in C. Rabin and Y. Yadin (eds.), *Aspects of the Dead Sea Scrolls, (Scripta Hierosolymitana* 4), Jerusalem, Magnes Press, 1958, pp. 36–55.

[3] See my 'Admonition and Error in Hebrews', *Westminster Theological Journal*, 39 (1976), 76, 79.

[4] Partly out of desire to connect Qumran and John the Baptist, there has been a tendency to try to make Qumran a very Palestinian movement. It has been depicted as an austere, pure faith of the Judean wilderness, connected in some fanciful treatments even with the Old Testament Rechabites! Consequently the question of contacts with diaspora Judaism has largely been ignored.

of Judaism, nothing much is to be gained by inventing hypothetical contacts, like making John the Baptist a member of the Qumran community. Rather it is better to compare the known examples of Qumran exegesis with New Testament exegesis. What characterizes Qumran exegesis is seeing the Old Testament prophetical text as a code which, with the right key to interpretation, describes events and personalities in the time of the Qumran community. It has been pointed out that they are interpreting Scripture the way Daniel interpreted dreams and visions.[1] That is, the Scripture text is a mystery which needs a special gift for interpretation. There is no obvious clue in the text itself.

Many people would suggest that this is the way the New Testament, especially the Gospels, uses the Old Testament. That is, that passages are applied to Jesus without consideration of their original context. Thus in Matthew 26:31 Jesus quotes Zechariah 13:7: 'I will strike down the shepherd, and the sheep of the flock shall be scattered.' One can ask: what basis in the text has Jesus for seeing a reference to himself? Is he not doing the same as the Qumran exegete?

Whereas the technical terminology of the Qumran commentaries gives us the clue that they were influenced by the picture of Daniel as interpreter of mysteries, we have no such clues for Jesus. He tends to use no such technical terminology but simply to introduce passages as Scripture now being fulfilled. Hence we have to look at the pattern of his use and the New Testament use of Scripture. There are several allusions to adjacent passages in Zechariah: Zechariah 11:12,13 (Matt. 27:9,10); Zechariah 12:10 (John 19:37). Why does the New Testament make frequent reference to these passages of Zechariah? The reason is fairly obvious. They all depict the rejection and affliction of the leader of the flock. The choice of passages to quote is not capricious. A number of passages from a connected section with a similar theme are being quoted.

This use of Zechariah does not stand alone. The sufferings of Jesus are commonly expressed in terms of psalms which

[1] F. F. Bruce, *Biblical Exegesis in the Qumran Texts*, The Hague, Uitgeverij van Keulen N.V., 1959, 1 ff. One of the best examples is the Commentary on Habakkuk. For a translation see G. Vermes, *The Dead Sea Scrolls in English*, Harmondsworth, Penguin, 1962, pp. 235 ff.

express David's experience as the rightful but rejected king of Israel. Further there are clear connections between this picture of Jesus and the suffering foretold for the servant in Isaiah 49:7;52:13–53:12 (cf. Acts 8:32–35).

Thus we are dealing not with an isolated quotation of a verse, but with a persistent tendency to apply to Jesus both the historical pattern of the true leader of Israel as the rejected one, and the prophecy that the same will be true of the leader promised in the future. As we have already seen in chapter 18, prophecy builds upon the pattern established by God in the past. The New Testament in using prophecy is picking up such patterns. When we find the quotation of passages which in the original context do not seem to be prophetic, then we are usually encountering the reference to such a pattern. Thus Matthew 15:7–9 quotes Isaiah 29:13 as a prophecy. From the context in Isaiah it would seem that the prophet was speaking, first of all, to his own contemporaries.

We have already seen that Jesus could see the experiences of David as proleptic of his own experience. Similarly the experience of the unrighteous in Old Testament times forms a prefiguring of the unrighteous during the gospel age.[1]

This tendency of the New Testament to see the Old Testament in terms of themes or patterns is frequently described as typological exegesis. It is hard to find clear evidence of typological exegesis in the Qumran texts. Conversely the New Testament does not represent the Old Testament text as a mystery which can be understood only by those possessing a special key of interpretation. It does say that the prophets did not know the details of person or time predicted by them (1 Peter 1:10–12). Nevertheless people can be rebuked for not believing what the Scriptures say and hence failing to understand the significance of Christ's death and resurrection (Luke 24:25–7). A common rebuke of Jesus was: 'Have you not read?' The patterns are there for all to see. Hence the Pharisees can be rebuked for failure to apply Scripture.

Thus there are significant differences between Qumran and the New Testament in their approach to Scripture. Certainly,

[1]For further comment on the typological use of the Old Testament by Jesus, see R. T. France, *Jesus and the Old Testament*, Grand Rapids, Baker, 1971, ch. 3.

as both were looking for the coming Messiah and the salvation promised in the Old Testament, both highlighted verses looking forward to that salvation. However the overall approach to Scripture interpretation differed. Hence there is no good reason for saying that Jesus or the Gospel writers derived their approach to Scripture from the circles of Qumran.

'ARBITRARY' EXEGESIS IN THE NEW TESTAMENT

The second reason for the claim that the New Testament was merely adopting the exegetical devices of its day is the cases in which its exegesis seems arbitrary or fanciful. As a way out of this problem it is suggested that the writers were merely adopting the methods of their opponents in order to refute them.

Sometimes the embarrassment is caused merely by failure to understand the passage. Thus Longenecker is embarrassed by Jesus' appeal to Exodus 3:6 in his argument for the resurrection.[1] Yet it is clear from his discussion that he has not caught the technical covenant force of 'I am the God of'.[2] Hence it is possible that some of our problems with New Testament exegesis come from our failure to appreciate the force and logic of the argument.

Of course, if we deny or play down the verbal character of inspiration, we are bound to have great problems with the way Jesus used Scripture. For to him, the actual wording of Scripture was significant. A good instance of this is another passage which causes problems for some, John 10:33–36.[3] The evidence that Jesus might be employing a typical argument of his opponents against them is found in several parts of what Jesus says. He calls the passage quoted 'your Law' and he makes the comment 'the Scripture cannot be broken'.

If Jesus was merely adopting his opponents' devices in order to refute them, such comments would certainly be in place. However they are also quite in place if Jesus himself would have accepted the validity of the argument he employs. There is

[1] *Op cit.*, pp. 68ff.
[2] See the discussion above in ch. 9.
[3] Longenecker, *op. cit.*, pp. 69 f.

rebuke in the term 'your Law'. His opponents had failed to mark what was said in the Scriptures God had provided to rule them. In John 8:17 Jesus also uses the term 'your law' and goes on to argue that he has fulfilled the requirement of that law, contrary to the Jews' attempt to use it against him. The statement 'the Scripture cannot be broken' is completely in accord with Jesus' other statements about Scripture and the use of Scripture. Thus nothing in the passage itself indicates that Jesus is merely arguing *ad hominem*.

Further, there are strong indications that he was not merely employing their devices. For the whole logical force of the argument depends upon his claim that he is greater than those referred to in the passage. We have already seen that Hillel, in the rabbinic tradition, is said to have listed an argument from a minor to a major in his exegetical rules. When Hillel actually does use such an argument,[1] he uses it to argue the legitimacy of a legal or ethical practice from the permission granted in Scripture for a less important practice. When Jesus uses it, here and in Matthew 12:5,6, he uses it to argue his own superiority to Old Testament institutions and people. An argument for the superiority of Jesus is not a mere debating device. Jesus asserts his superiority, just as he asserted his superiority over Jacob in the conversation with the Samaritan woman (John 4:12–14).

Thus the conclusion of the argument is in line with Jesus' whole tenor of argument. There is no evidence in the passage for seeing it as mere debating techniques.

We come back then to the basic question: has Jesus made arbitrary and illegitimate use of this text? The context of discussion was that he had called himself 'God'. He retorts that there is a Biblical instance of *God* himself calling people 'gods'. If it is a legitimate title for those who are addressed by the Word of God, is it not much more legitimate for the very Word of God himself, set apart and sent out by the Father? It can be objected that Jesus was proclaiming himself 'God' in a different way from that meant in the text. However that is covered in the discussion and indeed is part of the argument. Jesus claims a different and particular right to that title.

[1] To simplify the discussion, I am assuming that the traditions crediting these exegetical arguments to Hillel are correct. If Neusner is right the contrast is then between Jesus and *later* rabbinic practice.

The real crux of the matter is not the logic of Jesus' argument. It is the fact that Jesus built that argument on the literal wording of a text. That is contrary to our tendency to see the meaning of a statement somehow hiding behind and distinguished from the words which are used.

There is another way to check whether this is arbitrary 'literalistic' exegesis. Would it be open to anybody to use the same exegesis to claim that he was God? Clearly not! It is not man, according to Psalm 82 and Jesus' exegesis of it, who bestows the title 'God'. It is God. Further Jesus' right to the honour is bound up with the unique position he claims as one sent by the Father.

We have already seen in chapter 9 Paul's similar appeal to the very words of a text, when he argues from the refusal of Scripture to make the promise to Abraham to refer to his multiple seed. Other examples of Paul's exegesis have also been criticized. The accusations against his appeals to creation with regard to women's rôles in the church have been considered in Chapter 18.

It is not only Paul's 'literalistic' use of Scripture that has been attacked. He has also come under fire for his use of 'allegory' in Galatians 4:21–31. Since allegory as a method of Bible interpretation is so open to subjectivism and abuse, Paul's use of allegory comes in for criticism.

One of the first questions that has to be asked is whether Paul necessarily uses the term 'allegory' with all the definite and precise meaning it has come to have in our day. Certainly we have a good first-century example of developed allegorical exegesis in Philo. However we do not find in Paul the systematic reinterpretation of Scripture in Greek philosophical categories that characterizes Philo's allegories. Hence the charge that Paul was using allegorical exegesis must really stand on the form of the argument rather than on the term Paul used. We must not import technical meanings into words which may not have been used by the writer in a technical sense.

Paul builds his argument upon the contrast of the two children, Isaac and Ishmael, and their respective mothers. We meet elsewhere Paul's use of the example of Isaac. In Romans 4 Abraham's belief in the promise of children is treated as the

Old Testament equivalent of New Testament faith. In Romans 9:6–9 the promised birth of Isaac is treated as an example of God's freedom to choose freely and sovereignly those who are to be part of his people. Paul's discussion in Romans 9 is in the context of Jewish unbelief. He wants to demonstrate that the rejection of the message by many, and its acceptance by some, has antecedents in previous history. He begins that demonstration with Isaac. In verse 8 he says: 'it is not the children of the flesh who are children of God'. This has a double reference. It refers to those contemporary Jews who thought they had standing with God merely on the basis of physical descent. It refers also to those children that Abraham conceived without the aid of divine intervention to overcome the deadness of Sarah's womb. Thus in Romans we find many of the things we find also in the disputed passage in Galatians. Isaac as the child of the promise is related to those born to new life by God's grace. Ishmael is implicitly compared to those who rest their position on mere physical descent.

There is another aspect of the term 'children of the flesh' which we must consider. For Paul the antithesis to those who through grace receive faith are those who trust in the works of the law (Gal. 2:16). There is thus a contrast between what comes of grace through promise and what is achieved by human effort (cf. John 1:12,13). The birth of Ishmael fits in here as he was conceived through the efforts of Abraham without the need of divine power. Hence we have an association made between Isaac and Christians and, on the other hand, an association between Ishmael and unbelieving Jews.

Is Paul's treatment of these issues in Romans 'allegorical'? Much depends upon what we call allegory. What Paul argues in Romans 9 is that there is a pattern throughout the history of Israel of a distinction between those designated and chosen by grace and those according to the flesh. This is typology rather than allegory.

What do we find in Galatians 4:21–31 which we have not already found in Romans? We certainly find a difference in the way the material is utilized. Paul turns it into a vivid illustration, with much personification. However, what do we find that is really new? We find the introduction of Mount Sinai. Yet Mount Sinai is but a vivid symbol for the law and

[196]

Paul's treatment in Romans is already a sustained polemic against justification by law. Furthermore the idea of law as depriving of freedom is not new. It is introduced in Romans 7:1-3.

What is also new is the contrast between the two women, one free and one in bondage. This is developed by relating Hagar to Mount Sinai, or the Jerusalem of Paul's day, and Sarah to the heavenly Jerusalem. The antithesis of Mount Sinai and the heavenly Jerusalem is found also in Hebrews 12:18-25. This contrast itself cannot be called 'allegory'. It is a way of picturing the difference between legalistic Judaism and Christianity. The part of Paul's treatment that best qualifies as 'allegory' is the association of the bondwoman with legalism and Sarah with Christians.

If Paul's argument were put not in these pictures and symbols, but in theological terms, how would it run? Basically it would argue that those who depend on their own efforts have a long history. One would find included here Abraham's attempt to have a son. At the end of the history (in Paul's time) one would find those who rely upon the works of the law. In contrast one would find those who receive the promised blessing of grace. Further Paul would argue Scriptural evidence for God's choice of one over the other. That choice was shown by God's command that Ishmael must be cast out, for he could not share the inheritance with Isaac. None of this, either in its theological form or in the pictures of Galatians 4, can be called allegory without accusing the whole argument of Romans of being based on allegory.

Yet there is more than this in Paul's argument in Galatians. There is also the significance that Paul sees in the fact that Hagar was a slave and Sarah was free. His application to the contemporary situation is closely connected to the bound or free dichotomy. Hence the crucial question is: was the relative condition of Hagar and Sarah an incidental one, bearing no real connection to the real contrast between the child conceived by human effort and the child of the promise? In other words: has Paul allegorized an incidental part of the story?

It is fairly clear that Paul did not see it as incidental. His quotation of Genesis 21:10 in verse 30 is adapted to make the bond/free contrast even clearer. Paul's view of the Old

Testament history is much like his view of the text. The details are not trivial and unimportant. Just as the relative date of Abraham's circumcision is important (Rom. 4:10), so the legal status of Hagar is significant. There is an association between the efforts of the flesh and bondage in the past, as well as in the present history of Judaism.

Is this allegory, in a sense that a detail of the text is quite capriciously made the basis of a doctrine? Perhaps another Biblical example of such exegesis will make the issues clearer. In describing the final conflict of the people of God with the world, Revelation 11:8 says that the bodies of the two witnesses will lie in the street of the great city called 'Sodom and Egypt, where also their Lord was crucified'. Clearly there is something that links Sodom, Egypt, and Jerusalem. They can be related in terms of their corruption and their persecution of the righteous. In one sense this is allegory, making Sodom stand for all such instances. Yet it also flows from a reading of history which sees in it patterns, where similar characteristics are repeatedly found. It is this interpretation in terms of patterns that unifies New Testament exegesis and prevents it doing what allegory normally does, namely, spin this or that fantastic detail out of this or that isolated piece of the text.

Similarly we may put the question about Paul's use of Hagar. Was her slave status irrelevant to the story or is the story more than one of human effort versus grace? Was it also a story about the son of the free wife versus the son of the slave concubine? In the light of Genesis 17:18,19; 21:8–12; 25:5,6 we cannot exclude the contrast between the child of Sarah and the children of the concubine from the plot of Genesis. It may not be the main theme but it is a theme. That theme is then seen by Paul as significant and foreshadowing of a later conflict between those in bondage to human effort and those liberated by grace.

What do we call this sort of exegesis? It is not allegory as usually understood. It is not even typology as generally understood in terms of types of Christ and his priestly atonement. It is more extensive than that. It is a recognition of the patterned character of Biblical history. The typology of Christ is but one example of that patterned character. Through history runs an antithesis which places on one side of the divide human effort, bondage, and persecutors, while on the other side are grace, freedom, and righteous sufferers.

What does all this have to do with Jewish exegesis of the New Testament period? Practically nothing! While one could not say dogmatically that nobody in Judaism recognized such patterns, it is not what we find in extant examples of Jewish exegesis. It is significant that Longenecker has to create a hypothetical Jewish exegesis which Paul is then supposedly rebutting in *ad hominem* fashion. Rather than create imaginary Jewish exegesis, surely it is better to use Paul's other writings to try to come to an understanding of his mind. If we have to go beyond Paul, then it makes better sense to turn to other New Testament texts. Thus Hebrews 12:18–24 is relevant. One could also bring into the discussion the teaching of Jesus in John 8:35: 'the slave does not remain in the house forever; the son does remain forever.' This remark was in answer to the Jews' claim to being children of Abraham. In that context Jesus obviously has in mind the contrast of Isaac and Ishmael. Paul's treatment is an elaboration of the contrast indicated already by Jesus.

There is really little insight gained into the New Testament from comparison with contemporary Jewish exegesis. The New Testament has to be understood in its own terms.

🍥 23 🍥

Pseudepigraphy

Pseudepigraphy is the term used to describe the practice of publishing a work claiming it to be the work of an illustrious figure from the past. It has become common to charge that much of the Biblical text consists of instances of pseud-epigraphy.

Generally speaking, this practice has been denied by those who have claimed that the Scripture should be seen as the Word of God. One can expect, however, that this will not continue to be the case. There are several reasons why one can expect a willingness to accept pseudepigraphy amongst those who would otherwise yet want to be called evangelicals. We have already seen that connected with the unwillingness to affirm the inerrancy of Scripture is a view of God akin to a Deist view, that is, of a God who does not actively participate in the world he has created. His rôle is a more distant one. Among the arguments advanced in favour of calling Biblical books pseudepigraphic is the existence of detailed predictive prophecy. It is claimed that this must be really prophecy after the event. For example, Isaiah 'could not' have named Cyrus as the future conqueror of Babylon. Sections of Isaiah making such predictions must be from a later hand. Similarly Daniel's prophecies of Antiochus IV are used to prove that the book could not have come from the time of the purported author. Such a denial of the possibility of predictive prophecy is consistent with a denial that God acts to direct the course of human activity to accord perfectly with his plan. Those who have difficulty in affirming that God so acted with respect to the writing of Scripture will also have difficulty with respect to the history of empires and nations.

It is claimed that the practice of pseudepigraphy was a widespread and accepted one in the ancient world. As we have seen, part of the influence of historical relativism has been to picture the Bible as a pure product of its times. If pseudepigraphy was a common phenomenon of Biblical times, then it stands to reason, on a relativistic logic, that the Bible would also reveal that phenomenon.

There are more specific reasons why the idea of pseudepigraphy would be congenial to those holding to the idea of limited inspiration. They sometimes attempt to argue that the idea of the authority and inspiration of the Bible is an idea not found in the Bible itself. It is the creation of a post-Biblical (some would say post-Reformation or even nineteenth-century) orthodoxy which has artificially limited the freedom and flexibility of Scripture. Of course such a claim has great difficulty with the use of Scripture by Jesus and generally has to resort to the argument that Jesus simply was accommodating himself to the view of his time. However some of the most explicit statements about Scripture are found in books that have commonly been dubbed pseudepigraphic. Instances would be 2 Timothy 3:16 and 2 Peter 1:20, 21. If it can be argued that these works were written outside of the New Testament period, and thus represent a later orthodoxy foreign to the true spirit of the New Testament, then the testimony of Scripture is seriously weakened. Similarly the use of 1 Timothy 2:8–15 on the question of women teaching in the church would also be blunted.

PSEUDEPIGRAPHY AND RELIABILITY

If a person flatly denies the possibility of divine influence upon the world, then he must resort to pseudepigraphy to explain the Bible. Clearly it is not the evidence of Scripture that leads to the conclusion. It is his view of God. It is not my intention at this point to deal with such a position. Rather I am concerned with those who would claim to believe in the Bible in at least some sense, and yet want to find pseudepigraphy in it.

The argument for that position can be put as follows. Pseudepigraphy was an accepted device in the ancient world for putting across a message. If one had a point one wished to convey, one attached it to the name of a past luminary. Hence writers who did that were not stepping outside the bounds of what was considered proper. There was not an intent to deceive as the device was well accepted.

Furthermore, when the New Testament refers to such Old Testament works as the work of the nominal author, it is merely following convention. An analogy may strengthen this argument. Earlier[1] it was suggested that Matthew's reference to a passage of Zechariah as coming from the prophet Jeremiah could be explained as a result of naming the prophetic collection after Jeremiah, its first member at the time. What, it may be argued, is different between this and naming a Bible book after a supposed but fictional author?

To deal with such suggestions we have to take specific cases. However there is a problem with considering each alleged case of pseudepigraphy in isolation. As we shall see, a number of arguments presented to establish pseudepigraphy are mutually exclusive. There may be some cases in which an argument of the form outlined above could be made. Yet other books considered as being even more certainly pseudepigraphic do not lend themselves to the argument.

For example it has been argued that Ephesians was not written by Paul but by an admirer of Paul who was familiar with his writings and especially with Colossians. It thus presents Pauline ideas in what is more of a sermon than a letter. It lacks the address to a specific situation which characterizes other Pauline letters. There are formal references to Paul's knowledge of the readers and his concern for them but not the intimate involvement and personal detail that we find in the Corinthian letters or in Galatians. Here, it can be argued, is a good example of the working of the phenomenon of pseudepigraphy. A later devotee and disciple has clothed 'Pauline' ideas in the formal personal dress of the apostle without the marks of a genuine Pauline letter. It is argued that such practice was not regarded as objectionable in its day.

Let us, however, compare this with a letter generally regarded as much more certainly pseudepigraphic: 2 Timothy. This later letter is full of personal detail and indications of

[1]See chapter 6.

personal relationship between Paul and Timothy. If 2 Timothy is not from Paul then one conclusion is inescapable. Another writer has deliberately introduced all sorts of personal details and touches to make it appear that it came from Paul. This is more than a formal, conventional attachment to a homily in the 'Pauline' style. It is a deliberate fiction.[1]

The same point could be made by a comparison of 1 and 2 Peter. 2 Peter is the one which is much more confidently identified as not genuine. It is also the one which has more personal detail, such as the author's claim to have been an eyewitness to the majesty of Jesus (1:16) and Peter's knowledge of his impending death (1:14). He even claims that this is the second letter he has written to them (3:1), making an allusion to 1 Peter. Once again we have to say that if this is fiction it is deliberate intentional fiction. It sets out to convey the impression that the letter is from Peter.

A different but parallel point can be made from the Old Testament. It has been suggested that disciples of particular prophets were responsible for collecting and supplementing their masters' works. Thus a prophetic book may contain material from several authors. One of the cases where this phenomenon is suggested is the book of Isaiah. It is common to regard the section chapters 40 to 66 as coming from one or more later writers. It is argued that New Testament quotations from this later section as the work of the 'prophet Isaiah' are merely using the conventional and accepted term for the corpus.

We may compare this with Jonah or Daniel, both of which are claimed with equal or more certainty to be pseudepigraphic. Here there is not an original section claimed to be the genuine work of the original head of a school. The whole has been called in question. The problem is that both of them contain historical narrative. The message of the prophet is given in the context of a narrative of events in his life. Accepting that the text is fiction involves accepting that the events related did not happen.

In attempting to redefine 'infallibility' it has been suggested

___

[1]This point is not evaded by suggesting that 2 Timothy contains some genuine Pauline fragments which somebody has supplemented. For undoubtedly the intention was to convey the impression that the whole letter was from Paul.

that it should be taken not as meaning 'without error' but as meaning 'reliable', 'not misleading the one who follows it'. Is even such a redefinition of the infallibility of Scripture able to encompass pseudepigraphy? We have seen that acceptance of the allegation that Biblical books are pseudepigraphic means acceptance of a deliberate intent to deceive in the case of some New Testament epistles and acceptance that we have in the case of Daniel and Jonah the deliberate presentation of fiction as if it were history. Can that be included within a definition in terms of 'reliable' and 'not misleading'?

In other words it is very hard, if not impossible, to make any understanding of the Scripture as the authentic Word of God compatible with pseudepigraphy. The problem is that we are not merely faced with a formal name placed at the beginning of a work. We encounter books full of personal historical events and details. It is very hard to take the words of Jesus 'for just as Jonah was three days and three nights in the belly of the sea-monster; so shall the Son of Man be three days and three nights in the heart of the earth' (Matt. 12:40) as reference to a work of fiction conventionally regarded as the history of a prophet. That goes against the whole concern for historicity that we have already seen in the Biblical text.[1]

So far we have assumed for the sake of the argument that pseudepigraphy was a generally accepted device. It is time to consider that claim. What evidence is there for the claim? There is no evidence besides the fact that people did it. In a sinful world the existence of a practice neither proves its correctness nor its general acceptance.

We have already seen that saying that certain Biblical books are pseudepigraphic implies acceptance that certain persons went to the trouble of adding contrived personal details in order to deceive. If the device was generally recognized and accepted, why the need to deceive? In short the idea of an acceptance of this practice is contradicted by the works in question. Revelation 22:18 pronounces a curse on anybody who interpolates other material into that book. Once again this is hardly evidence of acceptance of the passing off of one man's work as another's.

[1]See chapter 10.

We know that in the early church the authenticity of certain works was called in question. 2 Peter is a good example.[1] If pseudepigraphy was so well accepted, why was there concern to question works whose authorship was in doubt?[2]

It is time to inject a little common sense into this discussion. It is clear that to be a witness at first hand to Christ's resurrection and to be commissioned by him was all-important in establishing apostolic authority. Paul's undisputed letters are full of his struggle to establish his own claim to such authority. Are we seriously to believe that it was considered proper in that environment for people to put forward their own writings as having that apostolic authority? In the modern discussions these people are referred to as admirers of Paul or Peter. But is that the admiration that would have been welcomed by the apostles or the churches they founded? It is one thing to say that somebody succeeded in deceiving the church. It is another to say that the church would have been content to be deceived.

Thus the claim that pseudepigraphy would have been understood and accepted is clearly unsustainable. The existence of such deliberate deception and falsehood within Scripture is incompatible with any regard for it as the reliable Word of God.

CONSISTENT CRITERIA FOR PSEUDEPIGRAPHY

What should count as significant evidence of pseudepigraphy? Many different forms of evidence are claimed but they are not treated consistently. For example, we have already mentioned that some reservations were entertained against 2 Peter in the early church. Is this weighty evidence against the book? If we take this seriously then we should also take seriously the affirmative evidence from the early church. It is therefore significant that 1 Peter and the Pastoral Epistles were

---

[1]For summaries of the evidence, with differing judgments of its significance, see D. Guthrie (*New Testament Introduction*, 3rd edition, London, Inter-Varsity, 1970, pp. 814ff.) and J. N. D. Kelly (*A Commentary on the Epistles of Peter and Jude*, Grand Rapids, Baker, 1969, pp. 234f.).

[2]For further evidence of a critical attitude in the early church towards pseudepigraphy, see Guthrie, *ibid.*, pp. 675ff.

uniformly received in the early church and that the doubts expressed about Jude seem to have followed an earlier period of acceptance. It is clear from reading the work both of those who accept pseudepigraphy and those who reject it, that neither party wants to take the evidence of the early church as concluding the matter. One of the difficulties with using early church evidence is that most of it is relatively late. The earliest evidence tends to derive from the second century and even later evidence is more common.

In claims that certain Old Testament books are pseudepigraphic, the charge of historical inaccuracy plays a prominent rôle. Yet one has to ask again whether the criterion is used consistently. For example, the mention of the name Belshazzar in Daniel used to be used as evidence of the book's historical unreliability. This 'error' was then explained in terms of the book being a late pseudepigraphic work written in the second century BC, rather than the sixth century as it purports. The mention of Belshazzar was considered an error because our other sources do not record his presence in Babylon. However we now have evidence from contemporary texts of his playing the rôle of regent during the absence of his father Nabonidas.[1]

Has the historicity of Belshazzar now been used as proof of the genuineness of Daniel and the idea of a pseudepigraphy been rejected? On the contrary, the argument for the historical unreliability of Daniel has simply shifted to other details, for example, the fact that Nebuchadnezzar is called Belshazzar's father.[2] Some have suggested that Belshazzar may have been Nebuchadnezzar's grandson, which would be quite within the range of meaning in the Bible of 'son' and hence not chargeable as an error.[3] Suppose this suggestion were to be confirmed, would we then have the last conclusive proof of the genuineness of Daniel? Certainly not, because 'Darius the Mede' is not attested in any extra-Biblical source. Is this therefore chargeable as an error?

[1] R. P. Dougherty, *Nabonidas and Belshazzar*, New Haven, Yale University Press, 1929.
[2] L. F. Hartman and A. A. Di Lella, *The Book of Daniel*, Garden City, Doubleday, 1978, p. 50.
[3] J. G. Baldwin, *Daniel*, Downers Grove, Ill., Inter-Varsity, 1978, pp. 22f.; Dougherty, *op. cit.*, pp. 6off.

Even if all these historical 'errors' were found not to be errors it would still be open for critics to claim that the earlier section of the book contains genuine historical traditions. To these a person centuries later had added the very detailed predictions of Antiochus IV as actually prophecies after the event. Is it really 'historical accuracy' which proves the work is pseudepigraphic?

Of course it could be argued that the number of claimed errors makes it unlikely that all these will eventually be proved not to be errors. However the real problem is our relative lack of detailed historical documentation for the late Neo-Babylonian and early Persian empires. Who would have anticipated the strange exile of Nabonidas[1] from his capital city before recent discoveries? To suit our own preconceptions we can overrate the problem or overrate the possibilities for their resolution. We are back with the problem discussed in chapter 10 of the incompleteness of our sources.

Historical linguistics shares the problems of sources with political history. It is easy to claim that a particular text is 'late' but such claims are often based upon incomplete knowledge of the language in its various stages and dialects. Once more the scholar seldom discourses on how little we know. Thus the language of Daniel has been confidently described as 'late' and others have pointed out the problems involved in such claims.[2]

One wonders if such arguments would be so forcefully presented if there were not other reasons for considering these books as pseudepigraphic. In the Old Testament the doubts expressed about particular books are very closely connected with the problem of prophecy or problems of the miraculous (e.g. Jonah). In the New Testament the problem revolves largely around the picture of the church and the Christian faith revealed in the disputed books.

THE PROBLEM OF PROPHECY

It has already been pointed out that a Deist conception of God

---

[1]See W. G. Lambert, 'Nabonidas in Arabia' in *Proceedings of the Seminar for Arabian Studies*, 1972.

[2]E. Y. Kutscher, 'Aramaic', *Current Trends in Linguistics*, 6 (1970), 399ff.

has particular problems with prophecy, except in the most vague and indefinite sense. However the concern with the disputed Old Testament books is often put more pointedly. It is not just prophecy. It is the very specific and detailed character of the prophecy. In Isaiah the clearest example of this is in the naming of Cyrus the deliverer. In Daniel it is the specific and detailed account of the conflicts of the Seleucids and the Ptolemies. It is sometimes argued that such specifics are contrary to the normal character of Biblical prophecy.

The problem with this argument is that if all examples of detailed prophecy are called pseudepigraphy then obviously there are no Biblical examples of genuine detailed prophecy. For example we have a case, besides Cyrus, of a figure being named in prophecy. Josiah is named in 1 Kings 13:2. However that can also be called prophecy after the event.

Thus the argument often makes no progress because the crucial evidence is defined as not being evidence.

We thus have to deal with the question in some other way. The disputed passages in both Isaiah and Daniel contain allusion to the fact that they contain prophecy. Isaiah 48:5ff. says that events have been foretold lest Israel attribute them to an idol. In Daniel 12:4 (cf. v.9) Daniel is commanded to seal up the prophecy until the end time in which it is to be fulfilled.

Whoever wrote these books included references to the fact that they contain prophecies for the future. We are faced with a similar issue posed by the personal details in the disputed New Testament books. This is either genuine or deliberate fraud. We have to imagine an author, writing after the 'prophecies' have been fulfilled, who carefully adds details to explain, in the Isaiah case, why such full 'predictions' have been given.

This makes the New Testament, and particularly Christ's acceptance of these books, significant. One can say that the New Testament is simply following the popular designation of 'Isaiah' or 'Daniel'. However if they are doing that and it is pseudepigraphy, then they are embracing a deliberate, conscious fraud as if it was genuine.

There are further problems for a Christian denying that these books really contain prophecy. Daniel contains visions of four world empires, of which the first must be the Babylonian (Dan. 2:37–8). That naturally suggests the sequence of the

Babylonian, Medo-Persian, Greek, and Roman empires. However on anybody's dating the book of Daniel predates the Middle Eastern conquests of the Roman empire. Hence to allow that the fourth empire is the Roman would be to admit an element of prophecy. Hence those who deny prophecy make the four empires the Babylonian, Median, Persian, and Greek. To add insult to injury the author is then charged with historical inaccuracy because there was no separate Median empire![1] So the basic question is whether the vision was meant to extend to Roman times or only Greek times.

In Daniel 2:44, immediately following the description of the fourth empire, we read: 'and in the days of those kings the God of heaven will set up a kingdom which will never be destroyed'. On the view that denies prophecy that must happen during the period of Greek domination. On the other view it would be during the Roman period. The Christian has to take this as a reference to Christ who lived in the Roman period. The Christian then must conclude that the fourth empire is the Roman and that the book does contain prophecy. This prophecy of an everlasting kingdom is obviously to be connected with the Son of Man whose reception of the kingdom is described in 7:13,14. We know that Jesus claimed to be this Son of Man (Matt. 24:30;26:63,64). If Jesus took these prophecies as applying to himself, then obviously we have to consider the book prophetic. Trying to date it in the second century BC, as those do who deny the genuineness of the prophecy, still cannot avoid the prophetic element.

A further element whose prophetic nature is very hard to deny occurs in 9:26. This whole passage is very difficult. Nevertheless there are two things of significance. The prophecy in question begins with the prospect that the time of Jerusalem's desolation is reaching its end. The prophecy of what lies ahead for Jerusalem tells us that 'the Messiah will be cut off and have nothing' and that 'the people of the prince who is to come will destroy the city and the sanctuary'. Does this, or does this not, refer to the death of Jesus and the subsequent destruction of Jerusalem? Those who deny the prophetic element try to find another interpretation.[2] Jesus' own

---

[1]Hartman and Di Lella, *op. cit.*, p. 30.
[2]*Ibid.*, pp. 250ff.

interpretation is very clear from Matthew 24:15.

The whole interpretation of the four kingdoms which makes the Median and Persian kingdoms separate is contradicted by the book itself which sees Media and Persia as one kingdom (8:20). Thus one cannot say that Jesus and the New Testament have misinterpreted passages which were meant to apply to an early period. It is those who want to avoid the possibility of prophecy who argue contrary to the book's own indications.

A similar argument can be presented for the book of Isaiah. Is Isaiah 52:13–53:12 a prophecy of the death of Jesus, or is it not? We know what the New Testament answer to that question was (Acts 8:32–35).

There are thus attempts to avoid the possibility of prophecy. To do this one must resort to pseudepigraphy as an explanation. The problem is that Jesus was foretold and nobody will argue that the Old Testament books were written after Jesus. Hence the whole attempt to escape the fact of prophecy has to be judged a failure.

Of course there will be other arguments put forward, as already noted. There will be historical and linguistic arguments. It will be argued that the fact that Daniel was not included amongst the prophets in the Hebrew Old Testament casts doubt upon it. Once again we meet an inconsistently used argument. If the book of Daniel is placed in doubt by its lack of inclusion amongst the prophets then are other disputed books confirmed by being placed in the prophetic corpus? Those who argue for pseudepigraphy will not say this, because they want to question other books in the prophetic corpus. What then is the value of inclusion in the corpus as a text? Some will argue that it is merely an indication of the time at which a book was regarded as canonical. At the time the corpus of the prophets was closed, Daniel was not yet considered canonical (or perhaps even written). As a matter of fact we do not know that the division of the Hebrew books represents no time of canonicity. Those who hold that parts of Isaiah and Jonah, etc., are pseudepigraphic yet must believe that they were canonized before any Psalms of David or Proverbs. For all we know, the division between the prophets and other writings may be on more literary grounds.

Given the dubious and uncertain character of such arguments, the question has to go back to the basics. Is God the God of the Bible or is he a Deist God?

ORDER AND ORTHODOXY IN THE NEW TESTAMENT

There are many and various arguments which have been forwarded for regarding certain of the New Testament letters as pseudepigraphy. Some have already been mentioned. We might mention others such as those based upon differences in vocabulary or style. Once again, these arguments are rather inconsistently applied. There is general acknowledgement that statistical analyses of language do not give unambiguous evidence of authorship, especially when used to prove that books are genuine![1] In effect those who use such arguments are claiming to know what range of vocabulary or style a given author might use under all conceivable circumstances. We really come against the same problem as arguments based upon historical 'problems' or historical linguistics. We are postulating fairly comprehensive knowledge on our part of the author, circumstances, argument, and language.

A different sort of argument for making some letters post-apostolic turns upon reconstructions of the situation of the early church. Commonly it is charged that letters like the Pastoral Epistles and 2 Peter show a concern with church order and doctrinal orthodoxy that is foreign to the genuine New Testament letters. A development is suggested whereby in church order the freedom of an unstructured church gave way to a church concerned with official positions and authority. The openness of doctrinal debate was superseded by the insistence on the apostolic tradition and apostolic orthodoxy. Whereas Paul argued with his opponents in his 'genuine' letters, the author of the Pastorals simply dismisses them.[2]

More is involved in this question than just the authorship of these letters. For what is being set up is a picture which makes

[1]See for example the dismissal of statistical arguments for the common authorship of 1 and 2 Peter in J. N. D. Kelly, *A Commentary on the Epistles of Peter and Jude*, Grand Rapids, Baker, 1969, p. 235. Note as an example of trying to use such arguments, while admitting problems, W. Dibelius and H. Conzelmann, *The Pastoral Epistles*, Philadelphia, Fortress, 1972, pp. 3f.

[2]Dibelius and Conzelmann, *ibid.*, p. 2.

order and orthodoxy foreign to genuine, original Christianity.

A discussion of this thesis is inhibited by varying definitions of the genuine 'Pauline' letters. For example, if Philippians is not a genuine letter, we lose a vital witness for the presence of bishops and deacons in an 'early' church as well as in the Pastorals (Phil. 1:1). If Ephesians is denied to Paul then its evidence for the existence of the presence of the teacher-pastor[1] alongside the charismatic prophet is removed (Eph. 4:11).

Yet if we remove these evidences, the evidence from Paul's eleven other letters gives overwhelming proof of his concern for order and orthodoxy. We have already seen in chapter 20 how adamantly he opposes any innovation in the worship of the church. 1 Corinthians is a very clear refutation of any idea that concern for order in the church was a late innovation.

Similarly, the Paul of Galatians and Romans is not a man indifferent to doctrinal orthodoxy. As a matter of fact Paul was not arguing with his opponents in these letters, if that means he considered they had a right to a position in the church and a right to hold their point of view. Consider the following statements: 'if any man is preaching to you a gospel contrary to that which you received, let him be accursed' (Gal. 1:9); 'Would that those who are troubling you would even mutilate themselves' (Gal. 5:12). These are not the words of a man unconcerned with heresy! Certainly Paul sets out arguments in letters like Galatians and Romans. These are to convince erring Christians. They are not part of a friendly, mutually tolerant discussion with the heretics. After Galatians, the Pastorals are not unexpectedly firm in their treatment of heresy.

If Paul in the Pastorals does not set out arguments against the heretics' teaching, there is an easy explanation. Writing to Timothy or Titus, he does not need to convince them that the heretics' position is wrong. Rather he needs to urge them to diligence in preventing the penetration of the church by false doctrine. In this respect the argument for pseudepigraphy is circular. If it is assumed that these letters are not written for

[1]'Pastors' and 'Teachers' probably refer to one, not two offices. See the discussion in W. Hendrikson, *Ephesians*, London, Banner of Truth, 1967, p. 197 and note the connections he points out between the joint pastoring, teaching role here and those roles in 1 Timothy (and we could add also 1 Peter 5:1–5 and Acts 20:18–35).

Paul's missionary associates, but, like his other letters, for congregations as a whole, then the differences from letters like Romans are obvious. The letters are ascribed to some later 'Paulist' who wants to put a message across to the whole church. Once the letters are treated as genuine, the problem disappears.

Certainly, as already mentioned, the evidence for Paul's concerns can be lessened by declaring this or that letter to be fictitious. However, if we take all the letters with a Pauline heading, we find a consistent concern for order and orthodoxy. Philippians 1:1 complements the church order of the Pastorals. The concerns of 1 Corinthians chapters 11–14 are the concerns of a man who did not believe that anything was permissible, but believed the church to be limited strictly by the pattern of Christ. The attitude to heretics in Galatians or Colossians is consistent with that in the Pastorals.

What is the basis for the argument that the 'real' Paul was not insistent upon order and orthodoxy? One wonders if it is a case of reading into Paul what some people want in the church today. That is, a freedom for all sorts of departures from orthodoxy. One suspects that in this lies the antipathy to letters like the Pastorals and 2 Peter. We thus come back to the question which was treated more fully in chapter 11. There is a tendency today to pick up Paul's teaching against legalism and his teaching on the freedom of the Spirit. These teachings are then placed in a foreign context and quoted as proving a Biblical antipathy to order and regulation. Yet when we do that we are falling into the very misinterpretation against which Paul himself warned his readers. 1 Corinthians is very important in this respect. It is a polemic against any idea that matters of morality are made irrelevant by the gospel (note especially chapters 5 and 6) and a polemic against departure from the traditions in the life of the church (chapters 11 to 14). It is only by pretending that such chapters and similar passages in other letters do not exist that we can then see the Pastorals as containing non-Pauline teaching.

๛ 24 ๛

Proving the Bible

Some may object that this work so far presented assumes the truth and authority of the Bible. It appeals to those who already, in some sense, accept the Scriptures. It may be countered that the acceptance of Scripture is itself in question. Or it may be argued that this does nothing to persuade a person who doubts the Bible.

Traditionally people have tried to present 'proofs' of the Bible. Is this what we should do?

THE PROBLEMS OF THE 'PROOFS'

Such 'proofs' may be questioned on a number of grounds. It may be reasonably doubted whether they serve to convince anybody of anything. Reliance on the proofs tends to give disproportionate emphasis to the rational factor when a person becomes a Christian.

There are other problems. Let us take as an example the 'historical proof' of the Bible. That is the attempt to prove that the Bible is true historically. Such a proof has to be distinguished from a refutation of alleged historical errors in the Bible. To show that an individual case of supposed error is explainable is not the same as proving the whole Bible to be true.

The problem of historical proof will be obvious from chapter 10. Our historical knowledge is so incomplete and deficient that it leaves us with many areas of ignorance. On reflection, we can see that this problem is inevitable. We prove something to be true by comparing it with known and certain truth. Our human historical scholarship cannot be called certain truth!

Obviously the same problem will arise with respect to any other proof. It assumes that we have at our disposal some store of truth against which we can compare the Bible. But we do not have such a store for many reasons, the most basic of which is man's condition as a sinner in a world still suffering the effects of sin and curse. Thus the so-called 'proofs' ignore what the Bible says about man. We can be thankful that no such satisfactory proofs can be produced. If they could be, then the Bible's description of man's condition would be shown to be false.

THE LEAP OF FAITH

This has caused others to picture believing in the Bible as a totally irrational act. It is a 'leap of faith' for which no rational reason can be given.

It is obvious that believing in the Bible and believing in God are closely connected. The same problem confronts those who are to decide on believing in God. What 'proofs' can be produced as to the existence and nature of God? Hence belief in God is often represented as a leap of faith.

This approach is closely connected with relativism. It sees a particular religious belief as the irrational choice of a particular group. As an irrational choice there is no good reason why others should make the same choice. Sometimes an argument is presented to justify such a leap. It is claimed that if somebody will but try such a leap, then he will find in his experience of Christ sufficient proof of the truth of God and of the Bible. Yet this still leaves the truth of God as something uncertain. Even if a man should take this leap and find his actions later confirmed, he can only say that for him it worked. There is still an element of relativism in his claim. If for him it worked, it still does not prove it will work for others.

The real problem with this advocacy of a leap of faith is its contrast with the Biblical proclamation of the gospel. The gospel is not, in Scripture, presented as something uncertain, as an irrational choice, to be proved only in the experience of the one making the leap. It is presented as a sure and definite truth, to which man is commanded to yield assent and obedience.

[215]

THE PROBLEM SUMMARIZED

Thus we find that the formal proofs of God or the Bible presuppose that man has access to full and certain knowledge. They ignore the sinful and fallen condition of man. Yet the gospel is preached not as hypothetical and relative truth with which man might experiment. It is proclaimed as certain truth to which man must yield.

This summary simply puts in another way a basic doctrine of the Christian faith. God, not man, is the standard of right and truth: 'let God be found true, though every man be found a liar' (Rom. 3:4).

Does that mean there is no possibility of man knowing God's truth? Of course it does not, because then no man could be converted. Does it mean that man does not in any sense know God's truth before he becomes a Christian? No, it does not, because man's guilt follows from transgression of the truth, or law, of God that he knows.

Thus the problem comes down to this: how do we understand man's knowledge of the truth, even when he is a sinner? How does the answer to this question shape our presentation of the gospel to man?

It should be noted that our consideration of presenting the truth of the Bible to man has become inter-twined with that of presenting the truth of God to man. That is because the New Testament proclamation does not separate the two. Wherever a Jewish audience is addressed, the sermon is full of Old Testament quotation and allusion (e.g. Acts 2:14–40; 7:2–53; 13:26–41, etc.). It is God who speaks in Scripture and therefore the warning of God and the warning of Scripture are one and the same thing (e.g. Acts 13:40,41; Heb. 3:7–13).

THE UNBELIEVER'S KNOWLEDGE OF THE TRUTH

When Paul set out in his letter to the Romans to prove that salvation for both Jew and Gentile had to be by grace through faith, he began by establishing the universal sinfulness of man. That is, he argued that all men were acting against their knowledge of God and his law. In 1:18–23 he argues that men have, from their observation of creation, sufficient knowledge to know the error of idolatry. We shall see below how Paul's own evangelization of pagans utilizes his theological understanding of paganism. Here Paul sees the depravity of conduct that characterizes paganism as a consequence of God's judicial act in removing his restraints. Since they refuse the true God, he leaves them without his merciful restraints. Yet even then, they still know that the practices they approve are deserving of the severest judgment (1:32). It might be objected that pagans show no such knowledge of God's judgments. That is, that they are bereft of any moral judgment or sensibilities. On the contrary, that they do have a knowledge of God's law is shown by their own conformity in some respects to it and by their own judicial debates.

Paul takes this up in chapter 2. In verse 14 he writes of the Gentiles doing 'by nature the things of the Law'. Their obedience, in some respects, to the Scriptural law shows some imprint of that law upon them. That imprint does not come from reading or hearing that law. It is 'by nature'. We saw in chapter 18 Paul's use of 'nature' to refer to the constitution of man that derives from creation.

Thus Scripture does not teach that the Gentile lives, in every respect, in disobedience to the provisions of God's law. Often his outward behaviour will conform to that law. This fact is often used today to deny his need for salvation. It is used as evidence of his innate goodness. However God's standard is not partial obedience. It is perfect obedience. When the Gentile, at one stage, lives in conformity to God's law, he shows some consciousness of that law. When, at another stage, he breaks that law, he is not acting in complete ignorance.

There is another way in which Gentiles show a moral consciousness, that is, in their own attempts to distinguish right from wrong. Paul speaks in 2:15 of 'their thoughts between themselves accusing or else defending them'. It is not clear whether Paul here refers to the debate of thoughts within an individual as that individual considers his own actions, or the moral debate between men. The same point is made whichever he intended. The debate shows a sensitivity to the requirements of law. That sensitivity will not be as developed as that of a person informed by God's written revelation. Nevertheless it exists. Sin is transgression of what is known by nature.

[217]

Thus in proving the sin of the person who is ignorant of God's written revelation, Paul appeals to that person's knowledge as a creature living in a creation. The conditions of the Jew and Gentile are not so different. Both act against what they know.

We have an example of Paul using his understanding of the Gentile condition in his speech at the Areopagus (Acts 17:22–31). This speech is often interpreted as an attempt by Paul to link Christianity to philosophical paganism or as an acceptance of elements of truth in paganism. Such interpretations ignore the critical element in Paul's address. He begins with the excessive religiosity of the Athenians. However he does not commend it. Rather he sees in the altar 'to an unknown god' evidence of ignorance. Did the Athenians mean this as a proof of ignorance? One doubts whether they did so. Paul is therefore turning an expression of pagan religion into proof that it could be characterized as a religion of ignorance.

It is part of the very nature of paganism to divide the divinity into many parts and thereby to render knowledge of God less certain and obtainable. When that crude paganism is subjected to philosophical development the result is not to make the divine better known. Rather the divine tends to become not just unknown but unknowable. Yet paganism also brings with it a lessening of the distance between God and man. The deity becomes an object dependent upon man for his needs and care. Thus the deity is both unknown and dependent.

Paul begins with their self-professed (even if not intended) confession of ignorance. He states boldly that he is in a position to counter and correct that ignorance (v.23). He flatly contradicts their practice of idol worship and proclaims that God is not dependent on man (vv.24,25). There is certainly nothing thus far which could be seen as a recognition of the elements of truth of paganism. Rather the reverse!

Paul, on the basis of the earlier part of the address, could well be accused of being a 'proclaimer of strange deities' (v.18). It could be charged that the Athenians had no basis for believing what he said to be true. That is, they would have no ground for being convinced that their behaviour was sinful. The quotations from the poets are designed to demonstrate that they had not sinned in complete ignorance. Polytheism generally shows two contradictory tendencies. One is the practice of idolatry and the consequent turning of God into an object made with human hands. The other is pantheism. The world, and man in particular, are seen as an emanation of the divine. The poets Paul quotes were probably meaning what they said in a pantheistic sense. Man is part of a cosmic divinity. However Paul is not quoting them out of context. His point is that even in its pantheistic form, man retains enough knowledge to know that he derives from God. Idolatry makes God derive from man. He is not commending the pantheists. Paul's whole argument is that they have sinned against their own judgment in practising idolatry.

Paul does not indicate the source of the knowledge which even in attenuated form is sufficient to condemn idolatry. From what he says in Romans, he would probably point to creation.

Paul thus drives at the contradiction between what man still knows as a creature and his practice. That knowledge will come through in weakened, reduced, and confused forms. Nevertheless it is sufficient to condemn men for their sin. Evangelism to such pagans is a matter of confronting them with such contradictions.

The gospel is not addressed to them as people who possess sufficient wisdom to judge it to be true. It is addressed to men who have acted contrary to the truth they have known. That truth may emerge only in their own internal debates and contradictions, or in their violation of their own standards. Nevertheless it is sufficient to render them guilty. The purpose of gospel presentation is to expose that guilt clearly to their own view in order that men may be moved to repentance and faith.

Hence one would not seek to prove the Bible to the pagan in some formal manner. One would seek to show him his guilt, on the basis of what he himself knows. Of course new knowledge should be added to the little he will have by nature. The distorting effects of paganism must be corrected, just as Paul showed in his Areopagus address.

THE MODERN RELIGIOUS PAGAN

How do we apply this to the modern pagan? In the case of the professed atheist or agnostic it will be by pointing out his particular contradictions. The modern atheistic view generally proclaims that man is nothing but a mass of chemicals or an evolved ape. But it also bestows upon man dignity and significance. Such qualities do not belong to chemicals. This contradiction derives from the fact that sinful man really knows he is a creature, no matter how much he may try to deny it.

The religious pagan presents a greater difficulty. Often he will profess to believe in a god, even the Christian God. However he will deny the comprehensive truth and authority of the Bible. His god really arises out of his own imagination. We either know God as he reveals himself in the Bible or as we ourselves imagine him to be. A god who does not reveal himself in Scripture is really a different god. Once a person admits that the true God reveals himself in the Bible, then the study of that revelation must lead him to accept the authority of Scripture. The real problem arises with other groups. There are those who claim to believe the Bible but who limit its authority, contrary to what the Bible itself says. Often such people are closer to those who deny revelation through the Bible. Some are willing to grant that God speaks through the Bible, so long as the Bible does not contradict what they already believe. Thus their real standard is not the Bible but their own beliefs.

Hence we have people who proclaim a faith independent of Scripture. Sometimes they will take a neo-orthodox position, saying that God reveals himself through his actions while the Bible is fallible man's account of those actions. Sometimes they will appeal to a 'deeper' truth behind, and contrary to, the actual words of Scripture.

For the New Testament proclamation of the gospel the essential question was the form in which man knew the truth. Was it such a knowledge as the Jews of the Scripture possessed or a creaturely knowledge possessed by Gentiles? The modern religious pagan does have some knowledge of the Bible. Yet he clearly attempts to limit the authority of the Bible.

We must ask for the basis of his faith and knowledge. For he is appealing to some standard of truth outside the Bible which allows him to pick and choose what parts of the Bible he will accept. In answer to this question he will respond in various ways and each of those ways must be answered differently.

Sometimes he will resort to pure subjectivism. He will say that a certain way is right for him and deny trying to force his view on others. Yet he remains a creature and as a creature he knows that there is a universal truth about God. Hence, quite inconsistently, he will turn to criticizing others. The only way you can criticize others is if there is something true for all men. Here is the contradiction we must point out as we seek to bring him to repentance.

Others will appeal to the academic disciplines of science and history as having disproved the Bible. Sometimes we are dealing with somebody who has simply been misled by teachers he thought worthy of trust. Or he may be motivated by the fear of the ridicule given in academic circles to the believer. Or this may be a cover for a more personal and moral rebellion against God. Nevertheless we may have to deal with his argument, whether it is the real reason or not. It is a profession that human scholarly judgments are the basis of truth. They take precedence over what God says about his word. Yet man as a creature knows that man is not the real authority. When it suits him he will turn around and cast aside the opinion of the scholarly experts. Or he will maintain the fiction of such a scholarly consensus even when he well knows that the scholars are in contradiction and confusion. If he is to be brought to see that he does know that truth lies not in men but in God, then this hypocritical, inconsistent appeal to scholarship has to be exposed. Often he will show the same inconsistency held by the unreligious pagan. That is, he accepts a framework of thought in which man is meaningless but lives as though man has significance and worth as a creature of God.

Often the rejection of the Bible is based upon a 'higher' truth that contradicts the Bible. It may be the Bible's insistence on God's order expressed in the divine judgment on sin or the prohibition of divorce, etc., that is the stumbling block. It may be the Bible's toleration of slavery. The Bible will be proclaimed as deficient in terms of a higher morality.

In essence the objection here is to the justice of God. This is one of the commonest objections to the truth of God today. Many want to recreate God with his justice removed but his grace retained. Thus the judgments and standards of Biblical law are rejected. However this new creation bears little relation to the Biblical God. The gospel that results is not a gospel. What point is there in man being freed from the guilt of sin if

God does not judge sin? Redemption has to become redemption from man's own sense of alienation or other psychological problems, or from political or economic oppression. Of course one has to ask what 'grace' means in this new theology. If man is not under judgment what can God's grace mean? What then was the purpose of Jesus' death?

Not everybody who begins raising questions about the Biblical judgments on sin, or on the institutions God devises for sinful men, intends to deny the gospel. We often have an adherence to a worldly wisdom that would reject the justice of God, combined with an insistent attempt to retain something akin to the Biblical gospel. The consistent denial of the justice of God is, in one way, easier to answer. For the man who makes that denial is still a creature of God. As such he knows that certain practices are wrong. He will be quite selective in the practices he chooses for condemnation. He may condemn racism but approve sexual immorality. Yet the very act of condemnation is inconsistent with what he proclaims about God. If God has no standards, then racism is not wrong. If God is the God of the Bible, then racism is wrong and sexual immorality is wrong also. We have in this case a very clear instance of Paul's argument in Romans chapter 2. It is when men pass judgment that they betray a knowledge of God and his law.

Let us then turn to the case of an inconsistent denial. A man may take something like what the Bible says about homosexuality and proclaim that no matter what the Bible text says, God really does not think that way. Yet on other issues he will say that the Bible is correct and an accurate reflection of God's standards.

In this case one can do no more than press home a man's fundamental inconsistency in his use of Scripture. Pressing the inconsistency will drive a man in one of two contrary ways. He may come to realize that his defence of homosexuality, or whatever, is contrary to Scripture and turn from it. Or he may decide that it is more important to persist in his denial of Scripture on this issue than to maintain the belief that the Bible is the Word of God. Thus he will move to the position of the religious pagan whose paganism has been influenced by contact with Christianity. Often this movement takes place over several generations. The first generation tries to hold the inconsistent position of approving what the Scripture condemns. The next generation abandons Scripture and thus resolves the contradiction. If we drive home to men's consciences the contradiction, then the resolution of that contradiction will happen more quickly. Men must decide whether they are for Scripture or against it.

Once a man has taken the position of a modern religious pagan, he has not escaped all contradiction. He has resolved the problem of rejecting the judgments of the Bible which he claimed to be the Word of God. He is then left with his own view of what God is 'really' like.

Let us say that this view proclaims a god with some resemblance to the Biblical God but denying the Biblical view of the sex rôles, with consequent departures on issues like homosexuality, sex outside marriage, divorce, etc. How can this man be brought to see that his rejection of Biblical teaching on these issues is sinful? We must go back to the fact that he is a creature. As a creature he exists within a created world in which sexual distinctions are very real, and as a creature he knows it. There will be a point where his actions and attitudes as a creature will contradict his proclaimed rejection of the Biblical teaching. We must bring such contradictions pointedly to his attention. Often they may be in things about which only he knows. Yet he has a conscience. We do not necessarily have to catch him in such a case of inconsistency. His conscience will be aware of his own hypocrisy.

If he is sophisticated in the arguments of relativism he will dismiss his own inconsistencies as the conditioning effects of a sexist and conservative culture or upbringing. Yet he only entangles himself in further contradiction by his argument. If his views are to be explained thus, then so can the 'sexist' view of his opponents who hold to the Biblical teaching. If a person's views are the product of a totally determining environment, then he can bear no guilt for those views. Hence there can be no moral attack brought against him for his views. Yet those who reject the Scripture on this subject regularly attack Christians on the issue. Their attacks prove that they really know that determinism is not true. Thus we come back to the truth that, in judging others, men condemn themselves.

[223]

They show that they really know the truth of God.

Determinism can be attacked another way. Suppose a man has resorted to the effects of environment to explain those ways in which he shows knowledge of Biblical teaching. Could not environment also explain his rejection of Biblical teaching? After all there are many influences in our culture against the Biblical view. The moment a man defends his rejection of the Bible as 'right' and not just as influenced, he rejects environmental determinism. But if he rejects it, he can no longer use it to explain away his actions when he acts in accord with the created and Biblically defined divisions of sexual rôle and function.

ASSUMING THE TRUTH

Thus our approach is not one of 'proving' the Bible. It is one of using what the Bible says about man so that men may see what they really are: sinners who really knew better. We can explain the unbeliever's contradictions. He can be brought to see that the truth he transgressed was part of a far bigger teaching. It was the particular part of Biblical teaching which remained in his consciousness.

How do we Christians know that the whole Biblical teaching is the truth? Essentially it has been by the same process. We came to realize that the truth which bothered our consciences and convicted us of sin was part of a Biblical truth. In arguing with an unbeliever as part of an abstract logical exercise we might divorce this or that aspect of Biblical truth and consider it in isolation. Yet what purpose or advantage is there in arguing that this detached portion is 'true' and trying to convince an unbeliever of it? The much more important truth for him is the one he already knows; the truth that God in his grace may use to bring him to repentance.

⧼ 25 ⧽

Freedom and Honesty

The debate over the authority of the Bible has included some highly emotional and emotive aspects. Those aspects derive partly from the fact that men are denying positions that have been expressed in creedal statements. In many cases they are denying creeds which they have sworn before men and God to defend. It is the insinuation that men have acted in a dishonest way which gave a particular edge to Harold Lindsell's book, *The Battle for the Bible.*

On the other hand those who question the accuracy and authority of Scripture see the commitment to a particular doctrine of Scripture as a restraint upon their freedom to be led by the Spirit of God into new truth. This argument is particularly pressed by those engaged in theological study and teaching. They claim that creedal positions restrict their research.

We have thus a conflict between the claims of honesty and those of freedom. Is there any prospect of accommodation between the two demands? Are they necessarily contrary principles?

There are two obvious extreme positions. One is to say that creeds may not be challenged or changed. The problem with this position is that it raises creeds to the level of Scripture. We have no warrant for doing this. The other extreme is to say that creeds should be abandoned. Sometimes people who argue against creeds will argue on the ground that particular creeds are outdated. Sometimes they argue against creeds as such. Hence there are different arguments which need to be considered.

An argument that creeds as such are inappropriate would

logically have to include all forms of doctrinal tests. There is no real difference between asking a man if he agrees with a written statement of doctrine and putting those same doctrines to him in oral form. It comes down to the question of whether it is wrong to require the passing of some test of doctrinal orthodoxy before a man has a specific responsibility. Attacking all doctrinal tests contradicts the requirements set in the New Testament. A deacon for example has to hold 'the mystery of the faith with a clear conscience' (1 Tim. 3:9). The elder according to Titus 1:9 has to hold 'fast the faithful word which is in accordance with the teaching, that he may be able both to exhort in sound doctrine and to refute those who contradict'. These requirements do not provide a defence for any particular creed. It could be argued that the creed contained unimportant or erroneous material. However, if it is always wrong to test a man's comprehension of Scriptural teaching, then Scripture is in error. That means the denial of creedal tests argues against Scripture.

The other common argument against creeds is that they represent the views of a particular age. They are inappropriate for our time or simply in error. Thus it may be charged that they embody common ideas of their time which are not Biblical. Once again there are two separate arguments here. One is a form of the historical relativism we have already considered. It is that truth can only be truth for a particular age. The argument applied against Scripture will also be used against creeds. If we reject historical relativism in the case of Scripture, then we should not accept it when used against creeds.

That does not mean that creeds should be uncritically accepted. They may well accept common ideas of their time. However, the real test of creeds must be Scripture. Dismissing them as being shaped by their times is often a way of avoiding the Scriptural test where it is realized that Scripture will confirm the creed. Attacks on the creed may be a way of attacking Scripture, but in a way that is less obvious to the church's members or the institution's supporters.

Thus creeds are not to be accepted uncritically nor dismissed in cavalier fashion. Both attitudes to creeds spring from a lack of respect for Scripture.

There is a further issue raised here. If a man has affirmed a creed, is it honest for him to attack creeds in general, or a particular creed as a product of its time? Here I do not refer to a specific objection to a creed. I refer to a general attitude to creeds or to the particular creed. Where there is a general undermining of the creed, how can a man affirm the creed? This question rises with even greater force if the affirmation of the creed also included a promise to teach and defend the creed. Thus attacks on creeds as such often raise the same questions of honesty as attacks on a specific doctrine.

THE PRACTICAL PROBLEMS

Suppose a man has particular problems with just one section of a creed. Or suppose he initially thought he accepted it all and then comes to doubt sections of it. What should he do, or what should others do in this case?

First, to regard such doubts as automatically and necessarily wrong is to accept the infallibility of a human creed. If we make Scripture our supreme authority, then we cannot have the attitude that a creed is unquestionable.

Here the road to be taken depends very much on the nature of creedal subscription in the particular church or institution. In some cases a church assembly interviewing the man may make a judgment that the point in issue does not touch the important doctrines of the confession. Other creedal subscriptions require subscription to the whole creed but allow for processes by which a creed may be changed. Sometimes there may be no machinery specified for a change or a change may be prohibited.

It is not my purpose here to debate which is the preferable approach to creedal subscription. Obviously, forbidding any change creates particular problems. It does so not just for the people who object to that creed but also for those required to uphold it. This problem will be taken up again later.

In most cases there is a way the problem can be addressed. There may need to be a creation of a procedure for dealing with a challenge to a creed. Nevertheless there is some way forward. That way forward generally involves raising the matter with others who have similar leading functions. Sometimes they may so instruct the person concerned that his objections are overcome.

However the real problems arise in a number of different but interrelated circumstances. Suppose the objector feels that others have closed minds on the issue. Suppose he finds that others have similar doubts but have done nothing about them. Suppose he finds strong disagreement from those he approaches. The crucial question then becomes: should the matter be pressed into an open proposal to change that part of the creed?

There may seem strong reasons against this course. The man in question may be convinced that the constituency as a whole is innately conservative. It sees the creed as a guarantee of orthodoxy and stability. It will resist any attempt to change without considering the arguments. Further, openly raising the subject may lead to a man being branded a 'heretic' and thus denied access to a position in the church or the organization.

There is thus a temptation to make or maintain a false affirmation. Is it right to do so? Obviously there is an element of dishonesty here. That is especially the case if a man is granted a position of trust or a salary on the basis of the creedal subscription.

Those caught in this ethical dilemma often feel that something unreasonable is being asked of them. This is particularly so where their freedom to do theological research is limited.

Obviously a different definition of the creedal subscription of theology teachers could be formulated. Yet constituencies are reluctant to make such concessions knowing full well that teachers of theology have played a major rôle in introducing heresy into the church. We come back to the anticipation that the constituency will resist change.

A proposal to alter the form of creedal subscription is thus rather similar to a proposal to alter a specific section of a creed. There can be the same pragmatic reasons for avoiding the attempt.

Yet there is a question that is unavoidable. Is it right to do evil that good may come? Can an anticipation of an unsuccessful outcome excuse one in doing wrong? Obviously not. If a man doubts, questions, or denies a doctrine that he publicly affirms, then he is a dishonest man. Such dishonesty is understandable but it is still dishonesty.

[228]

When one follows the history of churches and individuals one finds cases of men who first gradually and almost surreptitiously attack a doctrine they have sworn to uphold. This goes on for years until the church or institution finally ceases to hold that doctrine. Then they openly proclaim their rejection of the doctrine. One may grant that in the initial stage they may not have realized the full implications of their doubts. Yet at some point they must have realized that they doubted the creed. One can often see from the nature of their attacks, often involving the use of straw men, that they are well aware of the strategy they follow. Is this not dishonesty and duplicity? It may be well-motivated duplicity but it is still duplicity. It is this situation that produces in turn a reaction. There is an extreme fear of doctrinal deviation because the modern church has seen so much of it and seen it pursued with such little regard for openness and honesty. If teachers of theology feel inhibited, then rightly or wrongly, they are experiencing the consequences of breaches of trust by earlier teachers. The way to correct that situation is not to commit another act of betrayal of the constituency.

This general failure of people who have doubted doctrines to follow the accepted and open channels is a phenomenon which itself demands explanation. One can cite very few cases of men who early and openly brought action to change the relevant creed. How did (and do) such men live with their consciences?

One wonders if there is a connection between the nature of the doctrinal deviations and this failure to act openly. It has been pointed out that past deviations have created a suspicion of doctrinal change in the church. Humanly speaking, if an issue is raised while a church is still committed to doctrinal orthodoxy, there is little hope of changing its creed. It takes trust in the overruling providence of God for a man to undertake a course of action which seems doomed to failure.

We have seen that connected with modern attacks on Scripture is often a Deist theology. God is seen as uninvolved in the affairs of men. This has a consequence. The God who cannot send his Spirit to guide the writers of Scripture also cannot send his Spirit to guide the deliberations of church assemblies. Similarly, if Scripture originated purely through human agency, and a fallible human agency at that, is it not also to be expected that change is to be brought to the church by fallible human agency? The other side of the same coin is that the displeasure of a distant, uninvolved God is not feared like the displeasure of the Biblical God.

One cannot deny that the strategy of a quiet and dishonest attack often succeeds. This is especially so when it is carried out by teachers of theology who sow doubts in the minds of their students, who in turn undermine the church's confidence in the Scripture. Yet real success has to be measured not in the short term but in the long term. We shall all appear before God. Will we appear knowing that we have 'not walked in craftiness' but 'by the manifestation of truth' commended 'ourselves to every man's conscience in the sight of God' (2 Cor. 4:2)? The position of those who question the creedal affirmations on Scripture would be a lot more credible if one could look at a history of public, open, and honest dealing with the issue.

It may be objected that it is wrong to bring guilt by association upon those who are in this generation doubting the Scripture. If liberalism in former generations operated by stealth, that is no reason to assume it will do so today. The objection is perfectly valid. However, if history is not to repeat itself, the onus is on those who doubt creedal statements, particularly those relating to Scripture, to conduct themselves in an open and honest manner. If they fail to do so, then one must ask whether their conduct is such as to commend their doctrine.

THE CONCERNS OF THE CREED

It is often objected that the questions now being raised about Scripture were not in the mind of the formulators of the creeds. The authority of the Bible on religious, ethical, and liturgical matters may have been at issue, but not its authority on matters of history and science.

Of course one must respond to this differently, depending upon the creed in question. For every creed the story may be slightly different. I do not propose to deal with every creed. In general we may point to two particular periods of creed making. One is the Reformation and immediately post-

Reformation period. The other arises out of the combined phenomena of the spread of interdenominational organizations and the Fundamentals controversy late last century and early this century.

It is true that the Reformation and post-Reformation creeds were concerned to affirm the truth and authority of Scripture over against appeals to the church or tradition as a higher authority. Yet they do so in general terms. Thus we could quote the Belgic Confession Article v: 'We receive all these books and these only, as holy and canonical for regulation, foundation, and confirmation of our faith; believing without any doubt all things contained in them'; or the Westminster Confession Chapter i: vi 'The whole counsel of God, concerning all things necessary for his own glory, man's salvation, faith, and life, is either expressly set down in Scripture, or by good and necessary consequence may be deduced from Scripture.'

It is not consistent with the passage of the Belgic Confession quoted to say that the Bible made errors in matters of science and history. The Confession's statement is comprehensive. It is one thing to disagree openly and to alter the Confession to limit that truth to matters of ecclesiology and ethics. It is another to affirm the Confession while holding the Bible erroneous on some matters.

Further the matters in debate today are not just matters of history and science. They are ethical matters like a rejection of the Bible's position on homosexuality and divorce. They include ecclesiastical matters like the rôle of women in teaching/ruling offices in the church. The man who rejects the Biblical position on these matters cannot appeal to the fact that the Confession's concern was ethical and ecclesiastical.

There is another way in which appeal is sometimes made to the real concern of the Confession. It is when it is claimed that the Confession has a basic concern contrary to what the text of the Confession actually says. This is very similar to the way in which inconvenient teachings of Scripture are ignored in favour of a supposed basic message that is never overtly expressed.

Once again one must ask about the honesty of this approach. Suppose a man affirms a creed meaning that he affirms his own version of the creed's 'basic teaching' which is contrary to what the creed actually says. Will those who hear him make the affirmation understand that secret qualification? Once again we have a case of dishonesty.

Matters are somewhat simpler with the more modern creeds which have as their background the Modernist–Fundamentalist controversy. Matters of history and science were already in controversy last century. Such creeds often affirm the infallibility or inerrancy of Scripture, or both. In more recent times some people have wanted to distinguish infallibility from inerrancy. Yet originally the terms were understood to mean the same thing.

Some might refer to the common tendency of such creeds to refer to the Scripture's authority in 'matters of faith and conduct'. Some would want to restrict the Scripture's authority rather narrowly to such matters. However, once issues like homosexuality, divorce, or the rôle of women are raised, then such defences are shown to be obviously spurious.

THE FLOW-ON EFFECT

The concentration in this work has been upon the doctrine of Scripture. However the point has been repeatedly made that the positions being taken on Scripture have consequences for other doctrines. An example of this is the acceptance of the Deist view which would exclude God from immediate action upon men or other creatures. A man who takes such a position does not merely have problems with creedal statements on Scripture. Depending on how far he has moved in accepting the Deist position, he will also have trouble with creedal positions on matters like providence, regeneration, miracles, and the resurrection of Christ. A quotation of some creedal positions will illustrate this point:

'We believe that the same good God, after He had created all things, did not forsake them or give them up to fortune or chance, but that He rules and governs them according to His holy will, so that nothing happens in this world without His appointment . . .' (Belgic Confession, Article xiii).

'This effectual call is of God's free and special grace alone, not from any thing at all foreseen in man; who is altogether passive therein, until being quickened and renewed by the Holy Spirit, he is thereby enabled to answer this call, and to embrace the grace offered and conveyed in it' (Westminster Confession Chapter x: II).

'Christ did truly rise again from death, and took again his body, with flesh, bones, and all things appertaining to the perfection of Man's nature . . .' (Thirty-Nine Articles, Article IV).

The God of these creeds is not the distant God who is inactive in the world. He acts to direct each event for his purposes and to make the dead to live.

It is often a matter of astonishment to believers how quickly a church's position can change. At first there is only a little covert controversy, with positions presented without publicity for fear of attracting heresy trials. The controversy seems to touch only matters like Scripture and evolution. Once that agitation has succeeded in changing the church's stand on these matters, then rapid change takes place in other areas. The reason is that generally it was not specific doctrines which were initially questioned. It was a whole framework of thought. That framework came to expression particularly in rejecting Biblical and creedal teaching on Scripture and creation. These were the crucial test cases between two conflicting ways of viewing God and all that he does. The church by its failure to take a stand on the test areas declared the alternative framework to be permitted. What then happened was simply the carrying through of the new framework into all the other doctrinal and ethical areas.

It is because a framework is generally involved that there is often a degree of manoeuvre and sometimes dishonesty in presenting the problem as though it related only to questions like the historical accuracy of Scripture or the Biblical account of creation. The very same structure of thought which questions these teachings of Scripture will question many others as well.

A similar flow-on applies with the acceptance of historical relativism. Suppose it is argued that even though Paul appealed to creation to defend his view of women's rôle in the church, he was really just reflecting the sexist views of his time. That same way of dismissing Biblical positions which are unpopular in our day must flow on to other doctrines and ethical questions.

This whole point is important in another connection also. One regularly meets examples of fanciful, tortuous, and contrived exegesis designed to prove that the Bible does not really condemn divorce, women in teaching/ruling office, or homosexuality. Perhaps there is a level of deliberate fraud. One hopes there is not. One hopes it is rather a man faced with a dilemma. He is so influenced by conformity to our age that he is convinced there are 'truths' which the Bible could not possibly contradict. When he sees that the Bible does contradict the 'truths' he holds dear, he is convinced the Bible cannot say what it actually says. Fundamentalists are often criticized for going to ridiculous lengths in trying to harmonize seeming contradictions in the Bible. Yet they have good company in those who seek to explain away the clear ethical teaching of Scripture. These arguments strain the credulity. Nevertheless let us assume that many of the people who do this are sincerely wanting to accept the authority of Scripture. It is just that they cannot credit that it says what it says. For a time they may be able to hold this unnatural position, holding to Scripture and an ethical position contrary to Scripture. Yet the unnatural marriage must break under the strain. If conformity to the modern world wins over conformity to Scripture, then this will also have a flow-on effect.

TESTING A FRAMEWORK

The point has been made that what is often at issue is not this or that doctrine or practice but the whole framework within which the truth of God is viewed. Thus many portions of the creedal position are called into question because the Scripture is being approached in quite a different way from that used by those who have drafted the creeds.

Yet the question must be faced: could not the framework of interpretation used in the creeds be suspect? This charge is often made against the historic creeds. For example their appeal to specific verses of Scripture is dismissed by those who reject the exegetical methods employed by Jesus and the New Testament authors.

We have to admit that we cannot assume the framework of any creed to be correct any more than we can assume it is correct on every doctrine. Yet questioning the whole framework must raise even more objections to the specific teachings of the creed. If a man objects to the whole framework of the creed, as an honest man he could not affirm it and promise to teach it. That would be an instance of total and deliberate dishonesty.

This is not to say it does not happen. It is just that those who do this show total disregard for the standards of honesty expected in the world, let alone Christian standards.

It cannot be objected that there is no other option for those who have serious doubts about a Confession. They could refuse to take up any position in the Christian organization concerned or they could relinquish the position already held. Then, without their own position being ethically compromised by attacking what they have promised to defend, they are at least ethically free to put their views. Of course such a step may mean sacrifice both in terms of prestige and in financial terms. Yet is anybody seriously going to defend a person who acts dishonestly in the church because being honest is a costly matter?

Once again the problem will be raised particularly in terms of theological lecturers. Does this inhibit their freedom of research?

The framework within which the creeds have interpreted Scripture may be substantially correct or it may be substantially incorrect. If it is substantially correct but there are specific detailed problems, then let us go through the appropriate channels to change the details. If it is substantially incorrect, then nobody with any integrity would say he agreed with it. If the problem of the creeds is so bad, how is it that we have not had mass resignations from our theological faculties? We must conclude that either the creeds are correct and the theologians agree, or the faculties deserve only contempt.

What should a man do if he finds himself coming to doubt a substantial part or aspect of the creed? Surely in this matter he should not act differently from the office bearer in a local congregation who finds problems with a specific part of the creed. The ethical problem both face is no different. There are the appropriate channels to be followed.

Certainly there is a particular problem if a creed is

constitutionally established as unchangeable. Resignation seems the only alternative. It may seem a vain hope that everybody else will resign and the organization be reconstituted. Nevertheless, better what seems, in human terms, a vain hope, than a guilty conscience before God and man.

One wonders how seriously one should take the claim that these creedal positions are inhibitions to research. Research implies something individual and original. What we tend to see from theological faculties which reject the truth and authority of Scripture is the reverse. It is imitative. It is an imitation of what has been done in the liberal theological faculties which is itself an uncritical appropriation of ideas from secular scholars and faculties. Is this uncritical adoption of whatever counts as the latest fad to be called research? When one teaches in a secular university as I do, and reads, as I do, in a secular field that touches at many points on the Biblical field, then the originality of theological faculties is the last thing that strikes one. They repeat the commonplaces of secular scholarship, often after those positions have already been disproved by secular scholars.

One needs to ask whether the lack of originality and the lack of integrity are connected. Is the real issue for such men not what is true, but what is popular and respectable? Of course the same values rule the secular university. What is so sad is seeing popularity and respectability rule supposedly Christian institutions.

LOVE

The charge is often made that orthodoxy is synonymous with a lack of love. Any insistence that we adhere to Scripture and that God's law governs us, is attacked as being rigid and unloving.

There is the simple human fact that we get on better with those who agree with us. A man who has been resisted, rebuked, and admonished for his heretical views might well conclude that his opponents are 'unloving' while those who approve and encourage his heresy are loving and kind to him. Proponents of orthodox views find themselves similarly attracted by those who agree with them.

[236]

Beyond this natural selective affinity is there really anything in the charge that orthodoxy is unloving? Sometimes the charge is purely and simply an attempt to lay aside Biblical teaching. If it is claimed that to forbid divorce is unloving, then Jesus was unloving. Such arguments are really blasphemous and deserve straight rebuke.

However there is something more serious to be considered here. Is an attachment to orthodoxy necessarily accompanied by a rigid and unloving spirit? If we were to think of all the orthodox people we know then we might conclude that that is sometimes the case. If we recollect all the unorthodox people we know, then we might come to the same conclusion! The real question is whether there is any likely or necessary connection between orthodoxy and lack of love.

In this respect Christ's admonitions to the churches in Revelation 2 and 3 are particularly noteworthy. Christ rebuked the church of Ephesus for lack of love (2:4). Yet the same church is commended for orthodoxy and rejection of error (2:6). There is no suggestion here that their orthodoxy contributed to their lack of love. On the other side we should note that the church of Thyatira, whose love is mentioned by Christ (2:19) is strongly admonished for tolerating false teaching (2:20). Any idea that love and orthodoxy are antithetical to each other is foreign to the teaching of Christ. Our Lord requires both.

Let us therefore reject the sort of self-righteousness in which we congratulate ourselves on being orthodox and think that this somehow compensates for a lack of love. Similarly let us not think that Christ will overlook denials of his Word simply because we are loving.

The charge of lovelessness is often expressed psychologically. It is suggested that the orthodox are clinging to traditional positions out of fear of change. They cannot let go and reach out into the new age. As cramped, fearful personalities they are unable to love or to trust. No doubt one could make such a charge stick with certain people who are insistent on the teaching of Scripture. Yet people in glass houses should not throw stones. One could equally charge that those who want to cut us loose from Scripture are unstable people for whom the praise of the world means far too much. And there would be certain cases where a very plausible case could be made out for this interpretation.

What do we gain by exchanging psychological insults? Let us remember that we are to be judged by the measure we apply to others. If we have dwelt on the personality of others to avoid serious consideration of their views, then the Lord has every right to subject *our* personality to scrutiny. Let us remember that orthodoxy itself is not a substitute for the love and fervour of a genuine obedience to Christ. To the extent that we lack that, we deny the Scriptures we claim to defend. Let us also remember that those who freely brand the orthodox as unloving, Pharisaic, legalistic, sexist, etc., are in the act of such character assassination showing very little love. If we know the law of God sufficiently well to accuse others of having failed to keep it, then we should keep it ourselves.

Similarly the attempt to brand all those who hold the orthodox doctrine of Scripture as unacademic and obscurantist shows little wisdom. Much of what goes as the latest wisdom in science and history will yet be shown to be nonsense and those who embrace it enthusiastically will be viewed as dunces by a later age. This is not to say that we need not face the serious problems that are raised by secular scholarship. It is simply to say that a refusal to follow every latest fad of scholarship is not necessarily a sign of obscurantism. Often it shows more wisdom than blind faith. The naïve faith with which some theologians follow the uncertain course of secular scholarship is little less than pathetic.

DEALING WITH A HERETIC

It would be a great relief if men would follow the existing channels for dealing with doctrinal problems. If men had the integrity to vacate a position when they could no longer affirm a creed it would make the church much more peaceful. The sad fact is that they will not do so.

Sometimes it is because there is the unwillingness to risk the financial security and prestige they enjoy. They still their consciences and bite the hand that feeds them. Sometimes they can persuade themselves that their position really is almost creedal and Biblical, even if their hypocrisy is obvious to others.

Sometimes to leave would be to lose the very thing that motivates the heresy. That is 'to draw away the disciples after them' (Acts 20:30).

This means that the church cannot avoid dealing with such men. In our culture, in which tolerance and relativism are so widely taught, there are strong pressures against such action. An additional problem is the reverence with which ministers and theological teachers are often regarded. That reverence arises out of a desire on the part of many to avoid the labour of real thinking and Bible study. If they can trust implicitly in a man, they do not need to think. Christian leaders have sadly encouraged this attitude because of the respect and position it brings them. In this climate any opposition, any questioning of a prestigious figure, is resisted. People know it will place the responsibility upon them to think.

Nevertheless faithfulness to Christ and concern for his church obligates us to act. But it is important that we act in love and wisdom. We must act in love because those we class as heretics may be fighting a battle against temptations to conform to the wisdom of the world. They may yet be strengthened in their faith. We must act in wisdom because we may be confronted with men determined to use every trick and device to get their way. A heretic who has lied, and lied about his adherence to the confession and to his vows, will react in righteous indignation when brought to account. If any proof is needed of the strange perversity of the human character, it can be easily found in the fact that men can deny what they have sworn to defend but then react in outraged innocence when charged.

As we look at the recent history of the church, it is hard to argue that the general tendency has been a lack of love and tolerance. How many heresy cases and dismissals can one cite in comparison to the number of churches and organizations which have been drawn away from their original conviction of the complete truth and authority of Scripture? That fact in itself gives the lie to the claims that orthodoxy is characterized by a lack of tolerance. If anything it is the reverse. Even in those cases where a man has been dismissed, there has often been a rebound. In other words, when men have gone through the trauma of one such case and been vilified for standing for the truth, they are reluctant to try again. If we need anything at this crucial hour, it is courage and steadfastness.

The task is complicated by two factors. One is the deviousness of heresy. When a man thinks he has an opportunity to influence others, he will proclaim something quite contrary to the truth he has sworn to keep. When brought to account, he will deny that he meant what he clearly said. That is, he will deny it until opportunity arises to say it again, and, if the first challenge has been successfully blunted, to go much further.

A second problem is that a man may be influencing a wide circle with his heretical views while belonging to a congregation or fellowship apart from that circle. His own fellowship may be spiritually weak and indifferent to the destructive effect of his teaching.

A further problem has been touched upon in chapter 20. There is a strong desire on the part of men who doubt the truth of Scripture to create administrative positions for themselves out of the pastoral office. If successful they then proceed to create more such positions and staff them with people they find congenial with their views. This is not always their deliberate plan, though it may sometimes be so. A man who doubts the Scripture cannot bring the Word of God to men in face-to-face situations. He really has very little to say in the face of the every-day trials and temptations of the people of God. Further, the church which is beginning to doubt Scripture has a practical problem. It no longer has confidence in the power of the preached Word of Christ to advance the cause of God's kingdom. Hence it tends to create other agencies, which in turn tend to be staffed by men seeking escape from what they cannot do with confidence, namely, preach the Word. Thus churches drifting away from the Word tend to create administrations, agencies, and bureaucracies staffed by men with little confidence in Scripture. Even where these men are orthodox the administrative problem of keeping the organization running may come to count more to them than the spiritual problem of the health of that organization. Thus such men will resist dealing with heresy which they see as likely to be disruptive to the running of the machine. When such men come to have disproportionate influence in a church, then it becomes even harder to deal with heresy.

For some men teaching is a means of escape from a situation

in which they have nothing to say to a congregation. They will stress the academic side of theological teaching. What the students receive will be of little use in a pastoral situation. Yet the influence is disproportionate in undermining the confidence in Scripture which a student may have had before his theological training.

In this situation we must keep in mind several factors. Open error has to be rebuked openly. A favourite passage with those who deny Scripture is Matthew 18:15-20. According to them it means they are free to teach heresy publicly but must not be refuted publicly. Such a rule is a great help to them, especially where the man who objects belongs to a different congregation and fellowship and thus has difficulty in bringing the process of church discipline outlined below to bear or where the heretic's church tolerates error.

Is it consistent with the rest of Scripture to see this passage as teaching that open proclamation of heresy cannot be refuted openly? At issue is not only error in teaching, but any open sin. Jesus himself openly and publicly condemned the false teaching of the Jewish leadership. We have the example of Paul who publicly dissented from the practice of Peter (Gal. 2:11-14). We have the examples in Paul's letters of rebuke of specific sin in letters addressed to the whole congregation.

That is not to say we should not on occasion attempt a private meeting with the brother concerned. Often this is the best way. He may be simply swept along by the popular fads and may not have been challenged to subject them to the test of Scripture.

Again, Matthew 18:15-20 teaches that one discussion does not end our duty. If there is anything which we need to do in this situation, it is to go beyond the first step. Those who use this passage to condemn others who speak out against the promulgation of error ignore the end of the passage. For it teaches church discipline by excommunication. Generally, heretics are hostile to discipline while they are coming to power. When in power in a church they will sometimes use it against those who, on conscience grounds, will not participate in unbiblical practices. One can use the question of the ordination of women as an example of this. At first the argument turns upon the freedom to ordain women to teaching/ruling function in the church. Once this has been achieved it is then made a matter of confessional status. Those who refuse to do so are then excluded from office and refused the right to teach, and so on. This has happened in a number of fellowships. The concern of the unorthodox for freedom would be much more acceptable if they also had a concern to extend freedom to others. Without that concern it is exposed as empty hypocrisy.

If we are to take Matthew 18:15–20 seriously, it teaches the power of the church to act against a person who persists in a sinful practice. We have seen that involved in this whole issue are matters of denial of Biblical teaching and dishonesty in creedal affirmations. And the heretic is well aware of this situation. That is why he reacts with such righteous indignation when confronted with his duplicity. That is why it is so important to him to use parliamentary manoeuvre to prevent serious open and public debate on the issue. The church has to be kept from seeing clearly the contrast between what the Scriptures and creeds teach and what the heretic teaches. What we need to keep clearly before a man who is undermining the truth of God in the church is not the threat of church action. It is his own duplicity and dishonesty. Only by seeing his own action as sinful will he cease from trying to obtain his ends by underhanded means. Certainly the church may have to act, but let us be sure that the heretic knows in his own heart, despite his public howls of protest, that he acted dishonestly and now pays the price.

What has been said here could easily be understood as a statement that anybody who advocated that women should rule and teach is a heretic who should be dismissed at once from the church. That would be to oversimplify the situation. A man may have many different reasons. He may be honestly confused and swayed by the opinions of others. He may be struggling with his own personal problem of finding the weight of responsibility in a family situation to be more than he can handle. The real test of the heretic is the way he responds to private and public rebuke. We should not assume that he cannot be reclaimed any more than we should refuse to act if rebuke produces further hardening.

We have seen that there is a logic in heresy as there is in the

Biblical system. A man may claim that certain portions of Scripture should be set aside as only applicable to Biblical times. He may see that argument as merely a convenient device to avoid the unpopularity of refusing to adopt the customs of our age. His intent is not initially to conform the church totally to the world and to deny the authority of the rest of Scripture. Yet that is where the logic of the position leads. Confronted with the logic he will have to make a choice. That choice will pull him back to the authority of Scripture or drive him further away from it. The choice he ultimately makes will also reveal the state of his heart. What is more important to him: the authority of Christ speaking in his Word or the esteem of the world? Thus the process described will tend to drive a man in one of two directions. It is a polarizing process.

The description of this process of rebuke and discipline as polarizing will concern many. For them the primary need is peace and harmony at any cost. Therefore it must be pointed out that the gospel itself has this polarizing effect. It is a word of life unto life and death unto death (2 Cor. 2:15,16). Christ came to bring a sword and division (Matt. 10:34–7). We cannot use such passages of Scripture to justify division on false grounds; on the other hand we cannot set them aside. The administratively minded person, who has made the smooth running of the ecclesiastical machinery his only goal, has to be faced with his responsibility to the Lord and to the sheep who are being abandoned to false shepherds.

Once this process of rebuke and discipline has begun we cannot anticipate its conclusion. Indeed it is wrong to have our actions guided by an anticipation that the likely outcome must be this or that. Only our Lord knows the future. Our task is obedience.

THE PRIORITY OF THE PROCLAMATION OF JESUS

In the midst of such turmoil it is easy to lose sight of the whole picture. Preaching which has as its sole concern the protection of the flock against false teaching is unbalanced. There must be such preaching, but it does not exhaust the whole counsel of God. Let us remember that the heresy we are considering springs from two principal sources. One is the conviction that

God is an inactive God who intervenes little in the course of the world. The other is historical relativism which proclaims that anything written in the past cannot be an authority for us today. People with such convictions find it very difficult, if not impossible, to preach with conviction and with relevance. If they carefully limit the areas in which God is inactive, or the time-bound sections of Scripture, then they can continue to apply the Scripture. However, the more the logic of their position works on them, the less they can assure people of the power of God or apply the truth to their hearers. Those to whom they preach are starved of the comforting and motivating truths of God. This is a major factor in the decline of churches which have rejected Scripture, both in congregational numbers and in the numbers of preachers.

We cannot compete in terms of skill at parliamentary manoeuvre or in appeal to currently popular fads. But the people of God ultimately recognize when they are fed with the truth of the Word and when it is otherwise. Let the Word preached sincerely, searchingly, and forcefully be the mark of orthodoxy. We may lose many battles in church and organizations, but ultimately the power of the Word will prevail (Isa. 40:6–8).

Preaching the Word does not absolve us of our responsibility to deal with error. We cannot say that we are preaching the Word and leaving the results to God if by this we mean that we are allowing those gathered by the Word to be delivered to false teachers. That is a denial of the pastor's calling (Acts 20:28–31).

The priority on the preaching of the Word should alert us to the danger of the centralization of the church in massive and dangerous bureaucracies. We have seen that for some bureaucracy is a necessity. For us it is not. The real work of the church takes place not in central offices but out where men and women are discipled to follow Christ. Of course it is claimed that these bureaucrats assist in preparing and training the church for the discipling function. However one man giving an example of how it is actually done has a far more powerful impact than twenty men writing studies on how it should be done. Paul led the way to missionary work by example. It was as the problems arose in concrete situations that he dealt with them. That is the example we must also set.

This priority upon the real work of bringing men to Christ and teaching them will help us avoid the tendency to support and promote men according to parties. Sometimes men who are not really gifted in the major pastoral and evangelistic tasks have been promoted and supported for positions by an orthodox party. Such party-thinking is the denial of real orthodoxy. It is better to say openly that there is nobody presently suitable for a certain position than to appoint an ungifted man. It may be objected that to do such will ensure the appointment of an unorthodox man. But such political thinking is a denial of the power of God for which we claim to stand. Those whose concern is only party advantage, who constantly manoeuvre with that end in view, may win a few battles, but the final battle is decided by the Lord.

This does not exclude being wise as serpents as well as innocent as doves. There are manoeuvres we can anticipate and block. Yet to place an ungifted man in office is a denial of God's command. Since we rely upon God we cannot disobey him, no matter what the circumstances. To act pragmatically is to do what we accuse others of doing. Further we create future problems for the church. Our concern is not that our party win. It is that Christ be glorified through his people. We must remember that the battle is his, not ours.

Similarly, in other ways our concern must be for a clear conscience in the sight of God. Those for whom God is a distant God may take advantage of our scruples, but it will not be to their ultimate advantage. God and God alone controls the outcome.

❧ 26 ❧

The Political and Social Task of the Church

THE ALTERNATIVE MODEL

Those who reject the Scripture as their authority are not without an alternative rôle for the church. Indeed, that rôle is often very clear in their thinking and propaganda. It is essentially a political and social rôle.

This rôle follows as part of the system we have been considering. If God does not intervene in the world, how are the evils that beset the world to be corrected? It cannot be by God intervening in judgment, since his action is excluded in the theological system. It cannot be by the hearts of men being changed by the Spirit of God, because that once more would mean an action by God in the world. What then is the alternative? It must be by human action, that is to say, by concerted human political and social action. The rôle of the church becomes one of stimulating, facilitating, and participating in this political and social action.

There is a further problem which must be resolved. What direction should reform take? It is one thing to realize that the world is in a mess. It is another to decide on the direction which reform should take. Here the man who doubts Scripture has a problem. If the Bible is not accurate, how can it be used as a source of guidance on political and social reform? If it is bound to its own time and cultural situation, how can it give us guidance today?

This problem is rarely faced directly. Often the answer is supplied by another of those unexplained insights into the 'real' meaning of Scripture. By some intuition that is not concerned with what the text says (or fails to say) we learn what the

'Christian' political or socio-economic position is. The older liberalism was very much influenced by the conviction of the innate goodness of mankind. All men needed was to be told of the Fatherhood of God and the brotherhood of man. They would then want to do the right thing. More recent expressions of liberalism are aware that the problem is more difficult. Furthermore, they do not recognize the sinfulness of every man. Instead they attribute it to one particular group. Often they follow Marx and see this group as the capitalist or wealthy group.

We have to acknowledge the major influence of a general Christian world-view on Marx. His system hopes for a better future. In that sense it is reformist. Reformist movements in Europe generally arise from a secularization of Christian hope. Hence Marx's secularized hope is attractive to others with a secularized Christianity.

Marx's view, however, has some elements which are typically non-Christian. It is common for the non-Christian to locate the source of evil not in man but in the way the world is structured. Marxism is not as naïve as the old Liberalism. It does recognize that something is wrong. However it makes the wrong a structural matter – the present class structure and the economic system. The Marxist analysis of the cause of the evils of the modern world is attractive to those who generally feel that something is wrong and something needs to be done. Thus they have a reformist inclination. Yet because they have rejected Scripture, they lack a way to analyse the problem correctly.

There are several reasons why a right-wing view has no appeal for such people. One of them, paradoxically, stems from the strong Deist influence on right-wing thought.

We have seen that Deism is characterized by denial of God's direct action on the world. The Deists faced Christian objections that the world needed such intervention. The Deists argued that the world was made to run without interference and what we might call sins are necessary for its operation. Adam Smith turned these ideas into the classic defence of non-interventionist economics. He claimed that the economic system worked best when left to run by itself. What ensured its success when there was no intervention was human greed. The producer of goods, in order to maximize his own profit, is forced to make his wares as good as possible and as cheap as possible. Hence human sin, in this case greed, is turned from something requiring intervention to what will ensure that the system works without interferences. The whole tendency of the argument, therefore, is not to define a proper rôle for state interference. It is to deny the need for interference. Where this has influenced political thinking it has led to the attitude that things will operate pretty well as long as they are left to themselves. But this attitude is anathema to the person of reformist tendency. He also does not ask the question of the legitimate form of state action. He looks to the state as the saviour. Such hope in the state is but the logical extension of the idea that hope for mankind lies in human political action. Obviously the more power a saviour has, the better. Hence the hope for mankind is seen in the unlimited exercise of state power. Such thinking logically disposes a person to accept Marxism.

THE ALLEGED FAILURE OF ORTHODOXY

It is commonly asserted that religious orthodoxy has been oblivious to its social and political responsibilities, especially its responsibility to the needy and the oppressed. Often a contrast is drawn between caring for the material needs of the under-privileged and preaching the gospel to them.

A look at the record of orthodoxy would seem to be enough to refute this charge. One could list the rôle of Christians in establishing political freedom, in the antislavery crusade, in the reform of working conditions, in establishing schools and hospitals. The long history of medical and educational mission-ary work has its origins in orthodox, evangelical missions. Many of those missions or churches may now have been captured by unorthodox elements (and hence are finding it difficult to keep up the supply of missionaries) but the origins will time and time again prove to have been in groups who did make the Scripture their authority.

Why then the charge made repeatedly against orthodoxy? Part of it we can dismiss as simple debating tactics. It is repeated by people who have heard the charge and have not bothered to investigate the history of orthodox political and social concern.

Part of it is justified simply because we could have done more. There are many areas in which our human sloth and sinfulness have meant that the effort could have been greater. There has been in some quarters a reaction against the socio-political emphasis of those who deny the Bible. Rather than be seen to be theologically liberal, people have reacted against that concern. In some cases the influence of right-wing Deist thinking, as described above, has simply led to the assumption that all we have to do is to end state intervention in the economy and wealth will come to all.

Partly it is a take over of non-Christian accusations. Those who deny the truth of the Bible are cast adrift from it as their absolute standard. Thus they meet with difficulties when faced with the charges of the unbeliever. They cannot simply use the Scripture to determine whether the charges are false or not. The unbeliever often sees freedom as freedom from all re-straints on his behaviour. That means that even sinful conduct should be free from restraints. The Christian's insistence that man must obey God is then a denial of his freedom. This issue arises particularly in sexual matters. The Christian insists that God created men and women for separate rôles and tasks. He insists upon sexual fidelity within marriage and rejects homosexuality. This the unbeliever sees as a denial of freedom. He calls it sexist or discriminatory. Those within the church who are adrift from any really secure anchorage are perplexed at such questions. They generally do not want to go all the way with the promiscuous world. They retain enough of Biblical values to want to use words like 'love', 'faithfulness', 'enduring and stable relationships'. Yet they are uncertain how far to go in opening the door to an unbiblical confusion of rôles and sexual promiscuity. While trying to hold on to some values they are adrift in the current of non-Christian thinking. Hence they tend to repeat the non-Christian accusations against the Biblical position.

These are all reasons for the accusations against orthodoxy. Yet there is another, more basic and fundamental. It is that the form of orthodox action does not assume the priority of political action. It does not see the state as the great saviour. Another way of saying this is to say that its priority has been the preaching of the gospel. This is often called an individualistic approach since it has a concern for the conversion of the individual. The influence of Marx, even upon people who would not realize their debt to Marx, has been to see people in terms of groups – classes, workers, employers, etc. It has been to put emphasis upon institutions like the state and the trade unions. The gospel addressed to people, irrespective of their class position, as creatures responsible before a holy God, cuts across a whole way of thinking. It does not negate the state but defines its rôle in a very different way. Those who see the state as saviour are unwilling to go back to examine the whole basis of their faith in the state. It is much simpler to castigate the Christian position for ignoring the political. Similarly those who are unsure about the Scripture as a basis for our whole understanding of the rôle of the Christian in the world, who are unsure whether the preached gospel can bring real change because they doubt the work of the Spirit, are liable to repeat the charge that orthodoxy is ignoring its political and social responsibility.

THE PRIORITY OF THE GOSPEL

'Jesus came into Galilee, preaching the gospel of God, and saying, "The time is fulfilled, and the kingdom of God is at hand; repent and believe the gospel" ' (Mark 1:14,15).

Jesus came preaching and demanding repentance and faith. The apostles did the same. Where that is devalued, we have a departure from the Christian faith. Criticism of preaching is really criticism of Jesus. Certainly this does not exclude a rôle for Christian political and social action. As we shall see, it gives it a major rôle. However the primary point needs to be stressed. The gospel was originally brought to man by Jesus as a demand that men turn from their sin and turn to God.

This presupposes that men have a relationship with God their Creator and Lord. That presupposition is frequently denied today. It is asserted that men in poverty cannot understand the gospel until their physical needs have been met. It is asserted that men under political oppression cannot understand the gospel until they are politically free.

[250]

In order to discuss this contention we have to make a qualification. A man may be so sick from starvation that he cannot comprehend anything that is said to him, whether it is the gospel or anything else. If that is his condition he could not understand a call to political revolution either. Naturally food and medical attention come first in such a case.

The real issue is where men are not at the point of death. Can the gospel mean anything to a man in poverty or under political oppression? Another way of asking the same question is to ask whether his relationship to his physical circumstances must take priority over his relationship to God.

Scripture is very clear about the priority of the relationship to God. That was the issue in Jesus' first temptation (Matt. 4:1–4). Jesus criticized the Jews for seeking the bread that perishes. He said that the important thing was believing in the one God had sent (John 6:26–29). The purpose of Israel's sojourn in the wilderness was so that they could learn the right priorities: 'And He humbled you and let you be hungry, and fed you with manna . . . that He might make you understand that man does not live by bread alone, but man lives by everything that proceeds out of the mouth of the Lord' (Deut. 8:3). Elijah settled the question of who was the true God before the drought was broken (1 Kings 18).

Really the issue here is a very simple but fundamental one. Is man's relationship to the rest of creation more important than his relationship to God? That is what people are claiming who say that a man must be well provided for physically and politically before he can listen to God. It puts man's circumstances first and God second.

One can understand a Marxist saying such a thing. For somebody who claims to be a Christian to say it shows great confusion. Our first concern has to be God. The first commandment, as Jesus said, directs us to God (Matt. 22:34–40).

THE MAN ADDRESSED BY THE GOSPEL

The gospel comes with a demand for repentance. That is because it is addressed to a sinner. Those sins are not only against God. They are also against man. The gospel comes to a man who is in a network of responsibilities and relationships. It demands his repentance for what he has done in those situations.

Many examples could be given of this in Scripture. Thus Jesus welcomed Zacchaeus' decision to give to the poor and to restore what he had wrongly taken (Luke 19:1–10). John the Baptist told tax-gatherers and soldiers not to use their positions to extort money (Luke 3:12–14). When Paul had the opportunity to speak with Felix he talked about 'righteousness, self-control and the judgment to come' (Acts 24:25). James warned the rich of the judgment that must come to those who had defrauded a workman of his wages (James 5:1–6).

The gospel demands repentance from the way we have treated our fellow men. Instructions to Christians demand that we treat others in a way commensurate with the gospel. We have the instructions that specifically address men in their various family and other relationships (e.g. Eph. 5:22–6:9). Thus a gospel in which repentance from sin plays a rôle leads naturally to a Christian life in which obedience to God's law plays a rôle.

It has to be admitted that these notes have been lost or muted in certain sections of evangelicalism. Just as there is a temptation to accept the non-Christian view that man's problem is basically a political one, so there has been acceptance of the view that it is basically psychological. It consists in alienation and loneliness. Hence the exclusive portrayal of Jesus as a friend. Man is addressed as lost and confused and the aspect of his own responsibility is minimized as a result. This has combined with an antipathy to the law of God in some circles. But if there is no demand for repentance and no standard for the Christian life, then man's inhumanity to man goes uncondemned and unrebuked.

The answer to this is not to replace one un-Biblical emphasis by another. It is not to replace the exclusively inward and introspective emphasis of the psychological 'gospel' by the exclusively exterior and public emphasis of the political 'gospel'. God sets rules that cover everything from what a man thinks in his heart, to the way in which he acts in his intimate family circle, and to the way in which he acts to his workmen, and also to the way the ruler governs his kingdom. Many of the problems we are here considering flow from an attempt to restrict the law of God to part of this wide domain. There is teaching which would give the impression that all that matters is what goes on in the mind. If one's thoughts dwell upon Jesus all the time, then little more is asked. Other teaching makes Christianity an ethic of the family. Then again there are those who give the impression that the law of God addresses only corporate managers and leaders with a nuclear arsenal.

Each of these positions has its own moral agenda. Some delight in calling the others moralistic, Pharisaic, legalistic, and puritanical. When Christians speak of the violation of God's rules in sexual matters they are often scorned as legalistic by those who want a political ethic. Yet these latter are very moralistic when laying down the law to those whose political or ethical views disagree with their own. What is needed is not such hypocritical name-calling. What is needed is the application of the Word of God to all areas of life.

THE RÔLE OF THE STATE

We have seen that views influenced by Marxism look to the state as the saviour. We have also seen that right-wing views, influenced by Deism, tend to minimize the rôle of the state. The problem with both of these models is that they consider the state as an all-pervading entity. They do not ask the question of the purpose of the state.

When the author of Judges drew a moral from that period it was one of the need for kingship: 'In those days there was no king in Israel; everyone did what was right in his own eyes' (Judges 21:25). When Paul summed up the function of the ruler, his emphasis was also very much upon the judicial aspect (Rom. 13:1–7). This way of thinking of the state is consistent with the Biblical emphasis upon the sinfulness of man. There is need for a restraint upon the expression of that sinful nature. However the state cannot eradicate the sinful heart. All it can do is restrict its expression by punishing certain manifestations of it. To the extent that the sinfulness of man has led to the creation of unjust societal institutions, the state has a responsibility to abolish such abuses. However, changes to the structure of society will not deal with the problem in men's hearts. Hence the Biblical view does not at all support those whose faith is in the state. Yet neither may we approve the slogan, 'The best government is the government that governs least'. That comes out of a belief in the innate goodness of man.

THE CHURCH AND THE STATE

The state has to punish evil. To do this it has to know what evil is. Generally a state will act in terms of an understanding of sin found in its own particular society. This takes us back to the point made in chapter 24. Men have some understanding of the requirements of God's law. Hence there will be some overlap between the moral consciousness of the rulers and the law of God. Often very little of that overlap may seem obvious from the way he actually rules, but it is there. The church has the greatest impact upon the state when it awakens and develops that overlap. That is to say, when the church is preaching the full-orbed law of God as God's standard, it has its greatest impact upon the state.

Such witness involves an address to those in positions of authority, demanding that they rule justly. We have already seen examples of this. To these we might add Paul's constant attempt to call to his aid the principles of Roman law. Obviously it was to his advantage to do so. Yet his action was more than mere pragmatism. If the rôle of the state is to commend the righteous (Rom. 13:3), then it makes sense that the righteous call upon the state for support. One can note particularly Paul's strategy in demanding public exoneration when falsely punished (Acts 16:35–39).

Thus the church's address to the government, as to every man, is in terms of the rights and wrongs of God's law. The church loses its real impact when, accepting the priority of the political, it addresses the government in political terms. This happens when the church instead of warning of God's judgment merely warns of the loss of Christian votes! The church here has fallen into the trap often set by the non-Christian media. The media deliberately select the unbalanced, sensation-seeking elements of Christian opinion to interview on many moral issues. They give an unbalanced, extremist threat of judgment. Rather than appear like them, many Christians then try to speak the 'accepted' language and talk only in terms of Christian votes. But this reduces the church to just another pressure group among many.

The same thing is happening when speakers in the name of Christianity threaten violence. It means that they have accepted the priority of political means. It makes no difference if it is a right-wing person threatening to blow up an abortion clinic or a left-wing person supporting Marxist terrorist murders. Both have accepted that human force is the best means to achieve the church's ends.

When the church has become allied with a non-Christian political movement, it must also lose its impact. Politically it may gain a temporary advantage, since it makes that political movement appear stronger. Should the political movement it supports win, then it will not thank Christians for having realized its truth. It will expect the church to continue its uncritical support. Should it lose, the church also is discredited.

We have already seen the inability of many, who urge a political rôle for the church, to take a critical attitude to Marxism. They share too many of its premises to stand apart from it. Hence the liberal church, as represented by the World Council of Churches, seems incapable of bringing the law of God to bear against Communist countries. Their silence on the persecution of Christians in Communist lands, their acceptance of churches which refuse to side with persecuted fellow believers in their own lands, is a denial of Christian compassion. Certainly, being representatives of numerically large groups, World Council leaders will receive some political respect. Nevertheless the Communist must despise them in his heart for their abandonment of their fellow believers and their fear of criticizing left-wing causes. And the politicians of the West must despise their echoing of the Communist line. When those who advocate that the church should possess a greater political concern and political voice, and urge that it should do so by the World Council of Churches, then they lose all credibility. Theirs is not a voice. It is an echo.

That is not to say that the church should be afraid to speak God's Word to the rulers of the West. Ethically they are often no different from the Communist. The ultimate struggle is not East versus West. It is right versus wrong. Many in the West have seen the battle against Communism as the only battle.

Hence any means are legitimate in that battle. The support of governments and movements as unjust as any Communist government, simply because they are supposedly anti-Communist, is morally unjustifiable and hence politically foolish. Many Western leaders think tactically like Communists. They may be virulently anti-Communist but they have already lost the battle. If the church cannot bring God's Word to bear on that, even as it brings God's Word to bear on Communism, then the church has become trapped in a human political system.

THE SOCIAL RÔLE OF THE CHURCH

In the present debate it is hard to distinguish the church's rôle in social problems from its political rôle. That is because the assumption of many is that social problems are to be solved by government action. That thinking flows once more from the assumption that the state is the saviour. If the rôle of the state is to restrain evil rather than eradicate it, then the whole question has to be re-evaluated.

A further factor which has shaped opinions on social problems is belief in environmental determinism. It declares that people are incapable of doing anything about their situation. They are the victims of their environment. This leads to the idea that all that can be done for such people is to provide for their needs until the state changes their environment. When such groups in depressed environments are also racially distinct, a similarly defeatist view is taken by right-wing thought. There has been a debate this century over whether man's condition is determined by his environment or by his heredity.[1]

Left-wing thought has generally been inclined to see the environment as the determining factor. Hence there is hope that by changing the environment, man may be improved. Right-wing thought has tended to see heredity as crucial.

[1] For a survey of the conflict between hereditary and environment views see H. Cravens, *The Triumph of Evolution. American Scientists and the Heredity-Environment Controversy 1900–1941*, Philadelphia, Univ. of Pennsylvania, 1978. This work is somewhat inaccurate in suggesting that the environment view is more in line with Darwinian evolution.

Certain races or groups are doomed by their heredity to an inferior position.

Hence we find left-wing thought tending to say that such groups cannot change because they are environmentally determined. Right-wing thought tends to say they are shaped by their biological inheritance. So both come to the same conclusion. Their situation is practically hopeless. The people in the situation can do nothing.

If we are to take a view of the situation which is both Biblical and true to their situation, we will avoid determinisms. We will avoid a superficial assigning of blame. Such people may be the victims of oppression and exploitation by other elements in the population. They may be exploited by elements in their own social or racial sub-group. They may be the victims of their own sin. All these factors may be part of the situation in various degrees. Yet it is not true, whatever the situation, that there is nothing they can do. For God demands that all men everywhere repent and believe the gospel (Acts 17:30). That is the primary need they have. To make any physical or political need more important is to deny the gospel.

The consequences of that repentance and faith may be various. If their sin has contributed to their situation, then there may be a real and definite improvement in their physical situation. If they have been involved in the oppression and exploitation of others, their repentance may have a beneficial influence on the whole community. On the other hand, their becoming Christians may worsen their physical situation. They may be subjected to harassment, persecution, and the stealing of their goods. Notice the way the believers are commended in Hebrews 10:32–9. They had patiently endured persecution and robbery knowing that they had a better and abiding possession reserved for them. A believer may suffer a decline in his income simply because he now recognizes that some of the ways he formerly earned it were contrary to God's revealed will.

It is therefore superficial to suggest that if people would simply obey God, then their physical situation would automatically improve. Such attempts to blame people completely for their situations are as superficial as the attempt to absolve them automatically of all blame on the ground that they are the victims of the environment. The situation is complex. Yet whatever the situation the command of God is unchanged. God is to be feared, obeyed, and worshipped by men in whatever situation.

It is necessary to maintain that those in depressed situations have their own responsibilities to God. Nevertheless that is but part of the story. Their fellow Christians also have a responsibility to them. They are to share their riches with them in order to provide for their physical needs. If humanists have an emphasis on providing for people's physical needs, they have learned it from us. The Scripture is insistent that where there is no practical compassion for the needy there is also no real godliness or faith. This book is largely about the danger to the church of a departure from the doctrine taught in the Word of God. Yet it must be said that the danger of departure from the love of Christ to the needy is every bit as great. In his first letter John singles out two things which show that a man is not a Christian, no matter what he claims. One is doctrinal: denial that Jesus is the Christ, the Son of God (2:22,23;3:23). The second is practical: failure to demonstrate practical love to a brother in need (3:14–18; 4:7–12). Let it be said again: where there is not that ministry of compassion and love to fellow believers, there the Christian faith has been denied.

This ministry also needs to be a solidarity with those under oppression for their faith. The believers are commended in Hebrews 10:33, 34 because they shared with those who were persecuted and showed sympathy to prisoners. 'I was in prison, and you came to Me', says Jesus (Matt. 25:36). We have to acknowledge before God our sin in showing so little compassion to our impoverished fellow believers. And we have to acknowledge it also in showing so little compassion to our fellow Christians who suffer persecution. How have we shown our solidarity with them?

There are many who claim to be Christian and yet reject the Word of God. They much prefer a Marxist message. Their defence is to criticize the orthodox church for its lack of concern for the poor and needy. Some of that criticism is unjust. Yet we must acknowledge to our shame that some of it is just. Yet in their espousal of Marxism there is an obvious and glaring problem, for Marxist governments are some of the major persecutors of Christians. When such so-called Christians accept and extol Marxism, when they accept and embrace the official 'church' of Marxist lands that turns its back upon the persecuted believers in their own lands, where then is the compassion of Christ?

Thus the task of the church is to bring the gospel to man. Yet the moment the gospel is received, a responsibility is placed upon the whole Christian community. Here then is a Christian brother. He is to be taught and nurtured. If he is needy we must share with him. If he is oppressed we must stand with him. If he is sick we must seek to help him. The church cannot avoid a social concern and a ministry of mercy because it has brothers in all those who love Christ.

So far the emphasis has been upon the church's responsibility to fellow believers. What of its responsibility to men in general? Some would deny such general responsibility. Others would emphasize it to the extent that it absorbs specific responsibility to Christians. One passage of Scripture succinctly gives the answer. 'So then, while we have opportunity, let us do good to all men, and especially to those who are of the household of the faith' (Gal. 6:10). It is not wrong for the church to seek to meet the physical needs of men in general. Indeed the Christian is positively commanded to do so. However the fellow believer has the first demand upon his compassion. It is not a matter of either/or. It is a matter of priorities.

THE CHURCH'S RESPONSIBILITY TO THE CHURCH

So far the discussion has concerned the church's responsibility to a fellow believer. There is also another set of responsibilities. Suppose a church is not living up to its responsibilities, Suppose a church is discouraged. Suppose a church is in danger of falling away from the grace of Christ. Do other churches have a responsibility to that church?

We are our brother's keeper. We as Christians are part of one body. Suffering or weakness in a part has an effect on the whole. Hence we do have responsibilities to other parts of the body of Christ.

Yet how often do we see these exercised? Instead, there tends to prevail a spirit of indifference to others. One church will watch another decline and die, like a man watching another man drowning without doing a thing. Obviously this should not be.

In what areas should we be particularly concerned for the welfare of another church? Should it apply to doctrinal matters only? Should the church's political and social rôle also be included?

The answer to these questions is reasonably straightforward. Wherever obedience to Christ is concerned, there we have to encourage or admonish our brethren. Hence the range of concerns must be as wide as the teaching of God's Word.

This question has been raised particularly where it is felt that a church has not been faithful in suitably admonishing or opposing the government of its particular nation. Given the tendency of many churches to be uncritical of Marxist states this concern has often been expressed particularly where the state concerned is a right-wing one. The churches which do not admonish Marxist governments are less criticized.

Yet the question raised is one of principle. Is a church unfaithful if it does not admonish its government? Is it unfaithful if it does not advise its members to take political action against that government?

The difficulty with saying that a church must always admonish the state is that in certain states this will bring down even more persecution on the church. We can expect that they will show solidarity with fellow believers in prison or under persecution. We have no Biblical warrant for saying that the church must on every occasion admonish the state. The instructions in the New Testament letters do not indicate that the church was required or expected to take up every issue with the state.

However, where the church is not under persecution, the situation may be different. We in free states have an obligation to our persecuted brethren in other lands. We can address their persecutors with the requirements of God.

What is the responsibility of churches in free states to their own governments? Admonishing them does not expose us to the danger of seeking martyrdom. We do have a responsibility to bring the truth of God to all men, and rulers are obviously included in this. But when is the church bringing the truth of God and when is it echoing the clichés of a particular political position?

In general those churches which are favourable to left-wing political positions tend to raise such issues against right-wing governments as lack of government social services and discrimination. Those favourable to right-wing political positions tend to raise questions such as sexual issues and abortion. Can we escape from this obvious captivity of the church to political movements?

The only way we can escape is to apply the whole teaching of God's Word. Not until the church does that will it deserve respect from unbelieving governments.

To outline the way in which this should be done would take many chapters. All that I will do is give some illustrations. To some people these illustrations may not go far enough. Others may differ at particular points. My sole concern with these illustrations is to argue that there are ways to approach such subjects which attempt to be faithful to Scripture but do not bind us to a particular political camp.

(i) *Racism*

Scripture is emphatic that the church must be multi-racial (Col. 3:11; Gal. 3:28). A practical division can be defended on linguistic grounds where Christians cannot understand each other's language since the word has to be understood to edify (1 Cor. 14). But division on racial or cultural grounds alone can never be justified. If the state should by any law attempt directly or indirectly to prevent the church having a multi-racial character, then that must be opposed and resisted by the church.

When we pass to the question of a multi-racial state then the issues are not so clear. Should a multi-racial state aim at full integration or at the separate development of its racial groups? I do not think there is any warrant for saying the one is right and the other wrong. However the matter does not stop there. Suppose a state decides on either forced integration or forced segregation. How is it exercising its God-given rôle to suppress evil in so doing? Neither integration nor separate development can be called evil in themselves. Thus the moment the state applies force in this matter, it exceeds its authority and becomes an oppressor. The matter is aggravated if there are other clear transgressions of the law of God. For example if a state uses a racist doctrine to rupture a multi-racial church or a multi-racial family, then it would defy God and should be admonished by the church. If the state should show indifference to the matter of equal justice for all races or allow one race to exploit another, then it has failed in its task of administering justice.

(ii) *Private property*

One cannot say on the basis of Scripture that private property is of itself wrong. Neither may one say that it is wrong to hold property as community property. Suppose a government should attempt to force a tribal group to divide tribal land into individual portions. That would be an unjust act because the holding of tribal land is not wrong. Suppose a state, in the name of socialism, should try to appropriate all land. That would be equally wrong. In both cases the state has no authority for its action.

It is the unjustified force which creates problems with socialism or Communism. Yet that is not of itself a defence of capitalism as it presently operates. One of the major problems of Communism is found also in the capitalism of the large corporations. That is, both deny to the labourer a share in the products of his own labour. The labourer receives a fixed wage irrespective of the effort he expends or the profitability of the enterprise in which he is engaged. This is quite contrary to the Biblical principle (1 Cor.9:6–10). It would therefore be perfectly consistent with a Biblical view for the state to punish an employer who failed to share the profits of his enterprise with his workmen.

This case may serve as an illustration of the fact that a Biblical position sets us free from both wings of political thought. Right-wing thought has followed the Deist lead of Adam Smith into making greed a virtue. Therefore the employer is seen as having an absolute right to maximize profits. If the workman gets no reward for his particular industry, that is of no concern. Hence right-wing thought would reject the position proposed here. On the other hand left-wing theory has stressed the central rôle of the government.

That leads to a system of centralized wage fixing. What is suggested here runs counter to that because it allows a wide variation between rates of pay depending on the diligence of the workmen and the profitability of the particular enterprise. Of course there must also be opportunity for the owner to enjoy the fruits of his enterprise. Where that is taken away, as by socialism, then the same teaching of Scripture is violated. The way in which we should defend a non-socialist system is not by following the lead of Adam Smith and making greed a virtue. It is by appeal to the Biblical principle that every man has a right to enjoy the fruit of his labours.

(iii) *Sexual immorality*

One of the common characteristics of non-Christian thought in our day is the defence and promotion of sexual immorality. This promotion is both direct and indirect. There is the argument that people should not be bound by antiquated Christian taboos. There is also support for divorce, which is itself often a consequence of sexual unfaithfulness.

The law of God is very clear in these matters. Sexual relations outside marriage are forbidden, as is the breaking of marriage.

It is in matters like this that the question is often raised: should a Christian morality be forced upon non-Christians? This way of putting the question tends to prejudice the answer. It ignores the fact that the state has to enforce some sort of morality. The state may pretend to be enforcing a 'democratic' morality but it is never really doing so. Very few issues are ever solved by a referendum of the people on the specific issue. Given that man is sinful, and given the relative weakness and cowardice of the church in our day, such a referendum might result in more chaos than we already have. The state by its legislative and judicial actions does enforce a morality. The fact that it may be a very low level of morality should not blind us to the fact that it is a morality.

The question then becomes: what morality should the state enforce? The state may have to settle for less than it wants simply because of the hardness of men's hearts. We have an example of action taken to regulate a crime, rather than to eliminate it, in the Old Testament divorce law (Deut. 24:1–4).

How far law may go will in practice be linked to the diligence of the church in expounding the law of God in that nation.

Nevertheless the standard is clear. Sexual immorality is wrong and the rupture of marriage is wrong. That was the morality set by the one who created man. It is therefore the best morality for man. The fact that the non-Christian may not want to recognize that fact does not remove it as a fact. The state may find it practically difficult to enforce legislation based on the fact because of the hardness of men's hearts, but it still remains a fact.

Certainly the direction of any state programme on this matter should be towards discouraging the widespread immorality which prevails in our society. A closely connected matter is that of responsibility for the financial consequences of this immorality. A major part of government spending for the needy is spent to support illegitimate children and deserted or divorced families. In spite of all the rhetoric about women's rights and children's rights, we have created a system allowing men maximum sexual indulgence without their facing the responsibilities. Those who condone immorality or divorce are condoning the attitude of male society which wants pleasure but no responsibility. The problem is reaching such dimensions that the ability of the state to fulfil its other obligations is increasingly in question. The level of taxes needed to sustain this burden, in practice, tends to rob a man of the fruits of his labour. The question is becoming no longer one of whether the state can enforce a Christian morality in sexual matters. It is becoming one of whether the state can survive if it does not. Those who see a 'Christian' position as being simply to demand more payments by the state to the needy are being simplistic and failing to go to the root of the problem.

Scripture is very clear that a man has the responsibility to provide for his family. If a man engenders children, they are his responsibility. The modern state has allowed men to abdicate that responsibility and has shifted the burden on to the whole community. That becomes then a case of rewarding the unrighteous by removing his obligations and punishing the righteous. If the state is to perform its God-given functions of ensuring justice, it must attend to this matter.

[264]

CONCLUSION

The issues so far raised illustrate the complexity of the issue. It may be suggested that the suggestions made as to a Christian position on some of these issues are simplistic due to the complexity of the issues themselves. The objection certainly has weight, but where does it leave us? To take up issues not considered here and to ignore the one considered here would also be simplistic. We must remember also the context of this particular discussion: where is one church required to or justified in admonishing another church for failure to live up to responsibilities, especially responsibilities to admonish the state?

It is this uncertainty about the complexity of the issues which has tended to keep the church from speaking clearly and effectively on such issues. The confident voices have tended to be those motivated by a political philosophy and unwilling to face the differences between their philosophy and the teaching of Scripture.

We must remember that there is a connection between what God requires of the church and what the church says to the state. That is not because the tasks or laws for church and state are identical. It is because there is a congruence between them. Let us suppose the church has ignored Christ's injunction to preach the good news to the poor and afflicted. It has become a church consisting only of the affluent members of the society. If the position of that affluent element is linked with some injustice, it is difficult for the church to recognize and face the difficulties. Similarly, if the church has allowed itself, either because of political pressure, or purely social pressure, to be the church of one racial group alone, then its ability to speak is severely impaired. It is not merely that its credibility is impaired. It is also that it lacks the first-hand experience of the needs and the problems.

No amount of political posturing on the part of the church can really compensate for its failure. Much of the political and social criticism that comes from churches deserves to be ignored because it is an attempt to absolve the consciences of churches who have ignored their own responsibility. Of course an inter-relationship can develop here. There is a certain belief which leads to the preaching of the gospel. Where secular views undermine confidence in the power of God to change hearts, then the gospel is not preached, especially where it is anticipated that people may be hard to reach. If no change is being produced in society by the preaching of the gospel, then there is all the more reason to look to political action as the only hope.

If the gospel is preached with the genuine intent of establishing churches which are multi-racial and multi-class, then several things follow. When lives are changed and people live in obedience to God, many social problems are solved. Furthermore if Christians are living and working in such areas, many opportunities to do good to believers and unbelievers arise naturally. Finally if those who are oppressed and subjected to injustice are now believers, there is an increased obligation on the part of the whole church to stand with them. The church is better able, from involvement and experience, to discern who is actually at fault in these situations.

These advantages do not follow on the alternative model which substitutes political action for the gospel. People in the situation are not changed, and a first-hand involvement of Christians in the situation is absent. Of course, if the gospel is preached but believers fail to stand with fellow believers who are oppressed, then much of the politico-social consequences of the gospel are lost.

Thus if the church is performing its function, it not only has its own influence on society. It can speak more accurately and more assuredly to the state. It is in this sense that there is a congruence between the functions of state and church.

In other ways also the church has to be true to its calling. Suppose the church takes the attitude that sexual immorality amongst youth is a fact of life to be tolerated. Suppose it regards divorce amongst Christians as sad but inevitable. Then it obviously cannot address the state with any conviction in the areas of sexual immorality. It will be inclined to argue that the problems which follow from immorality should be resolved by more state financial aid to the illegitimate and the deserted.

A Biblical principle found in Deuteronomy 24:16 says that the child is not to suffer for the sins of his father. It is not right to demand that the illegitimate child live in poverty because of the

[266]

sins of the parent which brought him to life. The source of his support can itself be a question.

First call is upon the parents, then the wider community. The way the wider community meets that need, and the rôle of the government in meeting that need, is an issue which needs to be thought through. Yet whatever arrangement is made for meeting that need, ultimate success depends upon dealing with the problem itself. If illegitimacy and desertion continue at high rates, they will ultimately exceed the capacity or the willingness of the larger community to deal with the issue. If the church has accepted the inevitability of unfaithfulness within its own community, then it can say nothing to the wider community. If the church has lived according to God's law then it can hold forth that standard to others.[1]

The matter of the fair wage, or the fair reward for labour, might be one that would seem to affect the church less. Yet subtle influences are still there. Three sorts of wage-fixing principles are usually at work. One is the principle that encourages the employer to keep the wages as low as possible to maximize his profit. The second is what we often find when socialist governments are in power. The wage is fixed centrally according to the perceived need of the worker. The result is often that the employee is robbed of his incentive. Thirdly, Communist systems adjust wages according to the perceived needs of the state.

It has been suggested here that a system more in line with Biblical principles would allow for incentives for individual industry and for the sharing of profits between employers and workers. A Christian who attempted to put such a principle into action could find himself under fire from employers who felt the wages he paid were too high, from unions who resist the idea of workers being paid according to ability and initiative, or from the political supporters of each group. Obviously there

[1]What is said here is not meant to imply that the church cannot receive those who have formerly been unfaithful. Obviously forgiveness must extend to those who have sinned. The crucial point is whether they are expected to do what is humanly possible to restore the damage caused by their sin. For example, does the repentant person have a responsibility to attempt to mend a broken marriage or to care for an illegitimate child? As long as the church does not compromise that standard, it can still hold a standard before the community.

would be a need for Christian solidarity with the person attempting a better pay scale.

There is a subtler angle. Would those who are paid by the church desire that an element of flexibility be introduced into their arrangements? That is, that there be pay, in some degree, on the basis of performance? The difficulty men have in preaching and pastoring without a confidence in Scripture has already been emphasized. They do not produce and are perceived not to produce by those they serve. Hence liberal churches often have financial problems. Suppose a man knows that his members are reluctant to pay his salary. Suppose he knows they are reluctant to pay for the increasing number of bureaucrats his theological party desire. Will he approve introducing flexibility, incentive, and freedom into the way the church pays wages? Obviously that would threaten his liveli-hood. A man will naturally carry over his own fears about a non-centralized wage-fixing system into his thinking about the economy in general.

These examples all make the same point. If the church is obedient as the church, its opportunities for addressing the state increases. If it fails as a church, no amount of moralistic political pronouncements will compensate.

Hence our first question when we decide whether we should admonish another church should be a question about that church as a church, not as a political lobby group. Has it been living as the church lives? Or has it been influenced by racism, social prejudice, immorality, and greed? Has it sought, accord-ing to the means provided by Christ, to preach the gospel to all men? That is, not the false political 'gospel', but the Biblical gospel of freedom from sins through the sacrificial death and glorious physical resurrection of Christ.

Generally, if it has failed in these things, its message to the state, however shrill with the sounds of a loved political cause, will lack authenticity and power. If it has lived according to the gospel it may be expected to be a power in the state and an influence for good. If not, the problem is likely to be found in some misunderstanding: a belief that the law of God cannot apply to the unbeliever, an exaltation of suffering to the point that it excludes the importance of pressing for removal of injustice. However, such problems are the less common ones.

Hence in asking whether we should admonish another church, we need to ask whether it has been the church as Christ requires. Generally a failure to admonish the state will not stand alone. There will be other failures in the life of the church. We rarely need to admonish a church merely on political grounds.

If we ask whether the church has been true to its divine calling, it may also help us to avoid the hypocrisy into which we commonly fall. It is easy for a church to become activist in terms of a particular political philosophy. It then criticizes those who do not follow that party line. Our real concern should not be faithfulness to a particular line. It should be faithfulness to all that Christ requires of his church on earth.

27

Bible Translation

THE ISSUES

Bible translations can be controversial because of several issues. Discussion often turns on determining the Greek, Hebrew, or Aramaic manuscript which most faithfully preserves the original. Perhaps a majority of translation controversies have been on this issue. Those controversies are not the concern of this chapter. Rather the concern is with the principles to be used by the translator in translating the Bible into another language. It is with the discussion of whether a translation should be literal or idiomatic. Related to this are questions of how to render grammatical formations, concepts, cultural items, and so on, which are not known in the language or culture into which a translation is made.

How can we translate so as to do justice to the character and purpose of the Bible? How can we most effectively place the Bible in the hands of another language group? From this arise all sorts of issues of priority and choice. The translator faces the dilemma of choosing a translation which is closer to the natural idiom of the original language as opposed to adhering to the idiom of the language of the translation. (The language of the translation is commonly called the receptor language.) Within the group that speaks the receptor language the translator can choose to aim at satisfying the more literate or the less literate group of the population. He can aim at those with some experience of Biblical ideas through the church or those with no such experience.

Where translations already exist the issue can be further complicated. How much archaism can be tolerated in an old translation? When do we pass the point at which the disadvantage of its archaic language outweighs the advantage of its familiarity? Where several translations exist then the matter of comparison inevitably arises. The issues of style may also arise. One translation may be concerned to safeguard the euphony of the translation. Another may favour plainness rather than speech rhythms. These questions arise particularly with poetry. The particular images or the style of Hebrew poetry may be foreign to the poetic style of the receptor language. So the question arises of whether to retain the peculiarities of Biblical poetry or to make the translation more prosaic.

SOME PRELIMINARY QUESTIONS

We have already seen in chapter 9 the fact that Scripture is well equipped to survive translation. The basic truths are taught repeatedly in ways that refer back to one another and guard against distortion. The translated Word still remains the Word of God.

Therefore we need to approach the debate about translation with a sense of proportion. Sometimes translation theory and practice has been made too big an issue. Those concerned with the readability of the receptor translation have said that a more literal translation would be left unread. Those concerned with accuracy in translation have charged that less literal translations will obscure basic Christian truths. Both charges tend to exaggeration.

That does not mean we should not strive to come to the best possible method of translation. It means that the future of the gospel or of the church is not at stake. The Word will come through. But any translation is to avoid the introduction of any unnecessary hindrance to the clear hearing of the Word.

We must also remember that Scripture does not operate alone. It is accompanied by the Holy Spirit. Translators commonly attribute effects to their translation or their particular style of translation which are really due to the Holy Spirit. Given the power of the Word to survive distortion, we should be humble in claiming credit for a particular translation.

THE PROBLEM OF IMAGES

Given these preliminary considerations, one wonders why the matter has caused so much debate. Why have positions arisen defending quite firmly a particular approach to translation? One suspects that the debate is symbolic of something larger. Images and positions are caught up with the debate. Those who are making readability their criterion are reacting against a faith which they see as being shut off from living interaction with the world. If we are able to look back in say one hundred years' time, we might well describe evangelicalism (or Fundamentalism if you prefer that term) as experiencing an acute sense of isolation in the post-Second World War period. It feels that it has created a cocoon from which it cannot escape and into which those from the outside cannot enter. Communication across the divide between the church and the world becomes an extremely important issue. This issue particularly seems to bother those who grow up within the church. Those who come from outside into the church may be influenced by the general tone, but are less likely to be bothered. They know in their own experience that the barrier can be crossed and is being crossed.

For those who have this question of communication as a prime concern, the Bible has to be easily communicable. Readability comes to be very important.

Some would connect this concern with a new interest in evangelism. Certainly the discussion of evangelism tends to go along with it. However I am not convinced that the root issue is evangelism. Taking a broad perspective, it is hard to be convinced that the people who have this feeling of isolation are actually engaging in more evangelism than those who do not have an anxiety about being left out of the main stream. There is a whole lot of difference between talking about the church's isolation from the world and actually bringing former non-Christians into the church.

Those who tend to stress accuracy are also responding to a set of concerns. Their concern is with the loss of the quality of Christian discipleship. They are concerned about an ignorance of the Bible in the church. To them this is not inconsistent with evangelism because a well-taught church and a well-discipled church is a more effective evangelistic tool.

The pressure for a more readable translation has often come from those working with peoples to whom Christianity is quite new. Where it is a case of tribal people, their knowledge of some of the cultural items of Biblical times can also be limited. Hence there is an argument for substituting both ideas and objects which are more within their experience.

But such cases really do not solve the issue. For there is obviously another strategy which could be followed. The alternative strategy would put greater emphasis on teaching. Rather than limiting the Scripture translated to what the people can now comprehend, one could use Scripture as a means for raising their comprehension.

The difference has practical consequences. It means that we cannot simply rely upon the Bible translation itself to found a church. Church planters and teachers are essential. Hence the existence of the newly literate tribal person does not decide the case for a less literal translation.

I recognize the power of these images and their ability to influence the thinking of Christians on a wide range of issues. However I think issues should not be decided by such images. We need to find a way to choose between competing priorities in the matter of Bible translation.

THE TRANSLATOR'S DILEMMA

The problems facing a translator arise from the differences between languages. For convenience we may divide these roughly into differences which arise from the cultural history of the language group concerned and the differences in the structure of languages.

Some people may not have encountered many of the objects mentioned in the Bible. Hence their language has no word for these objects. For example we could think of peoples who were not familiar with bread, wine, figs, swords, and so on. The dilemma facing the translator is whether he substitutes something out of the people's culture which is roughly equivalent. For example, does he substitute yams for bread or some other fruit for figs? Related to this is the problem of idioms. Many metaphorical expressions are built upon some concrete object in the experience of Israel. An example would be the comparison of the people of God to sheep. Where sheep are unknown, should we seek an alternative picture?

Languages also differ in structure. One language may make exclusive, or almost exclusive, use of passive verbs; another may use few if any passives; while a third may use a fair mixture of passives and actives. One language may indicate emphasis by placing a word first in a sentence, even the object of the verb. In another language, the object may have to come in a particular place. The words of two languages do not completely overlap. They may overlap at some point in their range of meaning but they generally do not overlap for their complete range of meaning. A simple example would be the Hebrew word generally translated 'know'. Part of its use covers aspects of knowledge of people which we would commonly describe by words such as 'love'. In other languages the main word to 'know' may not cover such intimate and emotional forms of knowing.

Thus the translator rarely finds a perfect match between words and grammatical structures. He is forced to a choice which is well illustrated by the case of a people who know yams but not bread. Suppose he introduces a word for bread not previously present in the language. The people will not know what this word means and will need to be taught about it and the item it represents. The result is an obscurity in the translation for the native speaker who reads it. Let us suppose he replaces usages of 'bread' by 'yams'. He still has problems in his translations because much of the discussion of bread in Scripture has reference to leavened and unleavened bread. References to bread are connected to references to wheat as its primary ingredient. Substitution of 'yam' in such contexts leads to confusion also.

Similar problems may be more subtle. We have seen that the Hebrew word we translate 'know' has a wider range than our English word 'know'. One solution is for the translator to translate some passages with 'know' and others with 'love'. The problem with this is the fact that there are passages in which both the intellectual sense of 'know' and the emotional sense of 'love' are involved. As passages where the element of love is strong we could cite Genesis 18:19 where God says that he has 'known' Abraham and Amos 3:2 where he says that Israel is the only nation he has 'known'. In such contexts a word like 'love' would make sense. However what do we do with a passage like Hosea 8:2–4? Israel say, 'My God, we of Israel know Thee'. God describes their actions: 'They have appointed princes but I did not know'. Clearly this second use of 'know' means something like 'love'. God is aware of what they do but He does not approve it. How do we understand the first case where Israel claim to know God? We could also translate it as 'love' and make good sense in the context. Israel claim to 'love' God but in practice they disobey him. However Israel's claim to know God must be connected with all the things God did in order to make himself known to them (e.g. Ex. 6:7; Josh. 4:24; 1 Kings 18:37). A common theme of Biblical teaching is that God makes himself known to Israel in order that Israel may manifest its knowledge of God in love and service. We can arbitrarily decide that every time we find the verb in question followed by 'that' we will translate 'know that' and every time we find the verb with a person as object we translate 'love'. This breaks the natural connection between God's making himself known and the way Israel's knowledge should manifest itself. Yet it does not completely obscure the sense of the passages in question.

An alternative is to translate in such a way as to preserve the unity of ideas in the Biblical text and translate all cases as 'know'. The result for the reader unfamiliar with the Bible will probably be that he will miss the emotional dimension of 'know' in many of its usages. Instead he will read 'know' in terms of his normal use of the word. So we could translate according to context with 'know', 'love', or other words. There will be less initial confusion. In the longer term there will be less appreciation of the fact that there is an emotional dimension to knowledge in Scripture.

Thus we face a problem similar to that posed by our earlier example of bread and yams. A translation more in terms of the concepts of the receptor language will be more immediately understandable. To balance that immediate understandability we have the problem that such a translation gives less insight into the whole system of teaching in the Scriptures.

If we had just the case of 'bread' and the word for 'know',

then our problem would be minor. However, we must multiply this problem many times. There are many objects and many ranges of meaning which seem strange to another culture and another language.

Translations face a choice between preserving the culture and concepts of the original texts or preserving those of the receptor language. There are of course many gradations of approach in between the extremes. There is a logically consistent position which would attempt to retain the cultural objects of the original language but not retain the linguistic structure of the original. That is, in terms of the examples already given, which would use 'bread' but not attempt to translate Biblical usages of 'know' by the one word in the receptor language which came closest to 'know'. The reverse position is also logically possible.

Generally speaking the post-Reformation translation tradition tended to reflect the culture and language of the original texts. In English texts this tendency is represented by the tradition of the Authorized Version, English Revised, American Standard, and New American Standard. We have in recent years departures from this approach in many translations. The New International Version retains the cultural objects of the original but tries to choose the particular word that is most appropriate in the context rather than trying to reflect the word choice of the original. This principle, sometimes called 'dynamic equivalence', can be illustrated once again by the case of 'know'. Hosea 8:2b,4b in the New American Standard[1] reads

'My God, we of Israel know Thee!'
They have appointed princes, but I did not know *it*[2]

Contrast with this the New International translation:

'O our God, we acknowledge you'
they choose princes without my approval

[1]The New American Standard is not consistent. For example 'know' with sexual connotations is translated by 'had relations with' (e.g. Gen. 4:1) with 'knew' as a marginal reading. No translation represents the absolute example of either pole. It is a matter of degree.

[2]New American Standard follows the convention of putting in italics a word implied, but not explicit, in the original.

The problem with the New American Standard translation is that there appears to be a confession of ignorance on God's part. The problem of the New International translation is twofold. One wonders whether the translation 'acknowledge' is strong enough. 'Acknowledge' has something of a formal flavour in English. Perhaps Israel meant to claim more. However that problem is not the most important one.[1] The greater problem is that the contrast is lost which is clearer in the original between Israel's claimed 'knowledge' of God and God's statement that he did not 'know' Israel. Other translations go somewhat further in their rejection of literal translation and approach paraphrase. An example of this would be the Good News Bible.

The substitution of cultural equivalents for the unfamiliar objects of Biblical culture is particularly defended when translating for tribal groups. The more widely spoken languages often have words for things which are no longer in everyday use. Thus English has words for 'sword', 'winnowing', 'altar', etc. There is also more of a general, historical, cultural sense. There is a fair chance that a person will know what a sword is, though he may never have held one and is unlikely to have used one.

THE DEFENCE OF THE PRIORITY OF THE RECEPTOR LANGUAGE

There have been many defences of the approach to translation which tends, when faced with a choice, to err on the side of giving priority to the receptor language.[2] Their essential

---

[1] One sometimes sees in translations which have rejected the approach of translating the one original word by the one translation word, that there is something of a reaction to an extreme. One wonders why 'know' was not used here.

[2] Examples are: E. A. Nida, 'Translation or Paraphrase', *The Bible Translator*, 1 (1950), 97–106; R. G. Bratcher, 'Good News for Modern Man', *ibid.*, 17 (1966), 159–172; J. Beekman, '"Literalism" a Hindrance to Understanding', *ibid.*, 178–189; J. Beekman and J. Callow, *Translating the Word of God*, Grand Rapids, Zondervan, 1974; R. B. Dillard in J. H. Skilton and C. A. Ladley (eds.), *The New Testament Student and Bible Translation*, Phillipsburg, Presbyterian and Reformed, 1978, pp. 94–104, 109–118.

argument is easy to summarize. It is that the resultant translation is easier to understand. It does not impose upon the reader concepts and usages with which he will not be familiar. This defence is often supported by the claim that the Scriptures were originally written in idiomatic popular language. The translator should do the same.

This is not to imply that those who advocate this approach to translation ignore the problems. The difficulties they wrestle with, and the conflicts which result, will give a good indication of the problems.

(i) Concordance and meaning

A translation which tries to translate consistently the one original word by the same word is referred to as a concordant translation. The objection to such translations is that the original word may have different senses in different contexts.

A difficulty in this argument is that the original may use words in the same sense, yet these are treated by a receptor language as different words. An example would be languages in which God's actions and man's actions are described using different words. Thus in some languages different words are used for God's forgiveness[1] or God's love[2] as compared with man's. Of course such cases are probably a minority yet they illustrate a basic point. The problem is not simply the fact that a word in the original text will have different meanings in different contexts. It is the fact that a receptor language may make distinctions which the original does not make.

The priority of the context can produce some curious results. A number of phrases or sentences occur several times in Scripture. An example is the saying of Jesus: 'by what measure you measure, it will be measured to you' (Matt. 7:2; Mark 4:24; Luke 6:38). In Matthew the context is judgment and the point is that harshness in judgment will be appropriately recompensed. In Luke 6:38 the context is generosity and the point is that it also will have an equivalent recompense. In Mark 4:24 the context is the danger of being inclined to false judgments by gossip. It has been suggested that in cases like this it may be hard to translate the word for 'measure' by the

---

[1]Beekman and Callow, *op. cit.*, p. 155.
[2]*Ibid.*, p. 156.

same word in each case.[1]

This opinion may well be an extreme one, not shared by all who advocate dynamic equivalence as a translation principle. However it serves to illustrate an important problem. To what extent do statements stand alone and to what extent are statements part of the context in which they occur? We generally emphasize the importance of context because the danger is that words can be made to say something they do not say if context is ignored. Yet it is possible to have general truths which are stated and then given particular application in context. That is the case here. The general point is that we ourselves receive according to what we give to others. That can be applied to the case either of judgment or generosity. The general statement is not limited by the context. It is specifically applied in the context. Certainly there may be languages in which one would not use the same word for measuring our judgment and measuring our gifts. However that problem is created only by refusing to allow the general truth to stand on its own. These three passages are translated differently in the Good News Bible. In the Matthew (and Mark) cases where the context is judgment, the sentence in question has been translated to emphasize this. Hence Matthew 7:2: 'for God will judge you in the same way as you judge others, and he will apply to you the same rules you apply to others.' In contrast, in Luke 6:38 the sentence is brought into line with the context of generosity: 'The measure you use for others is the one that God will use for you.'

If one were to read each context in isolation, then one might find the passage comprehensible. Has anything been lost by this form of translation? It was pointed out earlier (ch. 2) that the form of Biblical teaching is very much one of stating a general law or principle and showing its particular applications. The reader who reads all of the Gospels is left without an appreciation of the general principle which rules both judgment and generosity.

What has happened in this case should make us look critically at the whole question of the priority of the context. Jesus gave a particular application of a general truth. He did

[1] *Ibid.*, p. 154n.

not modify the general truth to suit the context. That is what the translation has done. One could compare the situation with what a context does to a word. Sometimes a word has developed several quite distinct meanings with little obvious relationship between the meanings. An example would be the English word 'let' which from the same root in a much earlier stage of the development of the language has come to have the meanings of 'permit' and 'prevent' (the latter meaning is rare and archaic). In such a case the two meanings do not influence each other, except that to avoid ambiguity the use for 'prevent' is restricted in modern English to a few fixed usages. Thus in any given context only one meaning of the word can be in view. Other words have a range of related meanings. A particular context may use a word with emphasis on part of the range. Yet a connotation or flavour derived from other usages may still be there. An example is the word for 'know' already discussed. Even when the context is putting an emphasis on the intellectual side of knowing, there may be connotations of the emotional present. The emotional side may not be prominent in the context. Hence we can read Biblical passages which use the word for 'know' in terms of our use of the word for a purely intellectual cognitive phenomenon and find it to make sense. Yet we may have lost something of the original flavour.

It is wrong to leave to context the sole determination of the meaning of a word or a sentence. Context limits, focuses, and applies the meaning the word or sentence has in itself. The ignoring of context and the over-valuing of context are both wrong.

This means that the translator cannot simply choose the range of meaning of the word which fits well in our reading of that context. Attention must be given to the word's use in other contexts.

(ii) *'Cultural' differences*

To what extent is the Scripture simply reflecting a particular culture without giving any particular authority to that culture? To what extent does Scripture reflect a culture which has itself been shaped by God's revelation and is therefore a pattern for us? These questions are closely connected to the question of whether we may substitute cultural equivalents for things mentioned in Scripture.

We have already seen that the difficulty in this case is the unity of Scripture. Something like bread is mentioned frequently and in many different ways.

Other problems arise when we consider practices. In some cultures laying on of hands is a way of cursing. Hence it is suggested that the translator should not translate literally the passage where Jesus laid his hands on children. In those cultures the gesture will inevitably be misinterpreted.[1]

Here is a clear case where a choice has been made. Instead of using Scripture to correct the usages of the culture, the pagan usages are allowed to determine the translation. In every culture the practices of Scripture must be in conflict with the accepted. The Gospels are full of such clashes. The practices of Jesus and his disciples were not understood. The translator should not avoid such clashes between Scripture and pagan practice. That clash is one of the ways the gospel changes societies.

There are cases in which a question arises as to whether cultural practices are morally neutral. Beekman and Callow say that the method of disposing of the body of the dead is a matter of indifference. Burial, cremation, setting adrift on rafts, are equally valid.[2] This is a debatable point as shown by the many Christians who have rejected cremation. The translator should not decide such questions for himself. He owes it to the church to allow them to come to their own decision. The more the translator substitutes what he deems to be cultural equivalents, the less scope he leaves for the church to make up its own mind.

Certainly uncommon or unknown practices will create difficulties for the reader who is inexperienced in the Scriptures. However the mastering of such difficulties may be one of the ways in which the believers grow.[3]

(iii) *Metaphorical language*
The problem of metaphors is closely connected with the

---

[1] *Ibid.*, p. 122.

[2] *Ibid.*, pp. 201f.

[3] It is of interest that Beekman and Callow, while advocating some degree of cultural equivalence do concede that the problem is a lessening one as the readers become more familiar with Biblical culture (*ibid.*, pp. 208ff.).

previous topic, because many figures of speech allude to some object or practice of the times. However Biblical images are not just drawn from contemporary scenes. The Scripture builds up its own store of images by repetitive usage. For example, on a number of occasions Old Testament saints are described at their death as 'being gathered to their people' or 'gathered to their fathers' (e.g. Gen. 25:8; 35:29; 49:29; Judges 2:10). In Luke 16:22, in the story of the rich man and Lazarus, we are told of how Lazarus was carried by the angels to Abraham's bosom. These various images are testimony to a belief that believers are gathered with past saints at death. The picture of the story of the rich man and Lazarus is connected to the Old Testament pictures. The Good News Bible retains some of the idea at Luke 16:22 by paraphrasing 'to sit beside Abraham at the feast in heaven'. Yet in the Old Testament passages to which the picture relates, the literal wording has been replaced by a factual reference to death. Its rendering of Genesis 25:8 omits all reference to Abraham being gathered to his people.

Several things are happening in such cases. The reader's capacity to interpret Biblical images is being reduced by the elimination of other instances of the same image. Further, the richness of Biblical imagery is being reduced. In translating this idiom passage the Good News Bible is simply dull. Scripture was not written in a dull fashion. The translator does not really serve the reader by turning its intriguing pictures into commonplaces.

One of the ways words expand their range of meaning is by metaphorical use. Here a dilemma confronts those who oppose a literal translation of Scripture. They realize that suppression of all metaphors will lessen the message of Scripture. Yet their principle of translation according to context goes against a translation which would retain the original connection. An example is the treatment of 'flesh' by Beekman and Callow.[1] They see it as no longer a living metaphor. Hence there is no necessity, in translation, to try to retain the literal word. The New International Version translates 'flesh' in John 1:14 but 'sinful nature' or the like in the multiple occurrences in Romans

[1] *Ibid.*, p. 135.

7 and 8. The Good News Bible uses 'human being' in John 1:14 and 'human nature' in Romans 7 and 8. Thus both are making a distinction between John's usage in 1:14 where sin is not in view and Paul's usage where sin is very much a part of the picture.

How do we know for certain that for Paul and his readers, 'flesh' had lost its connection with its original meaning and become just a synonym for man's propensity to sin? In the context of Romans 7:7–25 Paul is building a contrast between the inner man of the mind and the body. In 8:23 he focuses on the redemption of the body as the object of Christian hope. Is not Paul saying that there is a sense in which sin has a particular hold on the appetites and desires of the body? Certainly he does not see the mind of the unbeliever as free from sin (Eph. 2:3; Rom. 1:21–23). But with the believer he pictures a process of regeneration stretching out from an initial root in the mind. How then can we be sure that Paul did not use the word 'flesh' because it suited his contrast of mind and body? Given the context it is more likely that we should retain the translation 'flesh' rather than the duller 'human nature'. Once more the attempt to avoid the literalness of Scripture results in a translation that lacks the vivid and concrete note of Scripture.

(iv) *Popular and technical language*

'There can be no other conclusion except that since the Holy Spirit chose to honour and employ the then current usage of the language, we should do likewise and use the form which is current and natural to the people.'[1]

Such arguments are commonly used to defend idiomatic translations. Are these arguments valid? They are probably generally valid. Unfortunately it is hard to establish whether they are completely valid. The problem is basically an historical one. We have very little Hebrew literature to compare with the Old Testament. With the New Testament we are somewhat better placed but even here there are uncertainties. For the New Testament was written, at least partially, in a dialect of Greek that is strongly influenced by Semitic language. Further, it is difficult to place both with respect to the colloquial and

---

[1] Beekman, *op. cit.*, p. 186. Similar ideas are found in Beekman and Callow, *op. cit.*, p. 346; Dillard, *op. cit.*, p. 102.

with respect to the literary language of its day. It cannot be identified with either.[1] It may well be that a dialect of Greek existed in Palestine which was strongly under Semitic influence. Men writing the profound truths of the New Testament in this dialect would produce work which lacks both the commonness of the colloquial language and the artificiality of the literary language.

Another factor must also be considered. The Greek of the New Testament is strongly influenced by the Septuagint. Thus the New Testament itself reflects the impact which a translation may make on a language.

Given the information available to us, the matter is not as simple as is often implied. The writers of Scripture may well have chosen, on occasion, a rare word to convey the precise meaning they wanted. Certainly they used a vocabulary shaped by Scriptural usage, not that of the most commonly used language of the day. They used loan words like 'sabbath rest' (Heb. 4:9).[2] Given the difficulty we find in determining the commonness or otherwise of much of Biblical vocabulary, we are forced to resort to internal comparisons to make more sense of what the Biblical writers were doing with language. Certainly some writers do use words in a way that tends towards the coining of a theological vocabulary. Paul is a clear example with his use of words like 'righteousness', 'flesh', etc. This does not mean that these words were uncommon words. But even common words can be given a technical flavour by consistent pattern of usage.

THE ARGUMENTS FOR A LITERAL TRANSLATION

The weakness in the arguments for an idiomatic translation are mostly related to a basic point. Biblical language has a history and a unity. There are patterns of usage and allusion in Scripture. Different contexts do not destroy that unity. This is true to some extent of the language as a whole. Words derive

[1]For a summary with references to further literature see J. H. Skilton, 'Future English Versions of the Bible and the Past', in J. H. Skilton and C. A. Ladley (eds.), *The New Testament Student and Bible Translation*, pp. 181ff.
[2]While attested in later Greek this certainly would qualify as a rarer and more technical word.

their meaning from a history of usage. However with Scripture this is true with particular force. For Scripture is self-interpreting. That imposes a unity upon the language of Scripture which will not be found in ordinary language. Certainly examples may be found in the language of Scripture comparable to the example of 'let' used earlier.[1] To deny the possibility of the development of such unrelated meanings is also to deny the history of language. Words can develop to the point where the meanings do not form a continuous range. The problem of the idiomatic approach, however, is its ignoring of the other common phenomenon illustrated by the discussion of the case of 'know'. Similarly the practice of cultural substitution often goes contrary to the unity of Biblical allusion and imagery.

Cultures also have a history. It is often the history of ignorance of the truth of God. As a result the language of that culture may be ill-prepared to receive the truth of God. That does not mean we should accommodate that truth to the culture. Rather we seek to use the truth to change the culture. That is no easy task. It may seem easier to ignore the many little points where Scripture conflicts with the culture or is simply incomprehensible in terms of that culture. Yet what is Scripture? Is it not given so that the man of God may be furnished for every good work (2 Tim. 3:17)? To remove the conflicts is to remove the incentives for change.

It can be quite validly argued that when it comes to evangelism the little points at which a culture clashes with Scripture are not important. We should hold to the more important issues. That is certainly true. Yet is it relevant for Bible translation? Should the translation of the Bible be determined by the capacity of the unbeliever to comprehend or by the needs of the church?

This question is easily answered by asking for whom the Bible was originally written. Was it written primarily for Gentiles or Jews? Is the New Testament directed to the world or the church? On balance one would have to answer that it is written for the people of God. Should not our translation practice reflect this fact? Even where we might argue for a wider

[1] For a discussion of possible examples see my 'Some Points for Defenders of Translations', in *The New Testament Student and Bible Translation*, pp. 122f.

audience, such as with John's Gospel, a mere glance at the first chapter shows that John has not avoided concepts or images that require a knowledge of the Old Testament for full comprehension.

LINGUISTIC THEORY

Bible translation has been much influenced by theories in linguistics. Obviously a better understanding of the nature of language could have a beneficial effect on our approach to translation. Just as obviously there could be a problem if linguistics is influenced by non-Christian ideas. The result would be a conflict between the translation theory, influenced by non-Christian ideas, and the nature of the Bible itself. Linguistic theory is trying to solve one aspect of a problem that has been considered earlier in Chapter 4. As part of creation, language partakes of the order of creation. However it has also something of the mystery of creation. All attempts to reduce language to one particular order, completely comprehensible to man, have failed. That should not surprise us. Physics and biology and many other disciplines face the same problem. There is order in creation but man does not succeed in reducing everything to the simple order that is comprehensible to the human mind.

There have been two primary ways in which linguistic theory during the present century has sought to understand language.[1] However, to understand the developments of this century we have to comprehend the distinction between linguistics this century and linguistics last century. Linguistics last century was very much under the influence of two factors. One was the realization that languages could be analysed as members of families, like Indo-European and Semitic, and that the histories of those families could be traced in some respects. The second was the influence of evolutionary theory. Both these led to a tendency to be interested in the development of languages. Hence linguistics was a historical study (often called diachronic linguistics).

[1] For a history of linguistics this century, with some criticisms, see G. Sampson, *Schools of Linguistics*, London, Hutchinson, 1980.

[286]

The emphasis this century has changed to an emphasis on the structure of a language as it exists at the present time (synchronic linguistics). The advantage of this approach is that it allows languages to be studied for which we lack evidence of development. Hence tribal languages have been considered far more seriously.

There is however a consequence. There is not the emphasis on a language as something shaped by its history. This has significance for Bible translation, as we shall see. Two schools have dominated the linguistics of this century. One was strongly influenced by empiricism and related ideas like behaviourism. Thus it sought to describe, analyse, and classify the data of language without any speculation as to what was going on in the mind of the speaker. It was also influenced by the work of Franz Boas.[1] Boas was reacting against a Euro-centric approach which would bring native languages and culture into comparison with those of Europe. The result of that approach was that the culture was not studied on its own terms. Its language would be analysed in terms of structures appropri-ate for European languages. Boas' views lead to a certain relativism. Culture and languages are to be analysed on their own terms. They are not to be evaluated with a view to establishing the superiority of one over another.

This approach had been particularly successful in phonetic and grammatical analysis of non-Indo-European languages. Its emphasis that no language was better than another served to correct tendencies to try to interpret other languages in terms of structures appropriate for more studied languages. Thus the phonetic and grammatical individuality of these languages could be better appreciated. Furthermore, phonetics and grammar lend themselves to an empirical study in which no questions are raised about the intention or meaning of the speaker.

The influence of this empiricist school upon Bible translation follows logically from the starting point. An emphasis upon the relativity of language counts against any attempt to conform one language to another. Certainly the areas in which conform-ing one language to another arise in Bible translation are not

[1]For the views of Boas see H. Cravens, *The Triumph of Evolution*, Philadelphia, University of Pennsylvania, 1978, pp. 92ff.

areas of phonetics and not commonly matters of grammar. They are more often matters of the meaning of words or 'semantics' (in the proper and not derogatory sense of 'semantics'). Nevertheless this strongly relativistic approach is inclined to carry over into semantics. Furthermore, the empiricist approach focused on languages as existing now, rather than as they had developed. Hence anybody coming to Bible translation out of this discipline would not be orientated towards the historically developed semantics of Biblical language.

The second main approach is philosophically opposed to the empiricist approach. This is the rationalist linguistics of Chomsky.[1] A normal child possesses a capacity to learn language. The empiricists would ascribe this to the influence of his environment. Chomsky, as a rationalist, sees it as evidence rather of an innate structure of the mind. Since the child may learn any one of thousands of different languages, this innate structure must not be specific for a particular language. Much of the research of Chomsky and his school is devoted to uncovering these universal innate structures. It is particularly syntax that has been studied to discern the relationship between the actual production of language and the deeper structures of the mind. Man is viewed as producing language from these deep structures by a series of transformations that are specific for the language in question. Amongst the consequences of this approach is that, within one language, different fiinal structures may express the same meaning. Similarly languages may differ markedly yet be seen as surface expressions of the same underlying deeper structure.

There are a number of consequences of such an approach to language. Just as with the empirical approach, these consequences may be as much a matter of attitude as of strict logical consequences of the theory. If different forms can be generated from the same deep structure, then the final expression or surface form is not so significant. In translation the important thing will not be a literal translation of the surface structure but an adequate representation of the deep structure

[1]As an introduction to Chomsky see his works: *Cartesian Linguistics: A Chapter in the History of Rationalist Thought*, New York, Harper and Row, 1966; *Reflections on Language*, London, Temple Smith, 1975.

which is behind it. Hence the translator's focus naturally moves from representation of the literal form to an attempt to represent the meaning he sees behind that form.

A second consequence is more closely connected to the rationalist view of a man. The rationalist sees man with innate powers and potentialities which he must be free to express. Thus Chomsky quotes with approval Humboldt's defence of man's rights: 'every individual enjoys the most absolute, unbounded freedom to develop himself out of himself, in true individuality.'[1] Obviously such an approach does not lead to the criticism of linguistic productions. It will not lead to questioning whether the existing forms of a language need expansion or modification in order to express a fundamental truth.

Chomsky's basic concern is with syntax. Indeed it has been pointed out that semantics is one of the weakest parts of his theory.[2] Just as with the empirical approach described earlier, there is not an emphasis on the history of language. Both these approaches are finding regularities in language which can be described and classified. One may focus somewhat more on phonetics and the other somewhat more on syntax. Each interprets the data in accord with its philosophical position.

We may freely admit that many of the regularities claimed do actually exist. However other aspects of language are not so easily classified and reduced to a system. Such aspects are inclined to be overlooked when the approach seeks a system. Meaning is one such aspect. We as Christians would not deny that language is an intrinsic part of man's constitution. Man has been created in the image of the God whose name is the Word. Yet we cannot assume that any part of man's initial constitution has been left untouched by sin. Languages may lack words or concepts to express certain Biblical truths, or the expression of them may be restricted by the lack of certain words. Thus the relative lack of words for expressing the ideas of sin and righteousness is a phenomenon recognized by translators.[3] Surely this lack has some connection to a lack of an

---

[1] *Cartesian Linguistics*, p. 25.

[2] J. Searle, 'Chomsky's Revolution in Linguistics', in G. Harman (ed.), *On Noam Chomsky*, Garden City, N.Y., Anchor, 1974.

[3] Beckman and Callow, *op. cit.*, pp. 180f.

influence of the law of God on the cultures in which those languages operate. Of course such words may occur in other cultures with different connotations. For example it would be possible to develop such a vocabulary where sin and righteousness are seen in purely human terms. Thus the existence of a vocabulary which can be appropriated and given new connotations in Christian use does not prove that such a culture is superior. The culture in which sin and righteousness are little mentioned and the culture in which they are secularized are both disobedient to God.

The point is that the word choices available in a language are strongly influenced by the history of that culture. Similarly cultures in which the church has been operative and the Scripture has been translated have their languages influenced by it. The prevailing schools of linguistics will not emphasize such effects. That is because their orientation is not historical and they are trying to reduce all to a logical system. In other words, however interesting their results with respect to this or that part of language, they are not dealing with the whole phenomenon of language. We should not allow this impoverished view of language to determine our translation practice.

In chapter 18 it was pointed out that the prophets drew their images from the past history of God's people. They wrote with their pictures already supplied to them. In a sense this is true also of all the Biblical writers. The semantic fields of their vocabulary were set by the previous use of that terminology and those metaphors. Certainly there were also new words and pictures. Yet the thread of continuity is what makes Biblical language and thought a unity. It is what gives the key to the interpretation of Scripture. We should translate so as to maintain that unity. The more literal approach to translation does that. The idiomatic approach, by giving the preference to the individual context and the receptor language, tends to obliterate those linking and interpretive themes.

CONCLUSION

THE PARADOXES OF LIMITED INSPIRATION

The attempt to limit the sphere in which the Scripture may speak produces a number of paradoxical results. These results may lead to internal inconsistencies in the whole position or go contrary to the proclaimed aims of advocates of the position.

There is widely expressed concern today that the evangelical church has been guilty of a retreat into the emotional, the private and the individual. Social and political concerns have been neglected.

Whatever the truth of the charge as a charge against evangelicalism, those making the charge are concerned that the church not abandon an important area of life and leave it to non-Christian forces.

Does not limited inspiration represent another form of retreat? In effect it says that the Scripture says nothing definite to the disciplines of science, history and so on. The Christian leaves these areas to be dominated by non-Christian approaches and assumptions.

That flight from the academic disciplines raises a question. Is the entry into the social and political spheres a flight from the academic areas? Is it just another form of retreat?

Raising these questions is not meant to criticize a Christian position in society or government. Rather it asks whether we should abandon any area to non-Christian concepts. That is what we are forced to do if we say the Bible is not our authority in these areas. We can talk all we like about Christians in the sciences and other disciplines but that does little good if once in position they have nothing distinctive to say as Christians. Similarly if we retreat from affirming what the Scripture says about marriage, we can say little useful or definite on the problems of society. Christians become the silent and ineffective presence in all these areas.

A different sort of paradox lies in the combination of arguments used to limit the areas in which Scripture may speak.

As outlined earlier there are two common arguments. One is that Scripture does not speak exhaustively on the matter in question. That argument assumes the possibility of exhaustive knowledge. That is, man may have a full and certain knowledge of things.

The second common way is a variety of relativism. Relativism says there is nothing sure and certain for all men. One culture or time has one set of values and those differ from another culture or time. The Bible is then seen as the expression of such a limited and relative position.

If man may have comprehensive knowledge, then relativism is false. If relativism is true then comprehensive knowledge cannot be set up as a standard.

A few examples of inconsistent arguments will make the paradoxes clearer. You cannot argue that the Bible does not give a full scientific account of creation, and is hence irrelevant to the scientist, if you also argue that Genesis is merely an example of the way that primitive culture looked at the world.

These two reasons for dismissing the creation narrative came from mutually exclusive philosophical positions. Alternatively you cannot say both that the Scripture does not consider constitutional homosexuality, so being irrelevant to the modern debate, and that it reflects a reaction against a society where sexual aberrations and pagan worship were linked, thus being irrelevant to a culture where sexual aberration has no religious connections.

Of course people do regularly combine both approaches, especially in arguing that Scripture was the product of a 'prescientific' age. The charge involves a confusion of two separate tests of truth. One is the appeal to objective scientific evidence. This is the older way of rejecting Scripture and reflects a belief in truth being factual and knowable. The second test says that a former age being culturally different cannot determine beliefs for the present age. As the attempt to disprove the Bible 'scientifically' fails, so the argument against the Bible has to resort more to relativistic arguments. If there is knowable truth valid for all cultures then it is irrelevant when that truth was first expressed. The dating of the Bible is unimportant. If no truth can cross cultural barriers, then standards of scientific truth cannot cross cultural barriers. Our trust in science must be valid for our culture alone and hence cannot be used to judge the products of another culture like the Bible.

That such paradoxes exist raises a basic problem: are people coming to belief in limited inspiration out of reasoning through from basic principles? Or is there another factor? It raises the suspicion that there is flight from beliefs and convictions which are rejected by non-Christian society as a whole. Popularity, not logic, determines the choice of what to believe.

CAN COMPARTMENTALIZATION SUCCEED?

What are we led to if we accept the idea of Scripture having nothing to say in important areas? People affirm that they believe in 'creation' but the mechanism proposed is indistinguishable from what is supposed to have happened without any God being involved. People affirm belief in the usefulness of prayer and a belief in conversion through the work of the Holy Spirit. Nevertheless they are embarrassed by the idea that God actually acts upon the world or upon people. They say that the Bible is the Word of God yet doubt what it says. They affirm Christian standards in sexuality and marriage but refuse to condemn sexual perversion and marriage-breaking.

Are such positions characterized by anything but weakness where the Biblical view confronts non-Christian views? Of course there are some who would limit the areas in which the Bible may not speak. Often they want to make it 'just science' or 'just science' *plus* some other academic disciplines. In those areas we are not to test truth claims by Scripture but readily take over non-Christian views.

Can science and other disciplines be so easily separated from the rest of human life and experience? There are several reasons why they cannot be. The basic one is that God and Christ are Creator and cosmic Lord. As already pointed out Colossians is a clear example of the Bible's combination of creation and 'religious' questions.

The Bible does not engage in such compartmentalization and neither do many dangerous non-Christian views. Racism this century has been characterized by appeal to 'scientific' and 'historical' arguments. If we are not meant to take Adam and Eve seriously as scientific data then it also follows that we cannot use the Bible to refute the alleged separate and animal origins of Semites and blacks. We should also not forget that 'history' was used by holders of prestigious university positions to prove that Jesus was not a Jew. Today such positions, in the light of the Nazi movement, are so embarrassing that these misuses are quietly forgotten. Nevertheless the truth remains that deadly error has sought endorsement from the very disciplines from which some would now remove any definite Christian position.

We must also ask whether appeal to 'science' to justify homosexuality is any different from appeal to 'science' to justify racism. In both cases the scientific evidence is simply not there. The appeal is an attempt to bolster what the Bible condemns. Homosexuality may be tolerated today and racism condemned but fifty years ago it was the reverse. Maybe in another fifty years the situation will reverse again or some other damnable error will seek 'scientific' basis.

The simple fact is that neither truth nor error fits into such neat boxes. All realms of life are involved in the warfare between Christ and Satan.

THE CONSEQUENCES

The 1960s and early 1970s showed the emergence and expression of great social concern, especially in the younger generation. It is a matter of simple observation (and of deep concern) that the dedication has dried up. A bored and cynical selfishness has replaced idealism. The movement lacked the motivation and conviction to sustain it through disappointments. Catching this mood rather belatedly, many Christians now advocate developing such social concern. The crucial question that is ignored is that of motive. What will keep Christians committed to such care for others? That it is fashionable will not do it. Being affluent, self-centred and comfortable is also fashionable. A distant God cannot motivate. A faith that does not teach the lordship of Christ in all areas leaves too many easy ways to escape from the demands of total discipleship.

Closely connected to this is evangelism. Evangelism that is Biblical has social impact because it commands men to yield all to Christ. It proclaims him as Lord of all. As already pointed out, the belief that God is distant and inactive undermines evangelism. True evangelism has social impact because it is not afraid to identify the typical sins and cruelties of a society and demand that men repent and turn from them.

Yet it also confronts man with the fact of creation. As we noted earlier, Paul's address to pagans appeals to creation and providence (Acts 14:15–17; 17:22–31). For it is as one who created and sustains that God has a claim on human life. Take away that claim and the gospel much more easily becomes an appeal to human psychological inadequacy.

There is a further consequence. If the Scripture is uncertain and indefinite, what can the Christian say in social and political areas? One of the things that is emerging is a new interest by Christians in the study of society. Often such study takes the form of sociological analysis. Producing a sociological analysis does not tell you what to do. Suppose we find deep racial antagonisms in society and a preference for relationships with people of the same racial group and income bracket. That does not of itself tell us whether the church should follow the trends or oppose them. The New Testament church set out to span the gaps. Paul laboured hard to overcome the tensions created by the presence of both Jews and Greeks in the congregation. James warned against social distinctions being imported into the church. However, they wrote to a different social context. The principle of relativism can be used to reject their example.

The combination of a conviction that Christians should have a social conscience and a relativistic uncertainty about the applicability of Scripture produces curious results. We have a lot of analysis and very little concrete action. Is uncertainty and inaction after social analysis that much better than the much criticized inaction of the church in social matters?

The church can easily fall into creating congregations which reflect the divisions of society. We can easily use sociology as an excuse for ignoring the poor and the outcast in our expansion of the church. We relegate them to their own groups, even their own churches and ignore the mutually upbuilding diversity that Scripture seeks.

There is a further consequence for the church. The issue of leadership is a major problem for God's people. From the question that begins Judges: 'Who shall go up first for us?', to Paul's rules for elders in 1 Timothy, the Scripture speaks to the problem. Leadership is a thing some men avoid because it demands sacrifices. Leadership is a thing some men seek because it gives power and glory. The church needs great wisdom to reject the power-hungry as well as encourage the timid. One of the consequences of reducing the domain of Scriptural authority is to reduce the cost of being a Christian. The conflict with the world is lessened. Willingness to bear ridicule is just one test of the genuineness of a man's call to Christian leadership. It is only one test as some will even seek the ridicule of the world so as to increase their prestige within the church. Nevertheless it is one important test. As the church narrows the areas in which Scripture may speak, it eliminates issues on which the world will ridicule it. It becomes more attractive to those who want leadership for the power, popularity and prestige it conveys. We have already observed how often such people reorganize the church along the lines of a centralized bureaucratic structure and away from real ministry to people. As long as such people are in control they will not identify the problem facing the church as one of leadership. Yet that is one issue the church must face. Such leaders will lead the church to conform to the world rather than seek to transform the world by the power of Christ.

CHRIST, LORD OF ALL

The task before the church is not one of becoming less vulnerable by jettisoning what the world rejects. Neither is it mere defence of precious inherited truths. Both those approaches do not recognize that the points of conflict are points where the world is departing from the truth of God and is therefore vulnerable to the proclamation of that truth. A survey of a few of the areas in dispute illustrates this.

Without the certainty provided by creation and by God's providential control of the world, the world becomes a very mysterious place. Older views misinterpreted the order provided by God's law to exclude God. However as the attempts to achieve total understanding have failed, and the element of mystery has become more obvious, so non-Christians' certainty and confidence have diminished. Only the Biblical view can give an understanding of both the order and the mystery of the universe. Creation and providence are not embarrassments for the Christian. They are the reverse. Further, as Paul teaches in Romans, man has a sense of the Creator. He may over-react against the guilt that derives from that sense, by vehemently attacking the teaching of creation. Nevertheless he is the one on the defensive, knowing the truth of what he suppresses and rejects. When the Christian proclaims Christ as Creator and Lord, he speaks to what the unbeliever knows.

Similarly relativism is useful to the unbeliever only as a defence against the universal claim of God's law. It does not give him any certainty. He shows that need for certainty when he must make ethical judgments. When the church proclaims the truth and certainty of Christ's law the unbeliever may reject it. He may accuse the church of dogmatism but he is still the one who knows the truth of what he attacks.

Finally the church can proclaim with confidence the mercy of Christ; mercy to those who have lived contrary to what they know in their hearts; mercy to the family members whose lives have been darkened by the world's indifference to sexual perversion and marital unfaithfulness; mercy to all who know their own poverty. To refuse to identify sin as sin is to give even more opportunity to those who in their sin exploit and hurt the poor and the weak. The church that proclaims the law of God to which all men must submit can also proclaim release to those held captive through their own sin or the sin of others.

To proclaim in such confident ways that Christ's lordship extends over all areas of human activity we need a Scripture that speaks to all those areas. The converse also applies. Since we have a Scripture which is sufficient to be an authority in all areas of life, let us proclaim with boldness that Christ is Lord of all and every area of man's life must be yielded to Christ's control.

INDEX

INDEX OF SCRIPTURES